THE GUERRILLA GUIDE TO MASTERING STUDENT LOAN DEBT

THE GUERRILLA GUIDE TO MASTERING STUDENT LOAN DEBT

EVERYTHING YOU SHOULD KNOW ABOUT
* NEGOTIATING THE RIGHT LOAN FOR YOU
* PAYING IT OFF
* PROTECTING YOUR FINANCIAL FUTURE

ANNE STOCKWELL

HarperPerennial
A Division of HarperCollinsPublishers

HarperCollins books may be purchased for educational, business, or sales promotional use. For information please write: Special Markets Department, HarperCollins Publishers, Inc., 10 East 53rd Street, New York, NY 10022.

FIRST EDITION

Designed by Irving Perkins Associates

Library of Congress Cataloging-in-Publication Data
Stockwell, Anne, 1953–
    The guerrilla guide to mastering student loan debt: everything you should know about negotiating the right loan for you, paying it off, protecting your financial future / Anne Stockwell. — 1st ed.
        p. cm.
    Includes index.
    ISBN 0-06-273435-0
    1. Student loan funds—United States. 2. Student aid—United States.
I. Title.
LB2340.2.S838 1997
378.3'62—DC21   97-2060

97 98 99 00 01 ❖ /RRD 10 9 8 7 6 5 4 3 2 1

CONTENTS

Part 2: How Did We Get Into All This Debt?

The rivals: The Federal Family Education Loan Program (FFELP) vs. Direct Lending * Opposites detract: two programs at war with us in the middle * FFELP's not-so-private enterprise * Lucky lenders: we students just keep coming * Conflicts of interest? * Direct Lending: a direct advantage to students . . . so far

The G.I. Bill: an all-American thank-you * The Great Society: getting us all into college * Guaranteed Student Loans: from middle class to freshman class * Sallie Mae: birth of a money machine * Pell Grants: needed then and now * The Carter years: everybody gets a loan! * The Reagan Years: no, everybody does not get a loan! * Everybody gets a monster loan, including your parents * The '90s: how much is this costing? We don't wanna know * GSL becomes FFELP: and now you can borrow more! * Direct Lending: better late than never * College now: a matter of life and debt * The future: demanding the best loan deal for our money

How your tax dollars became FFELP's treasure chest * How FFELP works * Banks: why lend money to students? * Guaranty agencies: the student loan cops * Secondary markets: holding loans for the loan haul * Loan servicers: doing the grunt work * Collection agencies: picking the leftovers * Cranking out loans, raking in money: the booming student loan business * The secret of the seed fund * Sitting pretty with money to burn * How to make a billion dollars disappear * The 800-pound gorilla * Audits point to conflicts of interest * Just one more chance for FFELP

Part 3: How Your Loan Works

CHAPTER 10: DEFAULT (YOU'LL LIVE)   172

Part 4: How to Live with Your Loans

CHAPTER 11: GIMME CREDIT: CONSUMER CREDIT IS THE OTHER HALF OF YOUR FINANCES   207

ACKNOWLEDGMENTS

I could not possibly have written this book alone. Many formidable people shared their time and expertise with me. A partial list: Suzanne Elusorr, Ernest T. Freeman, Fred Galloway, Lawrence Hough, Elizabeth Hicks, Elizabeth Imholz, David Longanecker, Barmak Nassirian, Sheila Ryan, Diane Saunders, Patricia Scherschel, Bob Shireman, and Gisela Vallandigham. I thank them for their generosity and their concern for students.

I'm especially grateful to my editors, Kristen Auclair and Peternelle van Arsdale; my agent, Eileen Cope; researchers Danielle Durkin, Bill Haugse, and Chuck Welch; and transcribers Howard Zilbert and Cindy Haney of Stereotypists in Los Angeles.

Friends and colleagues helped me keep this project going: Alan Berger, Abigail Bok, Alan Frutkin, Kathy Gori, Berta Hernandez, J. V. McAuley, Mary Morris, Dick Scanlan, Michele A.H. Smith, Sherry Sonnett, Judy Wieder, and Bruce Wright. Rita Williams gave me kindness, laughs, and roses.

During the two years I worked on this book—and the five years I studied in graduate school—my family stood behind me. Thanks, and love, to Carl Custer; Buddy Stockwell; Joe and Becky Stockwell; and most of all my mother, Marion, whose belief in me has so often made the difference.

HOW TO USE THIS BOOK

The most stressful part of owing a student loan is the feeling that you don't understand what's happening to you. Sure, people try to answer your questions. But half the time you don't even know what questions to ask.

The Guerrilla Guide to Mastering Student Loan Debt is here to help you change all that. This book contains everything you need to know in order to take power over your own student loan decisions.

It's designed so you can read as much, or as little, as you want. If you already know the basics about your loan, you can skip to the fine points. But if you're a beginner, you won't be confused because everything is explained, from the bottom up. You can find a quick fact about your student loan so you can handle a problem or get ready for an important conversation. Or you can get the big picture about your loan and your money as a whole, so you can start planning a financial future where you're the boss.

It's your book, your loan, your life. Do it your way.

PART 1

Opening Statements

CHAPTER 1

Why I Wrote This Book for You

On a gorgeous June day in 1990, I put on a pair of red shoes and went out to experience the dream of my lifetime. That morning, in a sea of students in purple caps and gowns, I stood and received my Master of Fine Arts degree from New York University's Graduate Film School.

Around me, in a wordless little knot, stood my classmates—my friends. We'd shared a five-year struggle that had shown us the best in ourselves. At that moment, we were connected by an inexpressible bond of love and pride. We were also connected by another bond that still joins us today: overwhelming student loan debt.

My classmates and I gave everything we had in order to pursue our dream. Actually, we gave a lot more than we had. To get through the program, most of us took out roughly $40,000 in student loans.

We knew the money would be tough to pay back. During the next few years, we began to learn how tough. We didn't realize that, counting interest charges, our loans would cost closer to $60,000—and then only if we could pay up within ten years. Some of us had to stretch our repayment schedules far into the future. With all that extra interest, paying off our $40,000 loans will probably cost $100,000 and more.

Compared to some of you in college now, we got off easy.

Believe me, I don't regret my education. My classmates and I are doing fine. We're working on our careers, making progress. Life is good. But it's also not how we thought it would be. Back when we were accepted to graduate school, we told ourselves we'd never really have to worry about repaying our student loans. We figured that with enough determination, we could outrun them. We'd put that education to work and start making big money before the loans really, really came due. That's what we hoped, but none of us managed it.

Does this sound discouraging? It's not meant to. The point is, we didn't know what to expect from our loans, and it made our journey tough. I wrote this book to help make your journey easier. Whether you're applying, in school, graduating, or years into repayment, you're not alone. There are more than 7 million of us student debtors now, and our numbers are growing all the time. By yourself, you might feel all this loan stuff is a little overwhelming. But you're not by yourself. You're a member of one of the biggest clubs in America.

You and I are America's student loan customers. The system is meant to serve us. But we need to keep a definite eye on things, because budgetary times in America are hard, and frankly, our access to affordable financial aid is dangerously close to drifting away.

I know you may have avoided learning very much about your loan. Maybe you're scared, or maybe you've decided all that financial stuff was too complicated. Big mistake. This is your life we're talking about. It's your future, and it's worth getting involved in. Don't be afraid to look, okay? You're going to be all right.

LET'S TALK NUMBERS

Most of us don't think it's polite to talk about our student loans. It's time we got over that, because we've got a major situation here. Looming student loan debts, sometimes shockingly large, are a fact of life for almost all students who earned an advanced university degree in the past ten years. For many of us, new cars, new homes, even new clothes are out of the question, now or ten years from now.

The problems may be much worse for our younger brothers and sisters. Student loans have increased like wildfire during the nineties. To get an idea what we're talking about, look at the numbers gathered by The Education Resources Institute (TERI), the nation's largest private student loan supplier, which in 1995 partnered with Washington's Institute for Higher Education Policy to publish a controversial report entitled *College Debt and the American Family.* "In the 1990s, American college students have borrowed as much as the amount borrowed in the 1960s, 1970s, and 1980s combined," reads the report. "This explosion in borrowing means that college students have borrowed over $100 billion in just six fiscal years. Even more astounding is that the majority of that increase took place in 1993 and 1994, when borrowing increased a total of 57% from 1992."

Let's hear that again. *Since 1990, we've borrowed more than $100 billion.* And the cost of education goes right on climbing.

That's got everybody scared. During the past five years literally hundreds of newspaper and magazine stories have warned us that ever-higher borrowing to pay for ever-more-expensive schooling is a trend that could cripple American buying power and threaten our economy into the next century.

"We are burdening lower-income families and students with loans," says TERI's chief executive officer, Ernest T. Freeman. "Maybe the students will be able to repay that loan and better their lifestyle, but maybe not."

A few more numbers from TERI's report: Our borrowing is increasing nearly three times faster than college costs, and four times faster than America's personal incomes. "At what point does the willingness to sacrifice get overtaken by the crushing reality of debt loads that inhibit other economic activities?" asks the TERI report. "This point may come sooner than we think." Sadly, our parents are a major part of this picture. Instead of looking toward their own retirement, our mothers and fathers are often borrowing for our educations, at an average of almost $4,000 per year back in 1993.

Former U.S. Rep. William Ford, for whom the Federal Direct Loan Program is named, has described the situation best: "We have created a new indentured class in the United States—the student debtor."

A GENERATION IN DEBT: OUR STUDENT LOANS JOIN US TOGETHER

In the dictionary, "indentured" means "bound into service"—and many of us are bound into a life of servicing our student loans, sometimes before we know it. We're predicted to owe $146.8 billion in outstanding student loans by the year 1999. With debts that size, we make a great target for preachy politicians of all stripes. For one thing, we student debtors rarely talk back. We're too young, too naive, and too overwhelmed.

"When legislators hear students can't make their payments, they just jump on this punishment thing, like, 'Let's punish the default-ers,'" says Kevin Boyer, executive director of the National Association of Graduate and Professional Students, a grassroots stu-dent group that uses an ingenious network of volunteers via the Internet to oppose education cutbacks in Washington.

What's shocking is that neither those antidefault legislators nor anybody else has a clue how much debt young Americans are really facing. Studies have been done, but as of this writing no truly current or accurate numbers exist.

How Much Do We Really Owe?

"There's been no study that gives a total picture," says economist and higher-education policy analyst Fred Galloway. "There've been studies asking about the level of student debt," he says, "but there's no current study that fully addresses the level of total debt, adding in credit cards, auto loans, and so on."

Diane L. Saunders agrees. As vice president for public affairs at Nellie Mae (the New England Education Loan Marketing Corporation), a major national handler of student loans, Saunders is spearheading a new study that for the first time will give Americans a clear look at total student indebtedness. But she's distressingly aware that many Americans, even in the financial aid business, still don't feel debt is that serious an issue for today's students. "Postponing an acknowledgment that we need to address the student loan debt issue is almost like trying to put off paying our tax returns," she says. "It's painful but inevitable, so why not pay up early?" Like Galloway, Saunders believes that student debt burden may be larger than past studies have shown: "There's also currently no definitive measure of the impact of private loan debt, which is now a significant percentage of graduate student debt."

In researching this book, I spoke to expert after expert who repeated the same mantra: "College debt is not out of control. Most students borrow about $11,000, and they can handle that." But a quick look through the numbers suggests that things aren't quite that rosy. "Average debt may be $11,000, but that's in the mid- to low-cost areas of the country," says Saunders. "That's not the case on the East Coast. No big national studies have been done that show exactly what students are facing today."

Grad Versus Undergrad

Another thing: that $11,000 figure is for undergraduate students. For many of us graduate and professional students, $11,000 is lunch money. Amazingly, no studies had attempted to gather the facts on graduate/professional indebtedness until TERI and The Institute for Higher Education Policy partnered once again to produce 1996's *Graduating Into Debt*. As with *College Debt and the American Family*, the numbers, though limited in scope, are arresting.

According to the report, two million of us pursue graduate or professional study every year, and our debt levels are scary. "In 1995, one million graduate and professional students borrowed $7.7 billion," notes the report. Our borrowing had increased 74 percent just since 1993.

How much are we borrowing as individuals? In 1995 our average loan was about $7,700 a year. Not so bad, until you start doing addition. At that rate, a two-year master's program would be about $15,600; a three-year Ph.D., $23,000. Add that to $20,000 of debt from undergraduate school, and you're looking at $43,000 of debt— a major life commitment.

We should know how to stop this, but we don't. The truth is, America's student loan crisis has exploded too suddenly. Students, parents, educators, and legislators, we're all unprepared. As the system hurtles toward critical mass, we students who are caught in the borrowing spiral have had to face a sobering truth. Nobody's really driving this bus. Nobody's in control. If we want answers, we've got to find our own.

As a reporter, I've found it natural to ask questions about my student loans, to get aggressive, to insist on hearing answers that made sense to me. But most of us aren't reporters; we do other things for a living. We've found that dealing with a student loan too often means groping through an overwhelming, endless maze of confusion. Phone lines are busy. Officials contradict each other. Errors go uncorrected. Outdated information goes unchanged. Helpful information goes unreported. Ask anybody who owes: our student loan system is an overcomplicated, ill-defined mess.

The Guerrilla Guide to Mastering Student Loan Debt is here to help you deal calmly and creatively with your own individual pay-back situation as you chart your financial future in the age of debt. Not everything in these pages is warm and fuzzy. That wouldn't be fair to you, because it wouldn't be truthful. But if you want to hear any lectures, any shame-on-yous, you'll have to read some other book. I'm on your side.

I've founded this book on a truth any businessperson can tell you: in this life, you don't get what you deserve; you get what you negotiate. It's critical that America's students learn to negotiate for our interests around student loans, both as individuals and as a national voting bloc. The deal we're getting leaves much to be desired, and the deal's getting worse.

"Regarding higher education, America stands at a crossroads," notes a 1994 story in *USA Today*. "In terms of preparing young people for a productive place in society, a college education is more crucial than ever before. Yet access to that same education is becoming steadily more difficult. For many students, it is drifting out of reach."

Will Your Education Guarantee You a Job?

In the brutal marketplace of the nineties, a degree is just the price of admission. It doesn't guarantee us job security or, for that matter, a job. Still, college expenses keep on climbing. According to the College Board, average 1995–96 undergraduate tuition plus expenses for resident students at private colleges is $20,361; for public universities, $9,649. Multiplied by four years, those figures rise to $81,444 and $38,596. And that's before graduate school.

The numbers keep climbing because colleges are floundering.

Traditional money pools have dried up. Strapped state legislatures have cut education subsidies. Grants for needy students are a fraction of what they were. Alumni giving is way down.

To fill the gap, nearly half of America's students now have to borrow money to attend school. With expanded eligibility granted by reauthorization of the Higher Education Act in 1992, the sums of money have shot up. In 1995–96, the pool of aid available to students grew to $50.3 billion. Of that total, $37 billion was awarded by the federal government, and three-quarters of the $37 billion was in loans. Subsidized student loans, on which the government pays interest while we're in school, still require us to prove financial need. But anybody can get an unsubsidized student loan, regardless of need, up to an amazing $138,500 for undergraduate and graduate school combined.

Some of us find that's not enough. If all else fails, our parents can borrow any amount, up to the whole cost of our educations. More and more students use their student loans for tuition and fees, and credit cards for living expenses—a phenomenon that neither government nor the private sector has yet found a way to measure.

Your Loan Means Big Profit for Big Business

This borrowed money has become a given; it's the grease that runs our higher education system. It also greases a billion-dollar financial industry that runs on us. Does this reflect some evil master plan? No. But the student-lending industry is a big, powerful business, not a charity. It's grown enormous exactly like the student-loan crisis: one step at a time.

Unfortunately, most of us student borrowers have stayed absolutely clueless about our loans and our lenders. We don't seem to realize any of what's going on. Ill-informed student borrowers are a chronic and frustrating fact of life for lenders in the education business. "I wish a book about loans would be required reading for every student," says Josh Dare, corporate communications officer of leading student loan marketing corporation Sallie Mae. "Lenders have assumed in the past that students were as well informed about borrowing as, say, somebody who was shopping for a home mortgage. That has turned out to be anything but true."

Time after time, lenders have told me the same story. They get on the phone with a young student borrower, and the kid says, "You mean I have to pay this back?" Hearing that, you can't blame loan professionals for being peeved. If we can manage to ignore the fact that our loans have to be repaid, we're in intense denial: we're literally imagining our loans as we want them to be, not as they are. But that's how scared we get over this stuff.

We student borrowers are in a uniquely vulnerable position. With our college careers just beginning and repayment years away, many of us have signed on the dotted line without really believing we were putting ourselves in jeopardy. But this doesn't mean we're irresponsible. Realistically, what else could we do? By definition, a student loan is a gamble: you have to sign without knowing your ability to pay. Certainly, in America, we're constantly told we mustn't be quitters. Turn down college because you wouldn't sign for a loan? What a loser!

The fact is, all of us—students and parents—feel enormous pressure to take the college plunge, no matter how expensive. So it's really not surprising that we don't ask for details about our loans. When you've already decided to go ahead, what do the details matter?

But more and more, the details do matter. In the nineties, we're facing a world of higher costs and more severely reduced expectations than our parents may realize. Americans have always believed that borrowing for an education is an investment that will pay for itself. Sadly, that equation may never add up again. According to the College Board, real salaries of recent college graduates actually fell by 2.6 percent between 1987 and 1991. You think every doctor still gets rich? Not anymore. True, during the past thirteen years medical students' first-year income has increased by 68 percent. But their debt on graduation has increased 248 percent. So how does that affect you? Ten years from now, you may look in vain for a family practitioner. G.P.s don't make enough money to pay back an $80,000 student loan.

Giving You the Facts You Need

In working on this project, I've tried to write exactly the book I would have wished for at graduation—or better yet, before going to graduate school at all. I'll give you all the facts about your loan, good, bad, and ugly—including the ones your lender doesn't want you to know.

I'll give you everything you need to start negotiating intelligently for yourself, with an understanding of your total debt picture, not just your student loan. I'll show you how to handle the aches and pains of repaying your student loan, including how to apply for deferments and forbearances. I'll share the facts on the "worst that can happen" stuff, like delinquency and default. In case you're drowning, I'll explain the basics of bankruptcy.

If you're caught between credit card and student loan debt (who isn't?), there's a section on handling credit, shopping for cheap credit, and—the big pain—cleaning up your credit report if it contains debris from your student loan. I'll also pass along ideas on how to cope if your monthly bills, student loan included, seem overwhelming.

Finally—and this may be most important of all—I've written you the clear, simple, and easy-to-understand story of how student loans got to be such an enormous part of all our lives. This is a story of politics, sometimes backdoor politics. You *must* understand it if you want to protect your own future, because what the politicians say decides how—and how much—we pay.

Why the Experts Can't Agree on the Best Loan for You

If student loans don't make sense to you, you probably think it's your fault. Not true. Student loans just don't make sense. By now I've put your questions—our questions—to a number of the people who really decide how we and our loans are treated. You know what? Often they're not talking to each other. Sometimes they despise each other. At best they're rivals who tend to push their own point of view and warn against the other guy's. What's so funny is that these ethical, estimable, and often brilliant people are not being dishonest. There really are no hard facts about student loans. Are there too many loans? Too few? Are they here to stay? Should you get one? Countless theories flying around Washington about our future are equally believable. No matter how violently they disagree politically or philosophically, everybody has great statistics to back them up.

In an odd way, that's good for us. The bad news is: our futures are linked to a system that's in chaos. The good news is: where there's chaos, we may manage to get in there and make things better for ourselves.

With that in mind, please don't swallow this book whole. First, the issue of student loans is immensely complicated, and it's evolving all the time. So some of the details you see here may already have changed (perhaps in your favor!). Second, this book reflects my opinions. I've tried to be fair to everybody's point of view, but if you violently disagree with me, you'll have plenty of good company. I hope you'll treat these pages as background material that will prepare you to ask tough questions of your own.

Of course, none of this information will erase your student loan debt. No matter what this book or any other advises, the fact remains that paying back a big student loan—or dodging it, for that matter—is tough. Realistically, a lot of us are going to have to live on less. But when you think about it, why should that be so terrifying? For my classmates and me, the secret of living with a big student loan has turned out to be simple: get the facts, including the worst that can happen. Make the best move you can. Let it go. Whatever happens, you'll live through it.

In that spirit, I offer you *The Guerrilla Guide to Mastering Student Loan Debt*. I hope it eases your way.

CHAPTER 2

Before You Sign on the Dotted Line

"What's wrong, honey?" says Nicki's mom. "You should be excited. You've been looking forward to college for years!" Sitting at the dinner table, Nicki is eyeing something frightening—her school's financial aid award letter.

"Yeah, *college,*" Nicki replies. "But I wasn't looking forward to this *loan.* I'm too young to be in debt, and this is a lot of money!"

"Well, you're growing up now," says Dad, laying a protective hand on Nicki's shoulder. "And learning how to manage your money is an important part of life as an adult."

Hi there. You're joining us in progress. We're watching the entrance counseling video for the U.S. Department of Education's Direct Lending program. You won't find this program on cable. It's playing in your new college's financial aid office. Why are you sitting here? You're required by law to watch this video, because you've just signed your name to a binding legal document: the promissory note for your federal direct student loan. The video is supposed to stand between you and unreasonable student loan debt.

Direct Lending is not the only loan program that has a video. So do companies like Sallie Mae, Nellie Mae, USA Funds, PHEAA, ASA, CHELA, and lots of others that buy and sell federally guaranteed student loans—companies you now know nothing about, but will soon discover. In fact, thousands of financial institutions big and small have student loans to offer you. Like college recruiting materials in general, student loan advertisements tend to sound inspirational. Just take a few simple precautions, you're told, and the dream of college can be yours.

Unfortunately, the truth about student loans is a bit more complicated than that.

In Direct Lending's video, Nicki's mom calms her daughter's fears by explaining the "basics" of successful student borrowing:

Plan ahead.
Don't borrow more than you need.
Make a budget and stick to it.

"I stuck to my budget," says Mom. "It's not that hard once you get into the habit."

For Nicki, that speech is all it takes. Next time we see her, she's in a cap and gown, waving madly to the camera. Her proud (and thrifty) mom is at her side. The whole thing's over in two minutes flat.

To be fair, Direct Lending's video mentions that when you graduate, you'll be hit with several big new expenses, not just your student loan payment. And though it doesn't try to talk you out of signing, why should it? It's designed for people who've already decided to borrow.

Still, Nicki's story offers more insight than it means to. If we watch objectively, what it really shows us is a young person being talked out of her own instincts as every well-meaning adult around her helps to lower her down into an ocean of student-loan debt.

Nicki, wherever you are, girlfriend, you *are* too young to be in debt, and it *is* a lot of money. Maybe your education turned out to be worth it. But you were right to be concerned.

There's one more thing the video doesn't cover. Wherever she is, Nicki's still paying. If she borrowed enough money, as the story says, to attend a four-year private college, Nicki will probably be paying for another twenty years, long after that snapshot of her in cap and gown has settled into a cardboard box in the back of the closet.

YOU DESERVE TO KNOW THE SCORE

Before we go any further, let me reassure you: I'm not going to try to scare you out of going to college. Believe me, I'm on your side. I wouldn't trade my education for anything. Still, when I signed my loans, I had no idea what to expect, and part of the reason is that nobody really told me. They mentioned facts, but that's not the same as telling the truth.

I didn't know how to judge whether I was spending too much or what I was getting in return. Experience has given me some answers to those questions, at least for myself. In writing this book, I want to share what I've learned with you.

Even in the age of big student loans, college can be the greatest investment you ever make. But since you're paying your way with debt, you need to choose carefully what you're going to spend the money on.

You deserve to hear the facts about student loans from a graduate who learned the ropes through experience. I want you to have a realistic picture of your situation. Not a discouraging picture, just realistic. I want you to go for a goal you can accomplish, and even more important, one that really pleases you. To do that, you have to be smart enough to separate the truth about college from the hype.

The American Dream, College, and You

You and I live in a country that's practically founded on the idea of doing the impossible. We have a term for it: the American Dream. You can shoot hoops right out of the inner city and into the NBA. You can rise from poverty and take command of a corporation. You can practice vogueing in an alley and wind up a supermodel.

There are probably seven people in America's history who have actually managed miracles like this, but we hear their stories so often that we think we'll rise just like them, if only we work hard enough. This is where student loans for college can be dangerous to your health.

It's tempting to think that a blue-chip degree will rocket you into that high life you see on TV. It's true, the right degree will help, but probably not in all the ways you think. If you borrow your way into an exclusive college, you'll cross paths with other young people who will grow up to be influential, in one field or another. But that doesn't mean you'll automatically be swept along with them. Your degree won't guarantee a thing in your quest to climb America's ladder of success. If you borrow too heavily to pay for it, it may actually slow you down later on.

The celebrities we read about and see on TV may have gone to good schools, but that's not what got them where they are. People climb in America when they have something juicy to sell, whether it's unusual knowledge, talent, or beauty. They also need one other quality: fiery, ulcer-causing ambition. This level of ambition is not something you should necessarily wish for. It's not pretty; it won't make you happy; and it has nothing to do with college.

If you're dreaming that college will change you into someone different, stop. You'll have lots of great adventures there, and you'll learn lots of wonderful things. But you'll still be you. If you weren't a ruthless tycoon before college, you won't be one afterward, either—and thank heaven. The world needs you, just the way you are.

I wrote this book to help you get real with yourself about college, student loans, and your future. Most of us who've been through the experience of college on loans don't talk about it, and that leaves you just where we were when we started: clueless.

Here's some real advice, from the other side of the diploma. Don't take out thousands of dollars' worth of loans to study something you're not sure you love. Don't sign those papers without knowing you'll get something you value in return. And if you want to take the college plunge, don't do it for anybody else. Do it for you.

Dream On: College Hype Can Backfire

The American Dream makes it especially lonely deciding where you'll go to college and how much you'll borrow to get there, partly because your parents very likely experience you as part of their American Dream. Where you go to college is a status symbol for them too, and if you want a particular school, they'll probably try to help you get there. But depending on how much that school costs, there may not be much they can do, except encourage you to sign student loans.

And they will. When it comes to college, everybody gets hypnotized all at once. The videos, the catalogs, the guidebooks, the recruiters, even your friends say the same things: Get out there; You can do it; Take your shot; Go for the gold. Those slogans are great, but they're empty. The danger is, when they fall through, you may feel it's your fault.

If you want to be happy out in the world, it's better to cultivate a philosophy that allows you to have slow days, low days, and bad hair days. It's very hard to do that if you're so overloaded with college debt that you must excel, every day and every moment.

In the Direct Lending video, all Nicki needed to hear were those three short sound bites of advice. Remember?

Plan ahead.
Don't borrow more than you need.
Make a budget and stick to it.

Those ideas are great as far as they go, but they certainly won't take you through just any college you choose. If your loan is large enough, you'll never pay it just by making a budget and sticking to it. Instead, you'll feel like an idiot as you watch the bills roll in. You'll be thinking, Why didn't I see this coming?

In this chapter, I'll show you some real numbers, not to scare you, but to help you understand the reality of your situation. When you know the score, you feel stronger, smarter, and more at peace with yourself. You also have a much better chance to get out of college what you really want, for you.

And here's a really radical thought: if you're not ready to go to college right now—don't.

HOW MUCH WILL COLLEGE COST, REALLY?

How much money is too much to borrow for college? Experts disagree. As you'll see throughout this book, both lenders and government suffer from a surprising lack of information about how we borrowers really manage during the years after we start paying our loans. Most of us don't default. But how much effort that costs us, how it gets in the way of our buying other things like cars and houses, nobody really knows. Frankly, until now, few people have asked.

Nobody knows how to make college cost any less. It's hard for us to face that, because we prize education so much. Politicians make noises about how the price of education must come down, but costs keep right on rising, and we keep paying.

We all agree on one thing, though: when you look at your loans in total, that number doesn't give you the real feeling of what you owe. In order to understand what you're really considering, it helps to look at your loans by breaking them down into monthly payments. Then, as the chart shows (see below), you can get a sense of how much money you'll need to make if you want to pay your loans off comfortably.

Most estimates I've encountered place the average college debt at close to $11,000. (Remember, this is undergraduate school. If you're looking at graduate school, the debt potential rises sharply.) According to a study done by USA Group Loan Services/USA Group, you'll be comfortable if you can keep your student loan payments at or below 8 percent of your monthly income. Here's an example: if you borrowed what they list as the average amount, $10,146, your monthly payment would be about $123. That's definitely manageable. You have to make more than $18,500 a year to keep it under 8 percent of your monthly income, but you can probably do that.

But let's skip down to $25,000 of debt, which many undergraduates face, and which graduates and professional students very likely face. There, in order to meet your $306.63 monthly payment as 8 percent of your income on a ten-year schedule, you'd have to make $46,050 a year. That's much higher than the starting salary for most professions.

You can see that in a lot of cases, we really have just one practical option. We can consolidate our loans, which means we'll now be paying for up to thirty years instead of ten. It also means that because of added interest, the loan is thousands of dollars bigger than we started out with. Our payments will still be in the $200 range, high enough to be an irritation, if not a major pain. And now we'll have them every month, for most of our lives.

What does it really mean, $200 a month? Try thinking of it this way. A typical car payment is $200 to $300 a month. If our salary is in the $30,000 range, that's about how much extra money most of us can afford to spend after we finish paying our other bills, and I don't mean $200 worth of credit card bills every month.

If you're paying your bills and going out on the weekends, and you're also paying $200 a month on your student loan, can you also buy a car? Here's the answer: you can't.

If you buy the car and put off the loan, the loan gets bigger. If you pay the loan and don't buy the car, you're riding the bus, or continuing to ask your parents for money. None of this is tragedy, granted. We're not talking about life-threatening problems. But it's a real situation to live with. It's an everyday presence in your life, and even if it's over in ten years, ten years is a long time. If you're a high school senior now, ten years ago you were in the second grade.

If you're getting a sense what it's like to owe $25,000, picture the situation for those of us who owe a lot more. The chart will give you an idea.

Monthly Payments and the Income They Require

Loan Size	10 yr. monthly payment	Consol. monthly payment	Income for 8% payment (10 yr.)	Income for 8% payment (consol.)
$15,000	$183.98	$145.52	$27,600	$21,900
$20,000	$245.31	$170.41	$36,750	$25,500
$25,000	$306.63	$213.02	$46,050	$31,950
$30,000	$367.96	$255.62	$55,200	$38,400
$35,000	$429.28	$298.22	$64,350	$44,700
$40,000	$490.61	$315.38	$75,650	$47,400
$45,000	$551.94	$354.80	$82,800	$53,250
$50,000	$613.26	$394.23	$91,950	$59,100
$60,000	$735.92	$450.76	$110,400	$67,650
$70,000	$858.57	$525.89	$128,850	$78,900
$80,000	$981.22	$601.01	$147,150	$90,150
$90,000	$1,103.87	$676.14	$165,600	$101,400
$100,000	$1,226.53	$751.27	$184,050	$112,650

Consolidated loan terms: up to 30 years.

Numbers rounded off to the nearest dollar.

(*Source:* Monthly loan payments from Sallie Mae's website)

Don't be horrified. You don't owe anything yet. What I want you to see is that—unless you are entering an unusually high-paying profession—if you borrow more than roughly $20,000, you will have a debt burden that's uncomfortable.

"But I'll just work harder and make better money," you say. I wish it were that easy. But the truth is, unless you're in one of a few select professions, you won't make that kind of money in the first few years after school. Depending on what you're studying, you may not make that much money ever.

You may be the exception to the rule, and that would be great. But let's start by looking at how it is for people who are right in the middle. According to the U.S. Census Bureau, these were our median incomes in 1995. ("Median" means right in the middle; half the people are above this mark, half are below.)

Americans' Median Income for 1995

Age	Number of people (thousands)	Income ($)	Standard Error ($)
Under 65 years	78,974	$24,470	$183
15 to 24 years	13,802	$6,913	$137
25 to 34 years	19,617	$23,609	$260
35 to 44 years	20,773	$31,420	$216
45 to 54 years	14,920	$35,586	$345
55 to 64 years	9,863	$28,980	$561
65 years and over	13,092	$16,484	$195
65 to 74 years	8,131	$18,347	$278
75 years and over	4,960	$14,160	$242

Occupation	Number of people	Income ($)	Standard Error ($)
Executive, adminis- trative, and managerial	8,013	$26,787	$288
Professional specialty	10,487	$27,234	$289
Technical and related support	2,515	$21,968	$343
Sales	9,056	$9,571	$242

Administrative support, including clerical	15,813	$16,292	$148
Precision production, craft, and repair	1,288	$16,792	$471
Machine operators, assemblers, and inspectors	3,573	$12,361	$267
Transportation and material moving	549	$12,787	$1,060
Handlers, equipment cleaners, helpers, and laborers	1,123	$9,686	$677
Service workers	12,294	$7,483	$153
Private households	1,007	$4,062	$434
Farming, forestry, and fishing	789	$5,015	$639

Educational Attainment	Number of people (thousands)	Income ($)	Standard Error ($)
Less than 9th grade	6,020	$7,096	$88
9th to 12th grade (no diploma)	8,122	$8,057	$160
High school graduate (includes equivalency)	28,785	$12,046	$116
Some college, no degree	14,619	$15,552	$224
Associate degree	6,642	$19,450	$426
Bachelor's degree	12,875	$24,065	$372
Master's degree	4,205	$33,509	$721
Professional degree	732	$38,588	$1,834
Doctorate degree	457	$39,821	$2,096

(*Source*: Statistics from U.S. Census Bureau)

Okay, just compare the charts we've got so far. They really show what you're up against. First of all, it's obvious that if you want a better income, you need a better degree. Even a bachelor's degree won't guarantee you more than a very modest standard of living. But now take a look at the income you're supposed to have in order to comfortably pay off your student loan versus the income you're likely to make if you do as well as most of us. They don't compute, do they? That's what nobody's telling you.

Do you know why nobody's telling you? It's illegal for providers to discourage you from taking out a student loan. Because student loans are an entitlement—by law, you must be given one if you apply—trying to wave you away would be interfering with your freedom. That's great, and neither you nor I would have it any other way. But on a practical level, it just reinforces the fact that from this moment on, you're on your own. When you borrow a student loan, it's not your parents' debt. This one is all yours.

Here's the truth about paying for your education with student loans. It's not easy. It's a big deal. If you borrowed more than, say, $30,000, you'll probably still be writing those checks (and wishing you could spend the money on something else) when you're the age your parents are now. So before you sign on the dotted line, let's go over your situation to make sure you're getting the deal you want.

WHO AM I, AND WHAT DO I WANT TO STUDY?

When I interviewed the film director Barry Sonnenfeld a few years ago, he joked about getting his bachelor's degree. "My parents sent me off to college," he said. "I had no idea what I wanted to do with my life. It was the world's most expensive sleepaway camp."

Up until the last few years, "sleepaway camp" was a pretty good definition of lots of college curricula. You went in order to "broaden your horizons," and that was fine. You didn't have to have a specific goal in mind. But college in the age of loans is exactly the opposite. Because it locks you into a major financial obligation, going to college on loans can actually narrow your options, not broaden them. So making the college decision is starting to be more like deciding to have a baby. Going ahead will mean real rough spots in your future, and unless you really wanted that degree, you're going to be one resentful graduate.

With that in mind, you need to think before choosing what you'll study in college, and where you'll apply. Doing this research can actually be fun. It'll show you some great things about yourself, and you may realize you've got strengths you weren't at all aware of. But remember: no cheating! What's important here is to be flat-out honest. Don't say what you think someone else would like to hear. This is your life, and you need to be true to yourself.

You've got an idea what you want to study? Great. Before you commit to a decision, ask yourself these questions.

1: Have I actually done this before? If you're paying for your training with a loan, this is no time to investigate something you've never tried. You need to invest in a skill that offers you a good chance to recoup your investment. If you want to try acting, for instance, great. But as things stand right now, it's dumb to enter college as a drama major just to see how you like it. You can take an acting class in your community for a fraction of the money. Only if you're sure that acting is how you want to make your living should you invest in it at the college level. (Even then, we'd have to have a stern talk.)

2: Am I really good at it? I wish it were otherwise, but enrolling in college on loans is no time for wishful thinking. Don't decide to major in architecture just because you think architects are cool. If you can't draw and can't count and can't put puzzles together, your talents lie elsewhere. You'll find it much harder to admit this after you've spent a couple of years paying for coursework you turned out to have no ability for and therefore never got to use. Instead, you may start to feel ashamed of yourself, like you should have known better. Not worth the hassle.

3: Do I really like it? This is the most important question so far. In the world of college on loans, getting your degree is just one more signpost in your effort to join your profession. After you graduate, you'll have to keep plugging, and some of the financial rewards you may have been dreaming of will go back toward paying your loan. So what's your reward? Doing the work you love.

"How do I know what I love?" I can hear you asking. "I'm too young!" Okay, but in your heart, you also know more than you think. Let's say you did great in math on your SAT, and your school career counselor says you have a shot at becoming a college math professor. Terrific. Now how do you decide whether that's a good idea for you? Granted, you've never been a math professor. But you can talk to a math professor, whether on your town's college campus or in a city nearby. You can ask that person what's really involved in his or her job, day to day. What are the rotten parts, as well as the fun parts? What are the skills they need to get by? What did they do to prepare when they were your age? And (don't forget this part) how much money do they make?

If you can talk to more than one math professor and compare their answers, so much the better. In comparing them, you're looking for the personality traits that made them right for their jobs—traits you may or may not share.

"I couldn't just go up to some strange professor and start asking personal questions!" you're protesting. No, and you won't. Instead, you pick the school, get the phone number, call for the address, get the correct spelling of the professor's name and his or her correct title, and write a courteous letter. It'll go like this:

Dear Dr. X:

I'm a high school senior who's interested in pursuing a career as a teacher of mathematics at the university level. My academic record suggests that I'd do well, but I don't feel I have enough facts about the business of teaching to make an informed choice. Could you spare half an hour to speak with me and give me a few descriptions about how your job actually works? I know you give classroom lectures, but I also know there's more to it than that. For example, how much time do you spend outside class grading papers? Do you continue to do research of your own? Do you get a three-month vacation in the summertime, or do you teach year-round? Would you be willing to tell me some of the drawbacks of your work? Finally, could you give me some general information on how much income I might expect to make in your profession?

Because my college plans will involve student loans, I want to be sure that I'm starting out on a path that's appropriate for me. Since I know you're busy, I'd be happy to speak with you on the phone if you're not able to meet with me in person. Thank you in advance for any insights you can give. I'll give you a call next week to follow up.

Sincerely,
(You!)

Next—and this is the hard part—make the follow-up call. Really make contact. Don't chicken out. Afraid the person on the other of the phone will laugh at you? So what if he did? Would you explode? Doubtful.

On the other hand, it's unlikely that the other person will be unpleasant, or find your letter unwelcome. Why? The answer is a secret of human nature that will rarely fail you. If you ask somebody how he became the big success that he is, he'll almost always fall all over himself giving you the answer. It's a fact: when a little flattering attention comes our way, most of us jump to give up our secrets. If you ask people questions about their profession, they will almost certainly be glad to give you information.

But How Can I Tell Beforehand Whether I'd Like the Job?

Well, you can't. But you can get an idea about what you do like, if you'll do a simple assignment I call "The Autobiography of Me." Here's how it works. Take an afternoon to spend quietly by yourself, in your room or the library or wherever. Think about your life so far. Be honest! You're not trying to impress anybody. Next to every year you can remember, write down what you wanted at that age, what you did about it, and whether it worked for you. You wanted to be a rapper? Great. Were you good at it? Did you connect with the kids who were watching you? Did that happen more than once? If so, then you know you have the gift of connecting with an audience. That's a skill that would be all too welcome in a math professor.

But just being able to connect with an audience, and even being gifted at math, is not enough when you're buying your education with loans. If you're going to enjoy being a math professor enough to pay for the privilege every month for years, you'd better really love math. Do you? Here you should take a minute and think about. . . exactly what you don't think about. When you stand in the supermarket checkout line, do you absentmindedly total up your items? Do you find yourself speculating how many people would be left in the room if everybody wearing brown suddenly left? This kind of "meaningless" buzz, the stuff your mind does to amuse itself while you're just woolgathering, will tell you a tremendous amount about yourself. It's an indication of where your strengths and talents really lie.

If doing math really amuses you, if you really enjoy it, then paying for a math degree with loans will probably turn out to be a good investment for you. You may not get rich (or you may!), but you'll be relatively happy in your choice.

HOW DO I PICK MY SCHOOL?

In the nineties, the art of picking a college is all about leaving your assumptions behind. You've grown up thinking college is sort of a noble place, where distinguished people impart a little culture to unfinished types like you and me.

At this point, that's like believing in Santa Claus. College stopped being that noble refined place, if indeed it ever was, when money got tight almost twenty years ago. Now, under cover of its old, laid-back identity, college has become an entirely different sort of business than what we'd expect.

Here's how it goes now. When you look at a college recruiter, think: *car salesman*.

Why do I say that? Not to offend either academics or auto dealers, but to give you an accurate idea of what to expect as you and your parents consider colleges. The reality of the nineties is that colleges are faced with tougher competition than ever before, and—just like every other business in America—they've tried to respond to the problem by getting lean, mean, and maybe even a little more creative with their admissions strategies than we might like.

In fact, shopping for a college has become a lot like shopping for a car. You'll meet a friendly salesman (your recruiter, or financial aid officer). You'll get a test drive (a campus tour). And you'll be quoted a sticker price. We don't need an equivalent for that term, because college pros talk about their product just like a new car—the sticker price. Everybody knows, of course, that the first price of a new car is meant to be negotiated downward. You're supposed to haggle, and you definitely don't settle for the sticker price.

But did you have any idea college is the same way? Just as with a car, you should ask if the college can cut you a better deal. Don't be shy about this: You can bet the college's representatives are trying to make a profit as they deal with you. In fact, they may be using sophisticated technology to estimate the lowest offer you'll accept. As financial reporter Linda Stern writes in a February 1997 issue of *Newsweek*, schools are "flocking to companies like the USA Group Noel Levitz, which uses computer models to profile which students will come at which price." Armed with that information, client schools won't "waste money on applicants who'll come anyway: they'll aim bigger bucks at fence sitters who'll contribute to the school's geographic, ethnic, or religious mix."

Colleges Aim to Make Money

In competing more and more aggressively for students, colleges have borrowed more and more bottom-line techniques from the corporate world. The press has had a field day in the past few years, reporting on how schools have begun to do things like check up on your parents' finances to determine whether they really have the money to send you. You'd figure that would mean you'd get less aid, right? Not necessarily! During the past few years, some institutions have quietly offered better aid packages to students with more money, and charged higher prices to those with less. Why would a college do this? Just business, ma'am. If you don't need money, you won't stiff them for the tuition bill. In return, they figure, you deserve a price break. That's a courtesy to an investor, which is what you are.

College recruiters from less-sought-after schools might even telephone your home, just like those people who call to say you've been pre-accepted for ninety free days of life insurance coverage. Having pitched you on his campus, the recruiter would invite you to come have a look. Your grades? Not an issue. Your parents' net worth? Bull's-eye.

Even Ivy League universities have pulled off some very creative moves regarding the prices you're asked to pay, writes Erik Larson in a March 1997 issue of *Time*. For years, he reveals, Harvard, M.I.T., the University of Pennsylvania, Princeton, Brown, Columbia, Cornell, Dartmouth, and Yale "shared information about future tuition rates and fees, agreed never to grant aid solely on the basis of a student's academic merit, and met to negotiate how much need-based financial aid should be offered to individual students accepted by two or more of the member institutions."

This concerted action was supposed to ensure us fair access to the Ivy League, but it seems to have enriched its member universities instead. Writes Larson: "Ostensibly the goal of this 'Overlap Group,' dismantled in 1991 after a two-year federal antitrust investigation, was to equalize the amount of money a given student's family would be required to contribute and thus keep price from clouding the student's decision. In practice, by liberating schools from price competition, the arrangement may have allowed them to boost tuitions to artificially high levels and, thanks to imitation by others, drive up tuition throughout the country."

Faced with tactics like these, you have to get smart. And for the past several years, parents and students have been learning to fight back.

What *Newsweek*'s Stern calls the "never-take-the-first-offer" era has been underway for quite some time. Many families now enlist the services of a college planner or counselor to help them zero in on the best deal. And they've succeeded often enough that, as of 1997, "many schools claim a defensive stance: no negotiating with terrorist dads or moms," writes Stern. "But there's a loophole. Schools still adjust awards upward for 'new information' like higher SAT scores or medical costs that don't show up on aid forms."

In other words, if you want to try for a better financial aid package, you should ask for a re-examination and then work to come up with some worse financial circumstances than the ones you first reported.

LET'S MAKE A DEAL: NEGOTIATING FOR FINANCIAL AID

I don't mean to put you off college. After all, the fact that we had to haggle for a car may mean that we enjoy it all the more, once the price is right. All I'm saying is, don't forget to kick the tires. When you're talking to the academic types at a school you're considering, it's easy to get intimidated and let them control the conversation. You mustn't let that happen.

You're in a negotiation. Each of you has things you want, things you're willing to offer, and things you're holding out on. At the end of your exchange, the school will (or won't) accept you, and along with that acceptance will come your financial aid package.

What's a financial aid package? From the time you express your interest in attending a certain school, that school's admissions office will be mulling you over. If you're asking for financial aid (and at this point, more than half of us do), the school's going to be cooking up a special offer, just for you. It will contain some combination of three kinds of aid: federal work-study, scholarship or grant money, and, of course, student loans.

You know the guy in the flea market booth who has a separate price for everybody? ("This priceless diamond ring? For you, darling, twenty dollars!") That's exactly the process you're involved in now. What you're trying to do now is get a package that's good for you, and good for you means more grants and scholarships, versus fewer loans.

But what makes you a desirable student? As in every negotiation, you need to have an accurate idea what you've really got to offer, neither underestimating nor overestimating. You may well have one or more skills or characteristics certain colleges need. They can become strengths in your negotiating position. To assess all your assets and come up with a winning admissions strategy, you'll want to do a lot more than read this book. You'll want to seek out personal professional advice. But just to get your feet wet, here are a few qualities you might decide to stress when you first contact the school you're considering:

1: Your academic record. Here's the reason you were supposed to be studying all this time. If you made outstanding SAT scores or won a National Merit Scholarship, you'll probably do well in college and make them look good. Conversely—and this is important!—if you don't have good grades, you probably don't love school. And if you don't love school, why should you pay to suffer through four more years of it? A two-year community college might feel more comfortable. And if you had a big transformation, you could always transfer to a four-year university later on.

2: Your talents, and I know you have some. We always hear (perhaps incorrectly?) about nine-foot-tall high school basketball stars who get BMWs in return for signing on with the college team. But if you don't happen to be nine feet tall, other accomplishments can recommend you. If you backpacked through the wilderness on an Outward Bound trip, or volunteered to deliver meals to homebound AIDS patients, or participated in student leadership training programs, or you speak a foreign language fluently, those are all bargaining chips of one strength or another. Be sure the people assessing you know about this stuff.

3: Are you applying to a school that's looking for students like you? Different universities have different academic goals, and they tend to spend most freely on programs that support those goals. What makes a particular school see you as a more desirable freshman than somebody else? It could be your major, or the area of the country you're from, or your ethnic origin, explains Stern. If you bring something to their plan, they'll give you a better deal. In the excellent Kaplan *Newsweek* guide *How to Get into College*, one counselor suggests that you look up two rival colleges and apply to both. How do you tell which colleges are in competition? Look for two schools with similar student SAT scores, costs, and academic rankings.

Early Admissions: Yes or No?

How aggressive should you be in your search for the best price on your education? That depends on what you're after. Thanks to all that horse-trading you and your parents have been doing during the past few years, more and more colleges are behaving like airlines who guarantee you a certain ticket price—but only if you confirm your reservation right then and there. In college lingo, this is called *early admissions*, and it involves promises of commitment on both sides. The school pledges to save your seat in the freshman class, and to reserve you a certain amount of aid. In return, you promise not to go comparison shopping for better deals at other campuses.

You may not get the lowest price this way. On the other hand, you may not care. Many of us want the prestige of a degree from a particular university, and we're willing to do whatever it takes to get it. How many of us feel that way? You'd be surprised. In fact, as tuitions shot through the roof during the 1980s, educators discovered what they now call the "Chivas Regal" effect: rationally or not, we Americans tend to feel that the more an education costs, the better it is.

If that's the way you feel in your heart, then your money is well spent. Just know that you'll probably revisit your youthful decision many times as you're paying your debts in years to come.

Comparison Shopping

If you're prepared to be more flexible about where you purchase those initials at the end of your name, then you'll want to comparison shop, by negotiating with several colleges at once. As you've already gathered, this takes nerve. It also takes a certain degree of savvy. Rather than trying to absorb all the ins and outs of the financial aid game on your own, you'll want to consult with a financial counselor who's done all this before.

Here's a simplified version of how it works: You pursue the application process very aggressively with at least three schools. Your object, naturally, is to get three competing offers, three different financial aid packages. That way you can start to play one college off against the other in order to chip away at your entrance price. The outcome can make a big difference in your level of indebtedness later on.

If you were buying a car, you'd comparison shop at three sales lots, insist on hearing all the price information right out in the open, and give your business to the dealer who offered you the lowest price.

Treat university recruiters and financial aid officers exactly the same way. If they aren't used to being questioned about the business propositions they offer you, it's time they learned.

Keep that in mind as you open up your financial aid package. Don't get into that attitude of begging for acceptance. If this college doesn't want you enough to cut you a good admissions deal, maybe it's really not the right place for you.

How can you tell whether you could be getting a better deal? Well, look at the mix of financial aid they've suggested for you. If you're getting the maximum loan amount for a college freshman, go back and ask for a better deal, with more grants and fewer loans. In fact, no matter what the school's first offer is, see if they'll top it. You'll never know if you don't ask.

It really is a battle of wits and wills. You want minimal loans on your record. Meanwhile, the university needs the federal loan money that only your signature will bring in. Those are opposite needs. But there is no reason for you to just go along with the school's needs, at the expense of your own.

In case you feel too shy to fight, stop and think: where would you find a spare $300 this month to pay a bill that just couldn't wait? Now think about finding that same $300 every month for ten years. (If you've got, say, $25,000 in loans, that's what you'll face.)

This is no joke. You want to do anything and everything you can to come out of college with $10,000 worth of loans or less.

If you want to have a say in the price of your education, the best strategy of all is to have three acceptance letters in hand and then play the schools off against each other. Low bidder gets the honor and privilege of having you join in the festivities this fall.

You're the Buyer, So Beware

While you're sizing up your negotiating position, here's a word to the wise. Like any manufacturer of a pricey, premium product, the school you're considering may be sorely tempted to be less than forthcoming about every single expense you'll encounter once you get there. Especially if you live far away from the college you want, it's a great idea to do just what you did with your math professor a few pages ago: track down a couple of living, breathing students and ask them whether the actual program they found when they unpacked their bags on campus lived up to its advertisements in the catalog.

The people who write university catalogs can be unaware of hidden expenses students might face. And besides, it's their responsibility to make their product seem attractive, so that they can get bodies into those chairs. It's up to you to decide whether what they're offering really meets your needs. This may seem obvious to you, but in researching this book, I spoke to a number of students who later realized—to their regret—that they'd been too excited, or too intimidated, to ask point blank what they were getting for their money. This is *your* education, and it's you who'll pay the bills.

DESIGNING YOUR PERSONAL GAME PLAN

With all this tough talk, am I saying you're supposed to be indifferent to where you go to school? No. We all know better than that. But here, as in every stage of your negotiation, you have to keep bringing yourself back to reality. You have to know what you really want, and remember that there's always more than one way to get it.

If you want to be an elementary school teacher, you already know you won't be making $60,000 a year. So if you're planning on getting your degree in elementary education with $40,000 in loans at an Ivy League college, you're making a lousy financial deal. If it's what you really want to do—or if you have a trust fund—go for it. But if you really want your degree from that school, isn't there a less expensive way to get it? Absolutely. You can do your first two years at a much less expensive public or community college, and then transfer. Bingo. You just found a half-price-off sale.

"But what if they don't take me?" you're wailing. Okay, there's an element of risk. But if you do your footwork and you're a good student—and your community college is reputable—there's a very good chance your plan will work out. By doing your footwork, I mean: at the beginning of your sophomore year, you visit the college you want to transfer to. (Wear something you've ironed.) Make appointments with admissions and financial aid officers of your particular college. Ask for their personal guidance. What applications should you file? What should you be reading? How should you prepare? By taking actions like these, you begin to work yourself into the identity of the school you want to be part of. (It won't hurt to have fabulous grades from your community college, either.) As you follow the advice they give you, write and say you're doing what was asked of you. In taking those actions and reporting back, you're accomplishing several goals at once. You're showing you're dependable. You're proving you can express yourself on paper. And, maybe most important, you're becoming familiar. By the time your application is up for a slot in the junior class, you won't be a stranger anymore.

What you will be is a shopper who was smart enough to get a prestige degree for half the money everybody else paid—and half the debt load everybody else is carrying.

You Don't Have to Be Miss Brilliant or Mister Know-It-All

Look. Not all of us like school. Not all of us were meant to sit in a chair and listen to facts out of books all day. Thank heaven, too, because if we were all the same, life wouldn't be much fun, would it?

There's nothing wrong with not being the scholarly type, so please be honest with yourself. If you never liked school before, taking out a bunch of student loans certainly won't make you like it any better. One of the biggest and most painful mistakes you can make is to let other people talk you into getting more education than you want or need. If you're good with cars, and you know you want to own your own service station one day, you'll make more money than most of the rest of us combined. But you will never, ever need to know what's in *The Canterbury Tales*.

On the other hand, if you're already working and you're interested in a particular job skill to advance or even change your career, you don't necessarily need a four-year college curriculum to help you do that. Because the traditional four-year model is so expensive, the trend in America today is toward more specialized two-year programs that keep the topic to what you really want to know.

Do This Your Way, Not Somebody Else's

It's a funny thing. In the Age of Information, we know less about each other than we ever have. As we Americans become less and less bonded through personal contact, and more and more connected through the filters of TV and the Internet, we start to believe tales about each other that aren't necessarily true. One of those tales is that we can't be successful without a college education. True, at least some college seems to be the path for most of us. But not all.

Just ask Amy Dacyczyn of Leeds, Maine (that's pronounced "deci-sion," by the way). Dacyczyn edits an amazing newsletter called *The Tightwad Gazette*. She and her husband and family are leading lights in something called the Voluntary Simplicity movement. Instead of splattering out into the typical nineties craziness of two jobs, daycare, and beepers, Dacyczyn and people like her are living life another way, moving back to the old American adages: "Use it up, wear it out, make it do, do without." By practicing extreme thrift, the Dacyczyn family has managed to do what they want with their time, without having to go out into the marketplace every day. And in so doing, they're ironically joined the circle of celebrity most of us aspire to. They live in a pre-1900 New England farmhouse with barn attached. Their newsletter is nationally read. And Amy's 1995 book-length compilation of her collected newsletter articles, also called *The Tightwad Gazette,* landed her on *The New York Times* best-seller list.

As you might imagine, Dacyczyn has some interesting thoughts on our national mania for pounding ourselves into debt in order to go to college. She says, "We're taking eighteen-year-old kids, who know nothing about life, and promising them that if they take this huge debt on, they'll be healthier, happier, and make more money. I think the whole process is getting so expensive that everybody needs to rethink it; we can't assume that spending this much money on college will necessarily pay off in the long run. In my personal life I see a lot of people in their fifties still paying off their college debts. I feel sorry for some of them. They're just burned out and trapped."

For Dacyczyn, plotting your course in college is like planning anything else: you have to be honest about the cost to you versus the benefit. "I think you have to look at the cost and the time required—the time out of your life—and look to see whether you will in fact recover that cost by earning more money," Dacyczyn says. "If you're going to be an engineer, you'll probably do well. But at this point, we have situations where people are absorbing huge debts, $60,000 and more, and not really thinking whether there's actually going to be a payoff. We say people with a college education are more well-rounded, that college 'teaches you how to think'—like if you didn't go to college, you wouldn't be able to think. If I want to know about anything, I just go to the library and read up on it."

Dacyczyn figures it this way: "To spend big money for information that you will use in an indirect way doesn't really make sense to me. To me, spending money for college is a good idea when you're getting information that you will directly apply to better your life."

READ THIS BOOK BEFORE YOU SIGN THAT LOAN!

Whether or not you're a thrifty type yourself, Dacyczyn's words make sense. What you and I are facing is a world where old ideas like four years of college for everybody have started to break down. But nobody's quite admitted it yet. If you go blindly into an expensive education that you've paid for with debt—and that education doesn't turn out to be what you really wanted—you're going to feel ripped off for a long time.

Each time I contacted someone new in the field of student loans, I was surprised how much they wanted to get this message through to you. There's a lot of concern for you out there, more than you think. Unfortunately, I can't keep you from getting hurt in this big, expensive transaction. But if you'll read this book before you sign on the dotted line, at least you'll have the advice of the experts behind you.

In the pages to come, I'll introduce you to the real story on student loans—the good, the bad, and the ugly. I'm not going to tell you how to get a loan. Thousands of institutions already compete to do that. I want to help you make the right moves after you've got your loans, because that's where your challenge really begins.

   Later, we'll talk in detail about how to keep your individual loan on track. But before we get to your loan, you need to understand a little more about the student loan business in general. You think this billion-dollar industry runs just to help you pursue your dreams?

   Read on. It's time you got an education.

PART 2

How Did We Get Into All This Debt?

CHAPTER 3

The Setup: Who Makes Money on Your Student Loan?

The more you learn about America's student loan system, the wilder it gets. It's like a mystery you can't put down. Sure, it's a story of high hopes and sweet dreams. But it's also about power, big money, and, unfortunately, the occasional victim.

This chapter is designed to keep you off the victim list.

If you owe a large student loan debt—or if you're about to sign on the dotted line—you'd better understand both the student loan players and the game they're playing, because what you don't know can make you miserable for years to come.

"Yeah, whatever," you're saying. "Just tell me how I can lower my payments."

You probably can lower your payments. The question is, how? Right now, you get to choose from two repayment programs, each with different strengths and appeals.

Whatever repayment plan you're in, it has a lot of enemies in Washington, because these rival programs have spent a lot of time trying to wipe each other out. Why should you care? Because the outcome of this battle can help you—or hurt you. Student loan law has always been subject to revision: Washington has often changed your legal options while you weren't even paying attention. But you need to pay attention, starting now. Bitter rivalry at the top levels of government has turned student loans into an emotional, volatile issue with an uncertain future. Major change is coming, and if you want to protect the student loan deal you've got, you'd better learn to open your mouth and say so.

The price of your loan—yours, not somebody else's—is decided by people very much like you, except that they happen to be in Congress. Until you know how to interact with them, and all the other people who handle your loan, you can't look out for yourself. It's that simple.

There's also another huge reason to learn about loans. When you realize what's actually gone on in the loan business while you've been struggling to make your payments, you may go ballistic. Considering that higher education loans were designed to be a service to you, it's sad to learn how many abuses have been linked to the student loan business, and how often politics and profit have undermined the service you get.

In the next few pages, I'll show you the bones of the student loan crisis: why the system is such a mess, how it all started, what it means to you. But this book is just a place to start. I've encountered few leaders in government or the financial aid industry who agree on what's best for you and me. There's no reason you should settle for their opinions—or mine. I hope you'll read, think, and come up with opinions of your own.

THE RIVALS: FFELP VERSUS DIRECT LENDING

In Washington, there's a war going on between two systems of lending. On one side is the traditional student loan system: FFELP, the Federal Family Education Loan Program. In one form or another, it's been around, constantly growing, for three decades. Opposing FFELP is a much newer lending system called the William D. Ford Federal Direct Loan Program, informally called Direct Lending. Issuing its first loan in July 1994, Direct Lending is barely out of diapers.

In general, Republicans support FFELP. Partly because President Bill Clinton has identified himself strongly with its competitor, Direct Lending, Democrats have been more aligned with Direct

Lending as well. After a bitter and drawn-out battle to win exclusivity in 1993, Direct Lending and FFELP are currently both in operation. And since neither party could muster the votes to ditch one system or the other, both are now struggling for the right to change their current restrictions and compete head to head by offering borrowers exactly the same benefits.

If your loan is small, your choice between programs is not as important. As time goes on, Direct Lending and FFELP will probably resemble each other more and more. But if your loan is large, the differences between these two programs can make a big difference in your life. Direct Lending offers the first-ever *income-contingent repayment* plan: no matter how little money you're making, your loan payment is figured as a percentage of your income. If you're making next to nothing, that's what you pay. This protects you from being required to make loan payments you can't possibly afford.

That doesn't mean Income Contingent Repayment is a gift. It's your most expensive option in terms of interest, and if you can't pay at least your interest charge each month, you'll run into a nasty thing called negative amortization, which means your loan actually gets bigger. Still, as the law stands now, after twenty-five years, any money you haven't repaid is written off Direct Lending's books. As the law stands now, you'll then owe taxes on that unpaid loan money—in a lump sum, too.

But you won't face the punishing experience of default.

If you have a FFELP loan—a Stafford, HEAL, or PLUS—your lender may offer various price breaks on fees and interest. And you can apply for *Income-Sensitive repayment*, FFELP's repayment option that lets you calculate your payment as a percentage of your income, but with the bottom line that you have to pay at least your interest charge each month. But if you're a large-loan borrower whose income is less than secure, those perks can't beat Direct Lending's income-contingent option. With FFELP, you can get deferments and delays. But there comes a point where you have to cough up the money you owe, whether you have it or not. Otherwise you face collection agencies, confiscation of your tax returns, and maybe garnishment of your salary. As for loan forgiveness, dream on.

Still, each loan program offers benefits the other doesn't. And since 1994, we've enjoyed the right to choose. The question is, who'd have a problem with that? Why would anybody in Washington fight to herd us all back into a single system? Why did the 104th Congress vow to kill Direct Lending in 1995—and why have FFELP agencies spent millions to help?

Opposites Detract: Two Programs at War with Us in the Middle

Though they hire some of the same servicing companies to help handle their loans, FFELP and Direct Lending are opposite in their philosophies, and each program makes a different bunch of people spitting mad. The battle between the two systems dredges up the whole spectrum of Republican-Democratic hatreds, from politics to the proper use of billions of taxpayer dollars.

Under FFELP, a bank lends you the money to go to school. With Direct Lending, your loan comes directly from the government.

On the surface, FFELP is what its supporters call "a successful public-private partnership." Direct Lending, on the other hand, looks like bloated big government. But though Direct Lending sounds like a Washington insider program, its supporters argue that it's simpler, more sensible, and—though this is disputed—a lot less expensive than its rival. In America's anti-government nineties, FFELP sounds like the righteous "private enterprise" alternative. But common sense suggests that its boosters love the program at least partly because it has brought them wealth—not from private profits but from government largesse.

FFELP'S NOT-SO-PRIVATE ENTERPRISE

The FFELP industry is a business run for profit, and boy, has it profited. During the three decades they've been around, some of the financial companies that head up the FFELP system have gotten very rich. Recent reforms have started to trim the industry's sails, and critics say those efforts are long overdue. As *U.S. News & World Report*'s Steven Waldman writes in his excellent 1995 book *The Bill*, our student loans have become huge moneymakers, "more consistently lucrative than even mortgages or car loans." A 1995 article in *Rolling Stone* agrees: between fees, built-in profits, bonuses, and collection bounties, the student loan industry has gotten gravy adding up to "an annual $638 million tax-free gift from the government."

When a business is making that kind of money, you assume it's private enterprise at work, and over the years, FFELP spokesmen have worked hard to reinforce that impression. But the FFELP program isn't really private, say critics; it just looks that way. The industry is actually fueled by billions of dollars' worth of government entitlements, in the form of various fees, profits, bounties, and operating reserves, which means Congress votes on how much money to give it each term, just as if FFELP were a government agency. This money comes from taxes paid by you and your parents.

You probably think "entitlements" means "welfare." More accurately, it means any government program where the money supply increases automatically along with demand. In an entitlement program, money must, by law, be parceled out to any applicant who qualifies, whether there are three applicants or three million.

Every American student who qualifies is entitled to a guaranteed, as well as a direct, student loan. As of this writing, that's more than seven million separate loans, all backed by the full faith and credit of the United States. In handling the distribution, maintenance, and collection of all these loans, FFELP lenders get to keep nearly all of their profits—but if they experience a failure, we taxpayers take nearly all the losses. As former Republican senator David Durenberger famously remarked during the first years of the student loan wars: "This is not the free market. It's a free lunch."

Lucky Lenders: We Students Just Keep Coming

This particular free lunch has worked because of FFELP's bizarre organizational setup. Dotted all over the country, FFELP has semi-independent branch offices called guaranty agencies. They're set up to back every federally guaranteed student loan in case anything goes wrong. (We'll talk more about them later.) To make sure they have the money to fix any problems, these guaranty agencies get federal entitlement money from the federal government, more than $150 million a year, whether they use it or not. If the money isn't needed, these agencies are trusted to just keep an eye on it. These funds are called "federal reserves." By now they're up to almost $2 billion.

Human nature being what it is, it's really not surprising that in the past, government audits have uncovered big problems with the handling of federal money in some of the FFELP industry's guaranty agencies. Nobody has ever proved that these problems were caused by intentional wrongdoing. And some guarantors are vastly better run than others. But common sense suggests that at least some guarantors had a chance to make out like bandits — and they took it.

Conflicts of Interest?

In several financial audits reported to Congress since 1993, the U.S. General Accounting Office (GAO) suggests that in the past few years, various student-loan guaranty agencies have found creative ways to make money: like reporting their records so as to suggest smaller default rates; and "borrowing" federal funds to invest in for-profit schemes of their own; and buying into businesses they're supposed to police. The amazing thing is, none of this was illegal. Not exactly, anyway.

"Come on," I hear you saying. "This is paranoid. I may not love government, but I don't believe they'd deliberately cheat me."

Well, no. It's not as simple as that. The crisis we're in now has been building for years, and as loan demand has exploded, the old industry rules and regulations have gotten less effective. What first worked so well for students has, not surprisingly, become a system that benefits the banks instead. In the face of pointed criticisms — and its first real competition — the FFELP industry has started trying to clean up its act. But observers say it has a long way to go.

Does this mean that student loans are all about FFELP's bad guys versus Direct Lending's good guys? Definitely not. For one thing, Direct Lending's advocates are also talking out of self-interest. Considering that Republicans have been threatening to eliminate it for several years now, it's not surprising that the Department of Education wants to hang onto Direct Lending. It gives the Department a reason to be.

For another thing, even if FFELP's guarantors have been in lots of hot water, that doesn't mean the system is all bad. FFELP's regulations are hellishly complicated—so much so, says one Department of Education official, that it's quite possible for a guarantor or other loan servicer to break some rule just by misinterpreting. And if professionals are confused, laymen—even laymen in government who have to make decisions about your loan—are often bewildered.

"We really have to educate everybody," says Ernest T. Freeman. As founder and CEO of The Education Resources Institute (TERI), which offers privately financed student loans, Freeman is an outspoken and candid observer of both FFELP and Direct Lending. "You would be amazed at how little members of Congress know about the student loan industry."

In fact, there's a lot of caring and compassion for students floating around on Capitol Hill. But where do these concerned legislators get most of their information on the very technical subject of student loans? From lobbyists on both sides of the student loan question. If a FFELP lobbyist says Direct Lending could hurt you, that's going to be very hard for your Congressman to ignore.

DIRECT LENDING: A DIRECT ADVANTAGE TO STUDENTS . . . SO FAR

We who owe a lot feel less cautious about Direct Lending, because we need the income-contingent repayment option that only Direct Lending has given us (so far, anyway). Some of us are graduating with literally four times the debt our big brothers and sisters faced. When debts were smaller, default wasn't such an issue, so income-contingent repayment wasn't necessary. You could reasonably pay what you owed in the ten years' time you were allotted.

But for those of us with the largest debts, traditional repayment options have become a joke. And without some major redesign, FFELP can't handle our needs. True, FFELP's Income-Sensitive Repayment plan offers interest-only payments. But the interest on a $50,000 loan can top $300 a month. That's just too much for some student debtors, a fact FFELP providers understand. "We'd offer income-contingent repayment in a heartbeat," says Lawrence Hough, CEO of FFELP industry leader Sallie Mae. "Don't you think we'd want to help? By law we're not allowed to."

"I love this new concern for students," retorts Diane Voigt, retired chair of the Direct Lending Task Force. "Before Direct Lending came along, the FFELP program's attitude was, 'This is the service you're getting. Take it or leave it.'"

Certainly, while Hough is frank about wishing FFELP could offer a sweeter deal, he also believes that we should simply sacrifice to pay our loans. "The average debt is about $10,000," says Hough. "If someone took a part-time job on weekends, and sincerely wanted to get rid of that debt, how soon could they do so? There are plenty of people who get a second job to pay for a car."

If you're having trouble paying your loan, it's easy to be cowed by messages like these. After all, they're true. Many of us borrowed too much for college and graduate school. Now that the deed is done, we feel guilty for wanting repayment terms that let us honor our debts *and* live our lives. But it's our job to get beyond all that. Whether or not it pleases anybody else, we have to come to terms with our loans in a way that works for us.

Since many thousands of us owe more than we can pay, we can't afford the luxury of ignoring the politics that surround student loans. Unless we want to risk falling helplessly into the seven years' bad luck of default, we have to protect our access to Direct Lending and Income Contingent Repayment. We also have to keep pushing FFELP to improve. For the next few years, that's our homework.

Frankly, if lenders disrespect us a little, it's not hard to understand. We students have not always been put-upon angels. Thousands of our older brothers and sisters ducked their loans by simply getting lost after graduation, or by going bankrupt while the ink on their diplomas was still wet. Plenty of us are still trying. (That's one reason that in 1991 Congress made it almost impossible to go bankrupt on a student loan for at least seven years after it comes due.) These lowlife strategies are costing us right now, because many lenders and legislators feel they know us already. We're deadbeats. When we students say we're being overburdened, it's easy for lawmakers and financial pros to shoot back, "Oh, grow up."

Before we pop off at each other, we all need to get a grip on the facts. You can hoot at the idiots in Congress if you want. But ask yourself this: How much do *you* know about the student loan industry? Before you go pointing your finger at anybody else, you'd better educate yourself.

CHAPTER 4

Till Debt Do Us Part: How Student Loan Debt Divides America

College has always been hugely important to Americans. That's a given. But how could we afford it, and how much should government help us? That's changed with every year and every president.

Our conventional wisdom has led us on a strangely circular path. At first, it was "tough luck, you can't afford an education." That became "come on, we'll give you a grant," which became "no grants, but here's a manageable loan," which became "no manageable loan, but here's a crushing loan!" Which is really just another way of saying "tough luck, you can't afford an education."

That's okay. We don't have to give up. Our old ideas about how to get to college are wearing out fast, but that just means we have to get sharper about what we borrow, what we pay, and what we demand in return.

THE G.I. BILL: AN ALL-AMERICAN THANK-YOU

Throughout most of our history, a college education has been a privilege pretty much reserved for Americans born to power—meaning wealthy, white, and male. Occasionally we'd hear about self-made men. But really universities existed to polish and groom our untitled but very real aristocracy. For the rest of us, college was just a dream. We didn't have the money to go, and that was that. We did okay without it. None of us dreamed that one day we'd sign a paper, and poof! Money would appear, and off we'd go to college.

If it hadn't been for World War II, we'd still be dreaming. Our idea of helping college students with government money really got rolling with the famous G.I. Bill. After the war, Congress rewarded veterans with a new kind of national thank-you: a ticket to college, to help them relaunch their interrupted lives. This first experiment in government aid for higher education was a grant, not a loan. It was a huge investment, the biggest social program of its day and bigger than anything we offer now.

Radical as it was, the G.I. Bill was a hit. It produced a tough, smart army of citizens who went right out and built America into the modern superpower we grew up with. Listen to just about any big shot of a certain age, and you'll hear, "It all started when I went to school on the G.I. Bill."

The G.I. Bill mixed social classes, spread wealth, and changed our lives. But that didn't automatically sell America on government aid for all students. G.I. Bill benefits were special, a gift in return for national service. Otherwise, Americans still saw college as something to be paid for by kids, families, and aid from colleges themselves.

So when did federal student loans come into the picture? The next time America got really scared. In 1957, Russia launched Sputnik, the first space satellite. We totally panicked. If Russia controlled space, would they use it to destroy us? We needed smart, well-educated young thinkers in a hurry. In case some needy student happened to be the genius who could whip Russia in the space race, Congress passed the National Defense Education Act in 1958. The first federal loans, NDEA loans, were created.

The ancestors of today's Perkins loans (named for former Congressman Carl D. Perkins), NDEA loans were handed out through schools. Like Perkins loans today, they were definitely for needy students only, and they carried much lower interest rates than most student loans. By 1993, Congress would be dispensing nineteen thousand a year.

THE GREAT SOCIETY: GETTING US ALL INTO COLLEGE

The door to college really flew open for young Americans during the activist presidency of Lyndon Johnson. His vision of a Great Society included the idea that college should be for anyone who wants it, not just anyone who can pay for it. He figured an educated citizen bene-fited society, and so society ought to invest in his education.

When today's budget-cutters fly into a rage about big government, President Johnson is often the guy they're mad at. As part of his ambitious War on Poverty, Johnson spearheaded practically all of the college federal financial aid programs we have now. In 1964, he enacted the College Work-Study Program. A year later came the Educational Opportunity Grant Program. We're still dealing with EOGP's descendants, Supplemental Educational Opportunity Grants (SEOG).

For poor kids, Johnson didn't stop at grants. Right from the get-go, his idea of aid included a push for kids without money or family behind them. Starting in 1964, government came up with TRIO, a cluster of extra-help programs that now serve more than six hundred thousand students. (Even so, they're losing ground, partly thanks to the soaring costs of college. Where a well-off kid used to be four times as likely to graduate from college as a poor kid, now he's ten times as likely to finish. Diploma or not, however, the poor kid still has to pay off his student loan.)

Guaranteed Student Loans: From Middle Class to Freshman Class

With aid available for poor kids, stressed-out middle-class families demanded help too. Johnson and Congress responded by passing 1965's landmark Higher Education Act, creating the program that would eventually change most of our lives: the Guaranteed Student Loan Program, or GSL.

From where we stand, the first GSLs were hilariously small. The government would pay your interest while you were in school—if your family's yearly income was under $15,000. If you were living large on $15,001, the interest was up to you. As for repayment time, it was just five years. (How these little baby loans mutated into today's wild and scary FFELP loans is a choice story by itself, as you'll see.)

In the sixties, the new GSL loans were gobbled up by a starving American public. Ironically, the man who signed them into law probably lived to regret it. By opening college campuses to thousands more (and more diverse) students, Johnson helped to hatch the rude, rowdy, and fabulous Woodstock generation, whose protests over his behavior in the Vietnam War eventually wrecked his presidency.

SALLIE MAE: BIRTH OF A MONEY MACHINE

Johnson went, but student loans thrived. In 1972, Richard Nixon attended the birth of what's now the most renowned name in the loan business: Sallie Mae. Structured as a private business yet implicitly backed by the feds, Sallie Mae (also known back then as the Student Loan Marketing Association) was the first *secondary market*.

Founded as a GSE (government-sponsored enterprise), Sallie Mae was a strange hybrid creature, free to raise money like a private corporation, but also free to draw on U.S. government backing in case of trouble. The object: to raise cheap money and buy up student loans, so lenders could recoup their money and recycle it into new loans.

Sallie Mae has charted a brilliant course throughout its history. Having started out with the tremendous advantage of implied federal backing, Sallie Mae got rich, then very rich. Its aggressive and creative marketing strategies have given it such high visibility—what advertising pros call "top-of-mind awareness"—that when you're starting to learn how loan issues work, you're likely to think the whole story amounts to one big grudge match between Direct Lending and Sallie Mae.

Sallie Mae's known for doing everything first class. You can view Sallie Mae videos on saving up money for your child's education. You can figure out your projected monthly payments on Sallie Mae's interactive website. You can call Sallie Mae's customer representatives anytime, all the time. You can even get Sallie Mae discount coupons, for various campus goods and services.

In fact, Sallie Mae has been doing so well for so long that in 1996 the company asked for and received permission from Congress to split off and become a totally private corporation.

As of 1997, Sallie Mae started life as an ultra-powerful new competitor against other privately run secondary markets, free to get into lots of new business activities that were formerly forbidden by its government charter.

PELL GRANTS: NEEDED THEN AND NOW

To get more money to students and deliver it better, Nixon and Congress also acted in 1972 to create need-based Basic Educational Opportunity Grants (BEOG), now renamed Pell Grants in honor of Sen. Claiborne Pell.

From the start, lawmakers have been less willing to fund grants than loans. Pell Grants have never been fully funded, though they're needed more than ever. "The maximum grant amounts are edging up, but they don't have the same purchasing power they had in the eighties," says Ann Coles, a senior vice president at TERI. Now that America is feeling pinched, Congress is less and less willing to give money outright for education, no matter how much a student might deserve it—and how hard it might be for him to repay a loan.

The Carter Years: Everybody Gets a Loan!

America was also feeling pinched in the era of President Jimmy Carter, and for the first time, we began to wonder if student loans were costing too much. Carter took office in a tough economic period when families were getting hammered by college costs. Carter and Congress tried to help out with 1978's Middle Income Student Assistance Act, which made Pell Grants available to more students and made Guaranteed Student Loans available to everyone, regardless of income.

Practically as soon as it passed, Carter's helpful legislation blew up in his face. Inflation went through the roof, and because Guaranteed Student Loans were fixed at a super-low interest rate, they were suddenly the sexiest deal around. Naturally there was a run on GSLs. With U.S. interest rates at an all-time high, the federal government was suddenly stuck paying GSL lenders appalling interest subsidies.

It wasn't pretty—and there was more. The Department of Education's first venture into a federally managed loan plan was completely mired in chaos. The Federally Insured Student Loan (FISL) program was such a mess that loan industry pros gleefully tagged it "Fizzle." These were the kinds of problems that set the stage for maybe the most charming opponent federal student aid ever had—Ronald Reagan.

The Reagan Years: No, Everybody Does Not Get a Loan!

President Reagan was not one bit sold on the idea that the federal government should help finance college for students. With his election in 1980, America's support of federal financial aid, at least conservative America's support, slowly began to reverse itself. Education really benefited the individual, not society, said conservatives. So the individual, not society, ought to pay.

True to his campaign promise to cut social spending to the bone, Reagan led eight years of efforts to reduce federal aid to college students. (First to go was Carter's expensive legislation.) Though Congress protected student aid from Reagan's more drastic cutbacks, he did succeed in stopping its growth. And as he also piled more expenses on the states, they in turn spent less on colleges.

Tuitions started rising. At some colleges, tuition increased 10 percent or more *each year* of the eighties. Though his social policies were surely a factor, Reagan can't be held responsible for all of the academic price-hiking that went on during that decade. Colleges and universities had made an amazing discovery: what they asked, students paid.

Maybe this would have been possible without student loans. But at the least, their availability was a very happy coincidence. With "free" money in free fall, schools offered new students a little work-study, a little scholarship money, and all the GSL loans the law allowed. Admissions rose. So did loan limits. In 1981, total loan limits were $12,500 for undergraduates and $25,000 for graduates. By 1987, the numbers were $17,250 for undergrads and $54,750 for grad students.

Loans this size are hard to pay back by anybody's standards. And this fact, combined with the brutal realities of a downsizing America, would be reflected in the nineties as whopping default statistics—almost 19 percent in 1993. Of course Congress went into shock at that point and decided students had forgotten their responsibilities, but the truth is a lot more complicated than that. Whether you saw Reagan as a freedom fighter or a scrooge, it was during his eight years in office that America's romance with college started degenerating into a fatal attraction.

Everybody Gets a Monster Loan, Including Your Parents

Maybe it was mass denial. Maybe it was something in the water. But as college costs kept shooting upward, we kept signing loan papers and showing up on campus. It seemed those enormous loans only made us more determined to beat the odds.

Mirroring the decade's widening gap between rich and poor Americans, college in the eighties began to foster the class divisions of pre–G.I. Bill America all over again—but in a silent and unacknowledged way. On the surface, both wealthy and unwealthy students were still managing to go to college. But without really comprehending it, we who were competing via larger and larger loans were setting ourselves up for life with a debt handicap that would actively hold us down.

"We've turned equal opportunity into a tollbooth," says Barmak Nassirian, director of policy analysis for the American Association of State Colleges and Universities (AASCU). "In the USA, the land of opportunity, we believe that everybody who has a theoretical shot at something ought to be given the chance to take it. The problem is that we used to finance it out of our wallets: 'Sure, you're not academically prepared, but this is America! If you fail, my expense, and if you make it, we all benefit.' Now we pull their wallet, unbeknownst to them. We pat the academically disadvantaged kid on the back, giving the illusion that, this being America, everything is possible—despite the fact that we know the odds are not very good. We send them out to win one for the Gipper, and most of them don't. That's how defaults happen."

In tune with the times, Reagan's administration saw the creation of new supplemental loans—to be borrowed when the GSL was not enough. Though they've been reborn under several names—ALAS loans in 1981, SLS loans in 1986, Unsubsidized Staffords in 1994— these loans share two things in common. First, you can get them no matter how much money you have; second, your bill starts ticking as soon as you get your check.

In 1981, your mom and dad also got a new way to sacrifice— Parent Loans for Undergraduate Students (PLUS). These loans let them borrow regardless of their income, at higher interest. The PLUS program, which is doing a roaring business today, is maybe the hardest for some of us to swallow. By the time we're in college, we'd rather see our parents planning their retirement, not going into hock for us all over again. But somehow we let them do it, and somehow they do.

By the last year of Reagan's presidency, as GSLs were becoming Stafford loans (in honor of Sen. Robert Stafford), Congress was starting to feel tweaked about growing student loan debt. In 1987, borrowers got the right to consolidate their loans, refinancing them at longer terms for higher interest. Starting in 1989, first-time borrowers were required to go through an entrance counseling session during which they were forced to look at how big their payments would be.

THE '90S: HOW MUCH IS THIS COSTING? WE DON'T WANNA KNOW

These little sessions in the woodshed definitely didn't slow anybody down. In terms of borrowing, the nineties have made the eighties look tame. More than half of all the money borrowed during the whole thirty-two-year history of the guaranteed student loan program has been borrowed since 1990—$100 billion and counting. This "run on the bank," coupled with a wave of tougher government regulations, shook up the student loan business. It also gave rise to tougher bankruptcy laws.

The amazing student loan boom wasn't exactly invisible, and soon entrepreneurs started cashing in. Privately financed student loan providers sprang up for students who couldn't qualify for government guaranteed loans, or—get this—who needed to borrow over and above their government loan limits. Founded in 1985, TERI quickly became the nation's largest private student loan guarantor and broker.

These and other privately funded loans got you over the last financial hurdles and landed you on campus. But when your bill came due, you owed your Stafford loan monthly payment plus the monthly payment on your private loan. And what about your parents, did they kick in for a PLUS loan? With nobody really noticing, the cost of professional schools was starting to billow out into a shadowy stratosphere where we were signing for the same loan amounts—but on three times as many loans.

Beyond Banks: Could Borrowing from the Feds Be Cheaper?

Back in Washington, people were seriously searching for ways to lower the cost of guaranteed loans, not to mention simplifying the loan process itself. There had to be some way around the more than seven thousand private financial organizations that currently had a finger in the student-loan pie.

Oddly, that way turned out to be a law called the Credit Reform Act of 1990. Credit Reform changed government's bookkeeping rules so that suddenly it was a bargain to lend students money directly from the federal government.

By 1992, President George Bush was faced with a strong surge of enthusiasm in Congress for Direct Lending. Naturally banks hated the idea, and did all they could to squash it. But in the end, despite Bush's veto threat, Direct Lending got its foot in the door.

GSL Becomes FFELP: And Now You Can Borrow More!

The Direct Lending experiment was just one of many changes in the Higher Education Amendments of 1992. Faced with evidence that college costs were pricing students out of the market, Congress stirred things up. Okay, some of it was window dressing—like all the loans got new names. The GSL program became FFELP, the Federal Family Education Loan Program.

The biggest immediate change was financial. Congress ripped the roof off borrowing limits. Total subsidized Stafford loan limits for undergraduates were raised to $23,000; the new limit for graduate students (including undergrad loans) was $65,000. Total unsubsidized Stafford loan limits were raised to $23,000 for undergraduate loans and $75,000 for combined grad and undergrad loans. In 1993, PLUS loans were reauthorized with higher limits still. Depending on their creditworthiness, your parents could (and still can) borrow up to the whole cost of your education, minus other aid—however many thousands of dollars that might be.

Other changes in the 1992 law tried to rein things in somehow. Consolidated-loan holders had to offer "income-sensitive" payment plans (different from income-contingent plans) that would swap lower payments now for higher payments later. Compassionate rulings helped students get their loans out of default. Other legislation dealt with men and women who had been bilked by trade schools; now their debts could be 100 percent forgiven.

Direct Lending: Better Late Than Never

All very nice. But by 1992 we were feeling dazed at the new burdens of college. The big loans were coming due, and the facts were coming clear. For a lot of us, college education was simply drifting out of reach. As a presidential candidate, Bill Clinton campaigned on a proposal for pay-as-you can student loans. Voters' enthusiasm for the pay-as-you-can part helped put him in office.

After Clinton's election, his campaign promise was nipped, tucked, diced, and sliced during a congressional brawl. What finally emerged was our current William D. Ford Federal Direct Loan

Program—Direct Lending. As Clinton had promised, it was the first student loan program ever to offer loan payments figured on a borrower's income, even if that meant not paying off the whole loan. At first, Clinton and his advisers wanted a total switch to Direct Lending: It was perceived as a thumb of the nose to America's wealthy and influential FFELP lenders, who stood to take drastic losses from the new program—and in a thumb of the nose to Clinton from the Republican leadership, Direct Lending was approved only as a phased-in program, to be tested against FFELP over several years.

At the moment, FFELP and Direct Lending are coexisting—uneasily. The cost of education keeps right on climbing. Today you can borrow up to $46,000 as an undergraduate. Half of that, $23,000, must be unsubsidized, meaning you pay interest from the get-go. More than half of your total graduate-undergraduate debt, or up to $73,000, must also be unsubsidized. Add in $65,500 of subsidized loans, and you hit your new limit: $138,500.

That's before your parents kick in.

COLLEGE NOW: A MATTER OF LIFE AND DEBT

If you don't count living expenses, 60 percent of all college students still pay less than $12,000 for four years of tuition, much lower than government's maximum loan limits. But many of us feel an intense pressure to go higher. When the G.I. Bill got started, college was still pitched at a level that required you to rise to the level of the very few. Now it's often observed that a college diploma basically means what a high-school diploma meant thirty years ago, except that we students are now going into debt to pay for what we used to get for free.

If we're ambitious, if we want to be lawyers, doctors, leaders, the asking price of that education may be $30,000, $50,000, $60,000, $100,000 of debt. Unless we're phenomenally successful—and I mean phenomenally, as in "in your dreams"—we're already signing away a part of our joy in the profession we wanted to pursue, because during our most productive years, one of our main goals is going to be paying back the money we owe.

And yet we need student loans. We're thankful for them, and for the chance at an education they provide—even if we pay forever. That's one reason it's hard for us to object to the level of debt we're now asked to shoulder. It seems ungrateful.

Everybody who deals with us has a strong motive to say things are fine. Educators need us, because they've used our loans to replace government money. Lenders want us, because student loans are their sweetest business. Legislators care about our needs, but they don't know us. They hear about us from loan providers who see us as opportunities for profit. Even our parents tell us things will work out—because that's what they hope.

"I just heard about a couple who owe $500,000!" a vice president of one of the nation's biggest student loan providers told me recently. "That's quite a figure," she chirped, "but technically it can be done!" Would she be so unconcerned if she owed the money?

Sooner or later, this system is going to collapse. Actually, for us who are already in it, that could be the good news. Whatever student-loan hole we're in at the moment, thousands of other Americans are in there with us.

The Future: Demanding the Best Loan Deal for Our Money

Direct Lending, with its income-contingent loans, feels like the most hopeful development in years for you and me. It puts us back in the college game, at least for a while. But we need to look past Direct Lending too. Its manageable payments may keep us out of trouble with credit bureaus, but they can also extend our indebtedness so far that we wind up paying more in interest than we borrowed in the first place. Anyway, financing higher education with always-mounting personal debt is a rotten way to sweep the cost of college under the rug. Is this really the best we can do?

Having hammered Direct Lending into existence, Bill Clinton introduced a series of additional ideas about how to get education rolling again. Two years of college for everybody, if they can keep up a B average. Tax credits of $1,500 per year for up to two years of college, tax deductions of up to $10,000 which can be used for more years of college. College IRAs, featuring withdrawal without penalty. And in a smart nod to the great tradition of the past, a "new G.I. Bill for American workers"—a $2,600 tax credit for anybody who wants retraining for another job.

It all sounded good. But the original G.I. Bill was money in your hand. Can tax breaks and tax credits reach past the middle class to help poor kids get all the way through college? Or are we really over that now? At any rate, as one Republican source commented, "Without some break in tuition, none of it's going to help."

If Democrats keep slugging for tax benefits and reasonable loan repayments—and Republicans choose instead to demand education at better prices—those are all steps in the right direction for students. Frankly, we can use all the friends we can get.

No matter how we feel about them, student loans are here to stay. With a $3.6 trillion national debt, America's definitely not going back to the free education of the original G.I. Bill. We all have to kick in and do our fair share.

But does that mean we can't improve the deal we're getting? No way. We need to be much sharper about what we're borrowing and what we're really getting in return. In this $100 billion business, we are the customers. We're the ones who have to be pleased.

At least now we can choose which loan provider we'll allow to service us. If you don't think that matters, read the next chapter.

CHAPTER 5

Attack of the Mutant Loans: How We Made the Student Loan Industry Rich

The story of the Federal Family Education Loan Program is exactly like one of those cheesy old science fiction movies. You know the kind, where a top secret experiment goes haywire and produces a giant mutant monster who stomps everything in sight.

You laugh at those movies on TV, because they're so silly they could never happen in real life. Well, quit laughing. The FFELP system probably handles your loan right now, and over the years it's become a mutant monster to rival anything you've seen on TV.

I'm not saying the FFELP program is evil. Obviously, it was designed to help us, and obviously it has. More than $200 billion in FFELP loans (or GSL loans, as they used to be called) have given nearly 77 million of us the boost we needed to go to college. But after nearly thirty-five years of tinkering and tweaking by the thousands of related businesses and political interests that own a piece of it, the FFELP system has become very much like those monsters you remember. An enormous and powerful creature, too weird to love and too big to shoot.

FFELP's service has been improving since Direct Lending hit the scene in 1994. But the tide could change. Your freedom of choice is not automatic. It's obviously difficult for government to run two massive student loan programs side by side, and FFELP leaders have been locked in a battle with Direct Lending advocates to see who'll be left standing in the end. Would we be better off in a Direct Lending world? It's too soon to know. Perhaps, since they've already started to hire the same servicing subcontractors, the two programs will eventually have all the same problems. One thing's for sure: remembering the old FFELP system when it was accountable to nobody, a lot of us aren't exactly thrilled about going back.

To be sure, most of us with FFELP loans have done just fine. But students who've had problems will never forget. Take the case of law student Shari Clair, as reported in the March 1996 issue of *Smart Money* magazine. Shari was already almost $25,000 in debt from undergrad loans when she enrolled in 1992 at the New College of California law school in San Francisco. To ease her debt load, she decided to cut back to half time in school and work more hours in her job as a paralegal. This meant changing her borrower status with AFSA Data, a New York loan servicer holding eight of her loans. Could she take care of her request with one form? Sorry. In typically overcomplicated FFELP fashion, Shari had to file eight separate forbearance requests every semester.

Only when she was turned down for a credit card in July 1993 did Shari learn that AFSA had listed one of her loans as seriously delinquent. The New York servicer claimed she hadn't turned in a necessary forbearance form. It then turned Shari's loan over to her guarantor, the California Student Aid Commission (CSAC), which slapped her right into default. What happened next? Shari's law school, New College, told her she was now ineligible for more financial aid. No more classes, no law degree, nothing.

Shari got an attorney, who discovered that AFSA had received, but not processed, Shari's forbearance form. But did CSAC apologize or move to help get Shari back into school? No way. Finally, after a personal appeal from the attorney, a CSAC official arranged to get Shari's loan out of default and have it bought by another agency. Shari took out a $6,000 commercial loan to pay her back tuition.

You'd think Shari finally got a happy ending, but no. After a year and a half of fighting the lenders, studying in school, and working as a paralegal, Shari was out of gas. She flunked the bar exam. Soon afterward, she started getting dunning notices again from AFSA. All her other loans had come due when CSAC put her in default. Shari had to start back down the path of asking AFSA for forbearances, but what did AFSA tell her? Her forbearances were all used up. Sorry about that.

Maybe the FFELP monster hasn't stomped you yet. If you have a dependable job that covers your loan payments, it never will. But if your loan is large and you're wondering what to do, you'd better learn all about FFELP, not just what they tell you in the financial aid office.

In 1965, the Guaranteed Student Loan program was an enlightened experiment designed with you in mind. Now, more than thirty years later, it's mutated into something very different—a massive industry that employs thousands of people, handles billions of dollars, and buys and sells millions of student loans. In the nineties, FFELP is big business, geared to its own survival, not yours. According to its enemies, the FFELP industry has grown rich by overcharging taxpayers and students. The industry's supporters laugh that off. From where they stand, no business could perfectly satisfy the limitless nitpicking of what Sallie Mae's Lawrence A. Hough likes to call government's "onerous regulations." Still, nobody denies that various entities in the student loan industry have had big troubles—and that some of those troubles have been ethical.

With our educations and our futures at stake, how did this happen? A little at a time. There wasn't some evil genius who planned it. Like any movie mutant, FFELP began to change when a seemingly innocent set of circumstances collided with one fateful accident.

HOW YOUR TAX DOLLARS BECAME FFELP'S TREASURE CHEST

Here's the problem. While government has been handing out billions of dollars for delivery to you, evidence suggests that some FFELP operations have used chunks of that money to line their own pockets instead. How much? Nobody knows, but this will give you an idea.

In 1996, President Clinton asked thirty-six FFELP guaranty agencies to return $1.1 billion worth of federal money. That's out of $1.8 billion they've been sitting on for so long that some of them claim it isn't federal anymore.

As of 1996, here are a few things that $1.1 billion might have bought: 470,085 Pell Grants; 419,047 first-year subsidized Stafford loans for undergraduate school; or 129,411 subsidized Stafford loans for graduate school. According to a 1993 U.S. General Accounting Office (GAO) audit, here are a few things the money has financed instead: posh offices, lavish salaries, Cadillacs, luxury vacations, and high-powered lobbyists to keep money flowing from Congress.

To be fair, the agencies didn't steal this money. It started with a seed fund advanced by Congress way back when FFELP was the Guaranteed Student Loan Program. Mostly consisting of the right to charge certain fees on every loan, the money was supposed to protect the agencies from business losses. Later this protection turned out to be unnecessary. But here was the fateful accident: Congress never asked for its money back. And poof! Suddenly the GSL program had its own private treasure chest.

In the next few years, strange things began to happen.

Throughout the nineties, FFELP's high-powered corporations have been under fire for all kinds of alleged misuse of the federal money in their care. But they hotly deny having done anything illegal, and the funny thing is, they're not lying. That's the beauty of the FFELP system. "No one understands how the program works," says Bob Shireman, who was a vocal opponent of FFELP in his former role as legislative director for now-retired Sen. Paul Simon of Illinois. "After years, I'm still not even sure I understand how it works."

One way FFELP doesn't work is free-market competition. In order to bankroll our student loans, the federal government pays FFELP loan providers millions of dollars every year in fees and bonuses and bounties and more. But has government been getting its money's worth? Within the FFELP program, there's never been a way to know for sure. FFELP lenders regularly get into big disputes with the federal government over whose money is whose. In 1996, for example, the nation's largest nonprofit guarantor, USA Funds, was ordered to return $43 million to its federal reserve. USA Funds had been using its federal money in order to pay its own for-profit sister companies. Unusual? Hardly. During the same year, multimillion-dollar settlements were also announced by American Student Assistance (ASA), of Massachusetts, and the California Student Aid Commission (CSAC).

As of this writing, FFELP's leaders say they know how to simplify and reform their system—but the Department of Education won't let them, because it really wants Direct Lending to prevail. And though the Department's top officials deny it, FFELP's claim can't be all that inaccurate: as of this writing, the same administrators oversee both FFELP and Direct Lending, and they openly prefer the latter.

Is FFELP getting a raw deal now? It's possible. Do students necessarily sympathize? Ask Shari Clair.

HOW FFELP WORKS

Banks: Why Lend Money to Students?

Maybe the student loan business is especially prone to scams because the whole idea of student loans was crazy from the start.

Remember, student loans didn't exist until just a few years ago, because nobody thought they'd work. A student loan is half cat, half bird: by definition, it's its own worst enemy. Like a scholarship, a student loan has to be there for anybody who needs it. But like a home loan, it has to make money for the lender. No way does that combination compute. Yeah, sure, it's noble to help kids get an education. But face it, from a bank's point of view, lending money to students is stupid. We have no collateral, no possessions, no experience, no track record. Not exactly a great risk.

In 1965, when Congress decided we should get loans for college, bankers thought that was a laugh riot. They weren't giving us credit, thanks, not unless somebody more responsible cosigned our loans. And that's exactly what happened: to reassure the banks and get the money flowing, Congress issued a *guarantee*: "Whatever student borrowers don't pay, the U.S. government will."

While they were at it, Congress also promised we could always get our student loans at a special low interest rate. This idea didn't thrill banks either, so Congress sweetened it with a *special interest allowance*: "If you issue this student a loan at a special low interest rate, the federal government will pay you extra interest so you're making your usual profit and even a little more."

Suddenly, student loans were looking like a very sweet deal. Government was taking on all the risks; banks were getting all the profit. But lenders were still nervous, so Congress started building an elaborate system of safeguards to make sure none of the banks got ripped off. Nobody could have known that the safeguards would one day become part of the problem.

Guaranty Agencies: The Student Loan Cops

When guaranteed student loans started, we were practically in the information Stone Age. There was nothing like the instant network of computers that connects us all today. Bankers involved in the new program really needed access to student loan officers that could handle problems in person. So Congress created *guaranty agencies*, also called guarantors.

Basically, guaranty agencies are the student loan police. Throughout the life of your loan, your guaranty agency is supposed to make sure everything is done according to the law. First, the agency cosigns your loan, literally stamping it with a guarantee that if you die, default, go bankrupt, or are disabled, the federal government will repay your debt. For this service, you pay an *origination fee* and an *insurance fee*—a total cost of up to 4 percent of your loan, lifted off the top before you ever see it.

Once you've got your loan, the guaranty agency is supposed to keep a sharp eye on your lender bank. Like if your lender reports you in default, your guaranty agency has to see that the bank really tried to contact you first. The same holds true if your loan is bought by a secondary market (more about them in a minute). By law, both lenders and secondary markets have to take certain actions to tell you if there's some problem with your loan. These actions are called *due diligence*.

If you default and it's all your fault, the guarantor pays off the bank that issued your loan, using its reserve fund of money provided by the federal government. No loss, either, because the guaranty agency turns around and gets almost all of its reserve money replenished by the government, in a policy called *reinsurance*.

Now the guaranty agency holds your loan. It sets out to recover the lost loan money by sending collectors to encourage you to pay. As of this writing, it's allowed to keep almost a third of whatever it gets back, with the rest going to the government. If the guarantor can't get your money, it sends your loan home to the U.S. Department of Education, which has collectors of its own. Since there's no statute of limitations on student loans, you may hear from different collectors for years after graduation.

Secondary Markets: Holding Loans for the Long Haul

In the first seven years of the guaranteed student loan program, demand was so explosive that banks were spread too thin. Student loan money took too long to come back home, and they needed it back sooner so they could make more student loans.

Congress made that happen in 1972, by creating *secondary markets*. These organizations buy your student loan, reimbursing your bank much sooner than you would. During the years you're making payments to the secondary market, your loan becomes part of its investment portfolio. Because it's cosigned by Uncle Sam, your loan is a valuable investment tool. By pooling it with many other student loans about the same "age," your secondary market can use your loan as an investment tool to raise more money and buy or originate more student loans. Many banks sell your loan to a secondary market as soon as you graduate. Or you can do the selling. If you have several loans, you can consolidate them with a secondary market or lender.

In buying your loan, the secondary market also takes over the busywork of servicing it: printing payment coupon books, sending you letters, and so on. This last refinement officially turned those impractical and unlikely student loans into one of the best bottom-line propositions banks had ever seen. Student loans were already totally safe. They already made money hand over fist. Now they involved no work. Was this heaven, or what?

Loan Servicers: Doing the Grunt Work

If banks were taking it easy, secondary markets were swamped. With student loans starting to number in the millions, they began to farm out their work of loan servicing. Not surprisingly, the organizations that handle this work are called *loan servicing centers*. You may notice that suddenly your loan-related mail is coming from somewhere you never heard of—the Loan Servicing Center of YouNameIt. That means you've been farmed out, babe! You're supposed to be told if your loan is moved, if it makes a difference in how you pay.

You may have learned the hard way that if you had four separate FFELP loans, they could be juggled to the four corners of the earth without your prior knowledge. It's been one of the FFELP system's most irritating—not to say damaging—design flaws. But even when confusing and confounding you, loan servicing centers are by no means the lowest species in the student loan jungle. As in every food chain, there are buzzards at the bottom.

Collection Agencies: Picking the Leftovers

When a student loan goes really wrong, *collection agents* are assigned to clean up the debris. Some agents are more reputable than others, but there's no telling which kind you'll get. Everybody uses collectors, from schools to guarantors to the Department of Education. No one realized in the beginning how important they would turn out to be in this whole process—or how important student loans would be to them. Now, according to financial counselor Jeni Tambash, the largest collection agencies may take in as much as $8 million a year in student loan revenue. Says Dr. Janice Shields of U.S. Public Information Research Group: "Student loans are the number one source of revenue for America's collection agencies."

For collectors, student loans truly turned out to be the banana split made from the endless banana. From the beginning, collectors have found students tasty prey: we're gullible, guilty, and easy to scare. If you haven't yet tangled with a collection agency, here's what they do: try to frighten you into paying your loan, whether you can or not. They might write you nasty letters on fake law-firm letterhead, threaten to have you arrested, or call your parents to scare the money out of them. If you run, they'll skip-trace you. (That's industry slang for tracking you down if you skip out on your loan.) There are limits to what collectors can do. But they won't tell you that.

CRANKING OUT LOANS, RAKING IN MONEY: THE BOOMING STUDENT LOAN BUSINESS

Each new entity in the GSL program may have answered a real need, but together, they cranked out loans in a hilariously unreal way. "At its best," says David Longanecker, the U.S. Assistant Secretary of Post-Secondary Education, "the guaranty system was an operation that just had too many moving parts." Streamlining was not a popular idea, though. Once created, each GSL entity became its own special interest group, fiercely trying to protect its piece of the pie. As of this writing, we're talking about a very big pie: seven thousand lenders, thirty-six guarantors, fifty secondary markets, and nobody even knows how many third-party servicers and collection agencies.

After years of political tinkering, the FFELP loan application process evolved into a wildly complicated ritual involving at least sixteen transactions between four kinds of institutions. "It's the most counterintuitive way the borrower, the school, and the federal government could interact," says AASCU's Barmak Nassirian.

Schools had to wade through paperwork on thousands of students with loans coming from thousands of lenders. FFELP players weren't required to standardize their operations, so in order to get the money flowing, students and school administrators had to deal with who knows how many different kinds of red tape. Naturally, this involved mistakes, misunderstandings, and lots of delays.

Only when Direct Lending came along to offer a simpler way did FFELP buckle down and start working to streamline its system. Now—finally—FFELP operations across the country are starting to adopt methods that will help you get your loan faster in the future.

Why couldn't the industry have made these improvements without a swift kick from the competition? Maybe they didn't want to mess up a good thing.

Sure, the FFELP system was too complicated if you were on the receiving end. But if you were one of the entities passing out the bucks, it was a sure-fire recipe for getting rich. Do you see why? Because every time a FFELP provider spent any money, it reappeared. The government replaced it, just like magic. In trying to assure banks that they'd be paid, government went too far and made the student loan business into a game where lenders really could not lose—no matter whether they were smart, stupid, dishonest, or even conscious. Instead of preventing problems, that magic stream of federal money helped to turn FFELP into the mutant monster that it is.

The problem with a 95 percent-plus guarantee on a loan, writes Bob Shireman, is that there is "little incentive for a lender to make a serious effort to collect payments from a reluctant borrower. For a small loan, a student loan provides a good rate of return to the lender. But for borrowers who require extra reminders, that profit can quickly be eaten up by collection costs. The way to maximize profits, therefore, is to accept the payments that come in easily, and have the government pay off the remaining defaults."

Obviously, if you're just not paying your loan—if you dodge your lender's efforts to contact you—you don't deserve to be coddled and protected. But to FFELP's critics, the system is designed all wrong, because continuing to contact you after a certain point actually cuts into your lender's profits. If you were a lender, would you care to watch your paycheck shrink while you tried calling that borrower just one more time? Doubtful.

As things stand today, your bank or secondary market declares you in default, knowing it will be repaid by your guaranty agency and, ultimately, by the federal government. Of course, the guarantor is supposed to challenge your bank's default claim. But in the end, accepting your default may be more profitable for the guarantor than trying to prevent it. Having repaid your bank, the guarantor turns around and gets largely reimbursed by the federal government—and under current law, the guarantor gets to come after you and keep 27 percent of whatever you cough up. (This money is added to the cost of your loan, by the way.) FFELP spokesmen insist that collecting loans is expensive, and 27 percent is only fair. But in recent years, the collection bounty has sometimes been much higher, *as high as 43 percent*. And the guarantor, along with its collection agency, gets it only if you default.

To keep guarantors from profiting too much from this arrangement, government laid down a rule: "The more your student borrowers default, the less money we'll pay you back when you ask to be reimbursed for a bad student loan." To enforce this regulation and others like it, FFELP's various agencies must do mountains of paperwork, submit to regular audits, and pay penalties if they're caught cutting corners. But underneath all the rules, say critics, there's still room to fudge. As of this writing, the guaranty agencies still aren't standardized under one system of electronic data entry, so they can't be accurately policed. In other words, maybe everything's fine. And maybe not.

The Secret of the Seed Fund

A collection bounty that's paid only on default isn't the only backwards incentive that drives FFELP's thirty-six guaranty agencies. Over time, they've become what Rep. Tom Petri calls "rogue mastodons"—massive and outdated, but continuing to rake in profits nonetheless. But they weren't that way in the beginning.

Remember, guaranty agencies were created to assure banks that if a student defaulted, his loan would be paid. To give the agencies the money to do this, Congress started them out with seed money of $190 million. Back then, though, *the federal government wasn't necessarily going to reimburse each default*. By charging an insurance fee on every loan, guarantors were supposed to build up a pool of money so that they could eventually make their own default reimbursements.

Since states were deriving some of the benefits of the new loans, federal lawmakers reasoned that they should also put up some of the money and share some of the risk. But as a practical matter, most states weren't interested. By 1967 thousands of students wanted new loans, but there were no state guarantors to back them. Finally Congress gave up and said the federal government would take over 100 percent of the guarantee.

But when it took on sole responsibility—here's that fateful science-fiction-movie accident again—government failed to revise the guaranty agencies' structure or ask for its seed money back. In so doing, Congress left the guarantors with a secret treasure chest that could do nothing but grow. It invited all-too-human error. "For anyone, the temptation involved in being responsible for a large quantity of federal money would be enormous," Shireman observes. "It is not just that the guaranty agencies have been given the keys to the treasury. They've been asked to work in the vault."

Sitting Pretty with Money to Burn

Partly because they were born a few at a time, guaranty agencies don't share organizational plans. Some are nonprofit organizations; some are state-run. They have just two things in common. They all have the power to write checks on the government's account, and they are all fueled by federal entitlement money. Guarantors still collect fees for every loan that comes their way. Originally these fees were supposed to offset losses from default and other expenses. But, since the federal government reimburses most losses, almost all the fees are profit.

Rep. Tom Petri—the Republican congressman who came up with the core concept behind Direct Lending—explained it well in a 1995 statement to the U.S. Congressional Opportunities Committee.

> [The guarantors] are sitting on a largely guaranteed stream of revenue with very little supervision from anyone over how they spend it. Congress is not directly looking over their shoulders because they are not federal entities. State legislatures are not much interested in them because they are not state funded. They have no stockholders to answer to. And the Department [of Education] has little leverage over them. They are an open invitation to abuse . . . the worst form of bureaucracy run amok.

How to Make a Billion Dollars Disappear

Guarantors are legally allowed to invest some of their reserve funds, so long as their investments are in the federal interest. And during the past few years, a number of FFELP guarantors branched out into a host of projects. Some were commendable. Others raised ethical questions. In fact, some guarantors may have begun, in Nassirian's words, to "play with federal reserve money as their own."

Whether to better serve students or to benefit themselves, guaranty agencies began to mutate. They began expanding their operations, founding spin-off companies that were structured to run on the federal reserve money in their care. This was done by turning the guaranty agency into a cluster of businesses, often sharing the same board of directors, whose members sometimes collected more than one salary.

These seemingly separate businesses were free to rent each other space, sell each other office equipment, and subcontract each other's data processing and software services, sometimes at jacked-up prices. By the time the federal government's money had made its way from Bob's Guaranty Agency to Bobby's Office Supplies to Robert's Data Processing, it wasn't federal anymore—and Bob was free to take it home.

This may have been inappropriate, but it wasn't illegal. Only in 1996 did government begin to pass regulations that touched on these issues. And the mutation didn't stop there. Remember, guaranty agencies were designed to be the student loan cops—to check, and check hard, to see if banks and secondary markets were treating you right. But in creating their clusters of related businesses, one guaranty agency after another started their own secondary markets.

That meant these guarantors now *owned* organizations they were supposed to *police*. Could this possibly be ethical?

Yes, says Sheila Ryan, director of policy and planning for the national FFELP loan handler Nellie Mae. She points to her own experience as proof. "I used to work at a guaranty agency [that also operated a secondary market]," Ryan recalls. "My experience when I was there is that claims filed by the folks down the hall were often treated more harshly. You really looked at everything very carefully to make certain that there wasn't any preferential treatment."

Unfortunately, the record suggests that not every guarantor was that careful. A 1993 Inspector General's audit examined twelve guaranty agencies and found that nine of them, holding about $40 billion in loan guarantees, were involved in business relationships that could damage their objectivity in dealing with us, the students. "But wait!" you say. "If there's a problem with my loan, who's on my side?" *You* are, kid. That's the point of this book.

The 800-Pound Gorilla

By now, some guarantors have grown so big that the idea of trying to shut them down is very painful. In 1990, the government got a graphic example, via a $280 million catastrophe. Partly because of conflict-of-interest problems, the Higher Education Assistance Foundation (HEAF), a huge national guarantor, became insolvent. Thousands of student loans were involved, and as the federal government reassigned and rescued them, a chilling fact became clear. There was no point in punishing HEAF for its poor judgment, because damaging the agency more would only make it more expensive to clean up the damage.

In other words, it may be cheaper to support a poorly run guarantor than to close it down. Maybe that's one reason why Congress jumped in to support the guarantors further, rather than backing away: as of 1992, every guarantor is backed by the full faith and credit of the United States.

AUDITS POINT TO CONFLICTS OF INTEREST

Government has long been aware that the guaranty system presented the opportunity for fancy footwork. "We have over the years performed reviews to try to detect any actual conflict that results in an increase in the government's costs," says Larry Oxendien, head of the Department of Education's Guarantor Lender Oversight Branch. "We have found no significant conflicts in terms of loss to the government, although I must acknowledge that those losses could be taking place and you'd simply be unable to find them.

"For example," he continues, "if you have a guaranty agency that is also running a lender servicer, there are certain shared expenses. It could be the building, could be certain employees, could be the computer system. It becomes very important how they set up their cost allocation plan for the cost of the various components. It would be possible to intentionally misallocate by one percentage point and drain a lot of money out of the guaranty agency, although one percentage point would be very, very difficult to detect."

By 1993, with the FFELP party in full swing, the industry had become distorted enough to cause alarm. Beginning in March, Congress began receiving some very damning financial audits from the U.S. General Accounting Office as well as the Department of Education. The auditors' findings provoked a fiery response in Congress.

For years, FFELP spokesmen had been insisting to Congress that their entitlement budgets barely covered their expenses. Now these revealing audits recorded on paper what many observers in Washington had long suspected. Here, based on a 1995 report by Bob Shireman, are a few creative uses some guarantors have reportedly found for taxpayer money.

- **Financial shell games:** Several guaranty agencies have created separate corporations that run on money from the guarantor's federal reserve fund. In at least one case, a state agency guarantor has contracted out *all* its activities to a separate nonprofit corporation. In another case, a guarantor opened a "separate" business and sold supplies to itself, at 10 percent over the market rate.

- **Questionable nonprofit status:** Many guarantors have entered businesses other than their guarantor functions, drifting away from the charter that originally got them their nonprofit status. These other activities often put the agencies in the position of regulating their own activity.

- **Mega-salaries:** Many nonprofit FFELP organizations pay huge salaries—as high as a reported $527,000 plus benefits [in 1995] for USA Group's CEO, Roy Nicholson. Is this appropriate for a charitable enterprise devoted to poor students?

- **Inside deals:** Some agency executives have guaranteed an income to their own businesses, which they've created on the side. This. . . violates nonprofit organization guidelines.

- **Big toys:** Nonprofit operations like USA Funds are known for their lavish offices and benefits. (Other FFELP providers sponsor lavish retreats and getaways to woo college financial aid officers.)

- **Lobbyists:** Because they so often depend on political entitlement money, guarantors make sure they're very well connected on Capitol Hill. Some agencies pay their own high-powered lobbyists, and nearly all pay membership dues to one or more Washington lobbying organizations. What kind of expenditures are we talking about? In 1993, USA Group alone reportedly budgeted $750,000 to fight Direct Lending.

JUST ONE MORE CHANCE FOR FFELP

It's ironic that conservatives in Congress should be so loyal to the FFELP program: Over the years, FFELP has fallen prey to all the same excesses and abuses they've sworn to eliminate from government. Yet in 1995, Republicans conducted a ferocious battle in Congress to kill Direct Lending and leave students stranded with FFELP once more. Even more surprising, considering the program's spotty history, the House tried to *cut* the federal funds that keep tabs on FFELP's operations.

Granted, many conservatives believe that FFELP's "private enterprise" system beats a government lending program no matter what. Besides, FFELP's corporate giants tend to be big Republican supporters.

At any rate, FFELP supporters have insisted that the industry is willing and able to reform itself, without competition from Direct Lending. But given its history with fraud and abuse, why should we students trust FFELP to be our only loan program again? Republican Rep. Howard "Buck" McKeon—chairman of the Congressional subcommittee on student loans—retorts, "That's like asking, 'When did you stop beating your wife?' The main problem with Medicare is fraud and abuse. You want to cut Medicare?"

Does this mean that Congress will aggressively attack FFELP's problems, even if that alienates the wealthy Republican powers that be? Even better, will FFELP's billion-dollar treasure chest eventually be recycled into Pell Grants? We'll see.

If the FFELP years have taught us anything, it's that we students need to keep a close eye on *whoever's* running around with our money. When a new lending alternative comes along—even one that seems to solve all our problems—we need to understand how it really works and what we're really getting.

Created in large part by conservative Republicans, Direct Lending was designed to be leaner, meaner, and cheaper than FFELP. Is it living up to its promises? And is it best for you and your loan? Read on, and decide for yourself.

CHAPTER 6

Direct Lending: How We Won the Power to Choose

If the story of FFELP is like bad science fiction, the rise of Direct Lending would have to be one of those weepy Hollywood movies where a school bus full of kids is saved from an oncoming train by a friendly angel. We student borrowers are the kids. The angel, of course, is played by Bill Clinton.

This picture's getting mixed reactions in the multiplex. Some people are crying their eyes out. Others think the plot is totally hokey, not to mention the casting, and they want to sneak back into the FFELP science-fiction movie next door.

Remember, the difference between the two programs is where the money comes from. FFELP loans come from banks. Direct loans come from the sale of U.S. Treasury bonds. Direct Lending was designed specifically to help students facing today's monster loans, and we stampeded to get in: Just two years after its creation in 1994, the program was handling billions of dollars' worth of loans—more than a third of our business. Still, that doesn't mean it will always be here for us. Congress has tried to kill Direct Lending several times. Why?

Before we start explaining the reasons, understand that in Washington, the debate over Direct Lending has been very intense. On both sides, it makes our elected representatives mad enough to spit. They get in that condition and then vote on our future.

That's why it's a good idea for us to eavesdrop on what they're up to. It's almost like we students are caught in a custody battle between two angry parents. The President and the Department of Education want us in Direct Lending; a passel of powerful financiers want us in FFELP. They're both promising us all kinds of benefits if we go with them. But we have to remember that whether they're aware of it or not, our parents use us to score points against each other. We have to choose what's best for *us*—not what brings them the most power, money, and prestige.

In order to choose for ourselves, we first have to figure out what they're all yelling about. This chapter will explain how Direct Lending works, how it could work for you, and why it makes your Congressman so crazy.

BILL CLINTON, DIRECT LENDING, AND THE CONSERVATIVE WAY

For Bill Clinton's political enemies, the success of Direct Lending is one more reason to detest him. Clinton didn't invent Direct Lending. Republicans did. He didn't even sign the first Direct Lending program into law. George Bush did that, though unwillingly. To some, it looks like one more case where someone else did the work, and Clinton grabbed the glory.

On the other hand, what Clinton did is memorable enough. He saw Direct Lending in a different light than its creators had. He and his advisors realized how to use the program not just to streamline government but also to give students a new way to deal with crippling debt—by letting us pay back our student loans as a portion of our income.

Both federal loan programs let you pay based on a percentage of what you earn. But Direct Lending offers you the most flexible loan terms yet. With FFELP's Income Sensitive Repayment plan, you have to pay at least your monthly interest charge. With Direct Lending's Income Contingent Repayment option (ICR), it doesn't matter how big your loan is. You pay a percentage of your monthly income, and that's it.

For your lender, ICR carries a risk. Maybe you'll never have the money. Maybe your loan will never get paid. Direct Lending is built to handle that possibility: if you make payments for twenty-five years but don't retire your whole balance, whatever's left of your student loan is officially forgiven. (This doesn't mean it's forgotten. Your unpaid balance becomes taxable income, so you'll probably owe a few thousand bucks to the IRS.)

Still, under ICR, you never have to go into default, no matter what. Some people think that's a rotten idea. "The idea that there's no default is just playing with semantics," protests Lawrence A. Hough of Sallie Mae. "If you look at it from the taxpayers' point of view, isn't the write-off of a loan equivalent to a default on that borrower's obligation to repay?"

It's not just money that makes the Direct Lending debate so angry. It goes beyond business, to people's core beliefs. When ICR implies that government will pay off your loan if you can't, many conservatives are deeply offended. Since the days of Ronald Reagan, they've been trying to detach government from any direct responsibility for financing your education. "You want it?" they say. "Go get it. We'll give you a break on the cost of the loan, but why should we actually hand you money? Your education is for you, not for all people in America."

For Direct Lending's advocates, the conservative point of view conveniently ignores reality. "While government has been saying 'Go buy it yourselves,'" they argue, "the cost of education has exploded. Now we're talking about a level of expense that can hobble students for life. Is this really a burden they ought to bear alone?"

We students could offer a ruder argument. "If you think our educations are for us alone," we might say, "try running corporate America in the next millennium without us."

Students Squeezed by Unmanageable Debt

For large-loan student debtors, the recession years of 1991–92 didn't exactly encourage our trust in a system with no safety net. We'd shelled out eighties prices for our degrees. Then, bang! *Dynasty* became *Roseanne*. Recession and the downsizing craze sucked the life out of the job market. We were left holding the sheepskin.

Lots of things weren't so great, but it was our FFELP loans that kept us awake at night, because they were totally beyond our control. Our options to postpone payment were all used up, but we couldn't pay in full. Could we send partial payments? Nope. Could we settle for part of the loan? Negative. Could we do *anything* but free-fall toward default? Sorry.

By offering us the option of Income Contingent Repayment, Direct Lending has helped to lift that weight off our shoulders, and every student debtor I know is grateful.

True, ICR has big drawbacks. Paying off your loan this way is probably the most expensive method you could choose. ("If you'd just buckle down," FFELP's spokesmen correctly point out, "you'd be free in ten years.") But for some of us whose debt has hit a really unmanageable level, the reality dawns that we may be paying for most of our lives. If our loans are a permanent expense, it makes sense to opt for manageable monthly payments rather than sacrificing to pay at any price. And that's an option conservative leaders feel is plain wrong—for government, and for us.

Because student loan law must be reauthorized (renegotiated) every five years, Direct loans will always be vulnerable to political attack. If Direct Lending ever went down, what would happen to Income Contingent Repayment? Nobody knows. But one thing is certain: as long as Direct Lending cuts into FFELP's profits, FFELP will try to defeat it.

With untold power and billions of dollars at stake, FFELP's corporate lords and Direct Lending's bureaucrats are competing all-out to dominate the lending game in the future. Their weapons are conflicting studies, confusing statistics, and contrasting predictions, expertly used to discredit each other. For us who actually owe student loans, it all boils down to gobbledygook. Will ICR save America, or drive us into the poorhouse? It depends entirely on whose paid spokesman you ask.

To get some idea which loan program you ought to invest in, you have to tune out all the competing voices and look for the truth on your own. Fortunately, the next few pages will help you get beyond what both sides have *said*—and tell you what they've *done*.

DL Meets ICR: Washington Power Couple

When we talk about what you and I now call Direct Lending, the first thing you need to see is that it's not really a single concept. It's a convenient name for the marriage of two intensely creative ideas—Income Contingent Repayment and Direct loans. Together, they form a powerful concept that has drastically improved the world for student debtors. Yet their marriage is not necessarily permanent. They're surrounded by rivals who would love to break them up.

Is this marriage strong enough to stand? Before you can judge, you have to know its partners better. Let's start by introducing the older one.

Income Contingent Repayment: An Idea with a Radical Past

Income Contingent Repayment has been around as an idea since thirty years ago, when libertarian economist Milton Friedman first put his finger on why it seems so funny to repay a student loan regardless of the value it brings you. For Friedman, it's a mistake to classify a student loan alongside fixed monthly debts, like home and auto loans. When you buy these possessions, you know what you're getting.

When you prepay for your education by signing loans, the situation is very different. You can't predict the value of what you're getting, because the whole experience of education takes place in your future. Will the curriculum be what you hoped? Will your training help you land a lucrative job? There's no way to know.

That's why Friedman thinks you ought to be treated as a start-up business, not an installment-loan borrower. For him, your student loan is an investment in which the lender is backing a new business: you. This means you should repay your debt not in set monthly installments but in dividends: a regular share of your profits, until the investment is paid back plus interest.

In the case of a student loan, this means your repayment would be contingent on your income. Hence, of course, the term *Income Contingent Repayment*.

"It's exactly the same as if you buy stock in a small enterprise," Friedman explains. "You're investing in a person's productivity. I start a company; you buy shares of stock in it. How do you get your return? Not by charging a fixed interest rate. You cannot start a new enterprise that way. It's too risky. The same thing goes for individual students. Some will become highly successful, some will be failures. You have to average the winners with the losers in order to make it a paying proposition."

On the other hand, counters Sallie Mae's Lawrence A. Hough, a purely income-contingent lending system would keep a lot of us from studying what we want, because our future earnings wouldn't cover the cost of our loans. "If you say, 'I'm going to be the world's greatest social worker, and the only thing that stands in my way is $100,000 for an education,'" says Hough, "an investor will answer, 'No amount of interest I can charge on $100,000 would allow me to invest in your future earnings as a social worker. Go find a school without a $100,000 price tag, because that tuition is all out of line with your earning potential.'"

Cracking the Code: How Government Lets You Pay Flexibly

That became the challenge: How could government give every student the option of flexible loan repayment, yet make enough profit to keep giving loans? It took a couple of government's most brilliant math whizzes years to crack the problem. But by the eighties, conservative Republican congressman Tom Petri of Vermont and his legislative director Joe Flader had invented a workable blueprint for the ICR plan we have now.

Back then, though, nobody was really interested.

As the ICR ball picked up speed, it was rolling toward a manhole, in the form of FFELP. Income Contingent Repayment wouldn't work within the bank-based system, because banks had no power to check upon our income and keep the weasels among us from underpaying. Realizing this, Petri and Flader figured the Internal Revenue Service should do the collecting on our income-contingent loans. It was already set up to take in money—and it already knew how much we made.

The IRS idea was gorgeously simple, but very bad for FFELP. This was territory where FFELP lenders couldn't go. Only government agencies have the right to swap information with the IRS. And worse trouble was on the way: as of 1990, other innovative thinkers in government were developing what would prove to be FFELP's nemesis and Income Contingent Repayment's happy home: Direct Lending.

Credit Reform: Direct Lending's Missing Link

Without an unsexy law called the Credit Reform Act of 1990, we wouldn't have Direct Lending today, because before Credit Reform, FFELP loans looked great, and Direct loans looked stupid.

Before Credit Reform, Congress counted the cost of a given cohort (group) of loans only during the year in which those loans were made. Any problem that might cost money later, over the long-term life of the loans, wasn't included and therefore didn't exist. (Among those "nonexistent" costs was the *huge* expense of reimbursing FFELP lenders for defaulted student loans.)

Under the old system, federally guaranteed FFELP loans looked dirt cheap. Why? "With a FFELP loan, you don't put out the money right away, the bank does," explains Barmak Nassirian of the American Association of State Colleges and Universities. "The bank, of course, is going to charge you up the wazoo later, but those charges will not come due within the next twelve months."

Conversely, continues Nassirian, the old rules made any direct loan (where money is lent directly from the government) look "horrendously expensive"—*because all the money goes out in the first twelve months*. "This loan was treated literally like a giveaway," he says, "because repayment occurs over the next twenty-five years, and we weren't taking that into account."

Under Congress's new bookkeeping rules, life is very different. Now if you decide to okay a cohort of loans, you have to figure in all their future costs—and profits. That's why FFELP loans suddenly looked expensive and Direct loans looked cheaper—even billions of dollars cheaper. Over the long-term life of the loan, government would be taking money in, not paying money out. There was also something else: In making direct loans, government could afford to be more flexible than banks. So truly flexible loan payments for students might be practical at last.

As of 1990 and 1991, Tom Petri and Joe Flader were no longer alone with their radical ideas about Income Contingent Repayment. "In the Bush White House," Flader remembers, "we made a determined push."

Nobody Likes a Smart Idea: Direct Lending Versus George Bush

Working in George Bush's Education Department and later in the Bush White House, Republican economist Charles Kolb came up with his own plan for Direct Lending. But his innovation fell on deaf ears. In his scathing memoir, *White House Daze: The Unmaking of Domestic Policy in the Bush Years,* Kolb tells all. (With apologies to Kolb, I've condensed his text.)

Kolb writes:

I co-chaired a task force to study reauthorizing the Higher Education Act. . . . The [FFELP] program had become unmanageable, unauditable, and unaccountable with the growth of a cottage industry of banks, guarantee agencies, and secondary markets that grew rich off the generous federal subsidy. Every effort was needed to simplify and streamline the program's operation. . . .

In April 1990, I outlined how a direct loan program might operate. The federal government would borrow directly from the Federal Financing Bank. The banks would be eliminated [because] Uncle Sam could raise the same money more cheaply.

With a direct loan program there would no longer be any need for guarantee agencies either. Secondary market entities like Sallie Mae could still function, primarily as contractors to service the loans. The complexity and indirect accountability of the existing program would be replaced by a streamlined system that maximized efficiency and minimized cost.

Can you imagine an idea that the FFELP industry would hate—or fear—more?

Naturally inclined to trust the bankers, Bush threatened to veto

Direct Lending. He relented only after a delegation of Republican Congressmen told him they would vote for the legislation anyway. In the end, Direct Lending was signed into law, but only as a limited pilot program. Not enough to change anything, really.

The next politician who got interested in Direct Lending changed things plenty. His name, of course, was Bill Clinton.

THE PRESIDENT WHO BORROWED A STUDENT LOAN: BILL CLINTON AND DIRECT LENDING

In the downsizing days of 1990 and 1991, students and their families were bruised and worried that worse was yet to come. The price of college, and of student loans, had become a source of smoldering resentment. Presidential candidate Clinton was listening. President Bush wasn't.

For Clinton, the issue of student loans was a natural. Affordable education was personal to him: he'd gone to Georgetown University on a National Defense loan and later worked part of it off as a teacher. Besides, every time he spoke of college loans for less on the campaign trail, people cheered.

Even so, Clinton was interested in more than low payments. He believed overwhelming debt was preventing us from going into public service. For Clinton, this was no way to do things. According to *The Bill,* Steven Waldman's fascinating account of the 1992 campaign and the new president's first months in office, Clinton was motivated by a lifelong love of national service programs like VISTA and the Peace Corps. He was determined to create a new program where all young Americans could work off a part of their loans by contributing two years of national service.

Drawing from several existing ideas, Clinton and his advisers came up with an elaborate "domestic G.I. Bill" that offered two years of national service to help pay back student loans. The plan also had a second offshoot: graduates whose loans were too big for their earnings could make payments equal to a small percentage of their income. For Clinton, Income Contingent Repayment would free us to pursue low-paying but useful work.

That was how, in September 1991, Income Contingent Repayment went from being a cool idea bouncing around Washington to a campaign promise that was heard by people like you and me.

Throughout the grueling 1992 presidential race, Clinton returned again and again to his three-part proposition: we should all be able to go to college; we should be able to pay back our loans as a percentage of our income; and we should be able to work off our loans through national service.

Clinton's visions of affordable student loans and meaningful national service helped to elect him. Making the visions come true would be another matter.

FFELP's Mean Machine: Fighting for Survival

During the campaign, as Clinton delighted crowds with promises to "scrap" the existing student loan system, FFELP leaders followed his every move. Clinton wasn't talking about coexistence. He wasn't going to call for a cleanup of the FFELP industry. He was simply going to replace FFELP with Direct Lending. He was planning their elimination. Understandably, they felt his elimination would be preferable.

Practically the minute Clinton was installed in the White House, panic hit the normally dignified atmosphere of FFELP power vortexes like Sallie Mae. Even before Clinton's inauguration, in January 1993, Washington was swept by the rumor that the new President would push for a complete switch over to Direct Lending.

Almost overnight, Sallie Mae's stock started dropping like a rock. In fact, after Clinton released his first budget, on February 17, Waldman notes, "panicked traders on Wall Street dumped so much Sallie Mae stock the New York Stock Exchange had to halt trading." If this wasn't war, it sure felt like it. Along with other FFELP powerhouses like USA Group, Sallie Mae retained a dream team of Washington lobbyists and prepared to wipe Direct Lending off the map.

The industry began by negotiating. Clinton wanted Income Contingent Repayment? FFELP would offer it. But Clinton's advisers had been doing their math, and they were convinced that Direct Lending would cost less. First, government can raise money to make loans more cheaply than private enterprise. Second, Direct Lending would hire loan servicers through competitive bidding, not through the political process. This meant that for the first time, the realities of free-market competition would drive down the cost of servicing our loans. It also meant the student-loan business might suddenly become a lot less profitable.

Writes Waldman:

> Politically, [ideas like these] meant that the fight over loan reform would not be a war of ideas about the best way to improve access to college or encourage public service. It would be a full-throttle, multi-front, high-stakes interest-group war over direct lending. The players would not be tweed-jacketed analysts with an intellectual interest in loan debt; they would be major financial institutions with a direct financial interest in preserving the status quo.

THE FIGHT FOR DIRECT LENDING IN CONGRESS

For the young President and his allies on Capitol Hill, fighting for both Direct Lending and national service was total war on two fronts, and, though he won, neither program retained anything like the scope Clinton had seen in his own mind back during the campaign.

Republican lawmakers dug in their heels and voted against Clinton to the end—even some who had voted for Direct Lending under Bush. It wasn't just the fact of Direct Lending that was being fought over. After all, it already existed. Clinton was seeking to win dominance for Direct Lending.

All the Republicans would agree to was a world in which Direct Lending and FFELP split the territory fifty-fifty.

While Congress was wrestling back and forth, FFELP and its lobbyists pulled out a whole array of sneaky tricks. Misleading polls were quoted. Frightening "studies" were released to university financial aid offices, purporting to show all the awful consequences that would follow if Direct Lending came to their campus.

For their part, Direct Lending's allies never missed a chance to paint FFELP's lenders as fat, greedy pigs. Even when their concerns were real and justifiable, bang! The bankers caught the pie in the face.

FFELP AND DIRECT LENDING ARE ORDERED TO COEXIST

Finally, on July 29, 1993, with every temper frayed and every last congressional nerve worked, the lawmakers finally pulled out a compromise that kept FFELP in the running but also saved Clinton's pride. The new Direct Lending program would be phased in, like so:

1994–95: 5% of schools switch to the Direct Lending program
1995–96: 40%
1996–97: 50+% (at least half of schools are in, and more can join if they want)
1997–98: 50+% again
1998–99: 60+% (at least 60% of schools are in, and more can join if they want)

Considering how sweet it sounded when you first heard your Direct loan might be forgiven after twenty-five years, you really won't believe how little thought went into giving us that blessing. According to Waldman, the figure popped out as just one more number in a legislative horse-trading session. In the Senate's version of the Direct Lending bill, there had been a twenty-year repayment limit. On the House side, there had been no limit at all. They compromised at twenty-five years, and threw in the part about your leftover loan becoming taxable income.

That was that. The Student Loan Reform Act of 1993 became law. And as of July 1994, we could pay back our loans as a percentage of our income.

Waldman points out the irony in all this: in the midst of posturing and bluffing and working out win-lose percentages, hardly anybody on Capitol Hill paid real attention to the point that, for us students, far outweighs where the money comes from: with the right to pay back our loans as a percentage of our income, we could start moving forward again. If we'd borrowed too much for our education, at least we could work to get our lives back on track without suffering the additional punishment of default.

WAS DIRECT LENDING A SUCCESS?

Once off the ground, Direct Lending took off like gangbusters. Given the option of consolidating their existing FFELP loans into Direct Lending, students jumped on the chance. Its first year in operation, Direct Lending consolidated 25,000 loans worth $200 million. And though Congress had paid scarcely any mind to Income Contingent Repayment during the Direct Lending wars, students immediately recognized its star quality. Thirty-seven percent of us chose it during the first year; in year two, the number shot to almost half.

Hearing the vast sucking sound of customers jumping ship, FFELP lenders suddenly got very concerned about our satisfaction. They started figuring out ways to lower their profits a little and give us the benefits. From our end, things were definitely looking up. Of course, FFELP's leaders weren't thrilled. Though they had been defeated big-time, they accepted it. After all, you can't turn back the clock.

Except, as it turned out, you could. In November 1994, Democrats watched in horror as Republicans swept their way into majorities in both houses of Congress, carried along by the super-simple language of Newt Gingrich's Contract with America. It seemed impossible, but it was true.

FFELP's corporate leaders read that contract and saw a piece of fine print all their own. It said: Rematch.

CHAPTER 7

The Showdown: How Students Saved Access to Our Aid

In January 1995, nobody in Washington knew which end was up. Dazed Democrats were packing their belongings in offices all over town. Equally dazed Republicans were trying to get used to the feeling of being on top.

Newly elected Speaker of the House Newt Gingrich was not dazed. Along with his Contract with America, he had triumphed with voters, in a spectacular victory worthy of the great military generals whose exploits he loved to study. Now Gingrich told his congressional troops to march. His new military objective was to pass the Contract in one hundred days. He meant to lead America to a balanced budget in seven years. Why seven? According to *Newsweek,* Gingrich picked the number because he found it "mystical."

Waste of all kinds in government would have to go. Every program would be inspected, judged, put through the wringer. Nobody in government disagreed with that. It was the same language politicians always use: let's trim the fat, cut the waste, curb spending, root out fraud and abuse. Generally, wrangling between the parties guaranteed that nothing too drastic would be done.

But in January, it seemed anything could happen. Washington was suddenly full of first-time congressmen and congresswomen who saw themselves as a wrecking crew. They had come to tear the corrupt old system apart and start again from the rubble, reinventing the federal government as a much smaller, much less powerful entity, a different animal altogether.

Now, finally, Americans would get down to business and balance our budget no matter what. If student loans had to be gutted, so be it. But the budget-slashers of the 104th Congress were forced to back off their decisions to drastically reduce student aid primarily because thousands of students jumped into the political debate and told them: no.

You've heard about the famous 1995 Christmas government-shutdown budget standoff between Newt Gingrich and Bill Clinton. You probably haven't heard how student groups got together and used their brains, guts, and superior nimbleness on the Internet to defy Congress and protect our access to education.

By the time Congress and the President reached a budget agreement in 1996, the most drastic cuts in education had been eased. Direct Lending was still standing. So was FFELP, complete with some welcome improvements. As a result, we've had the benefits of both programs, and competition has helped to keep them on the level.

Understanding how this happened will show you better than anything else could how fragile our rights are as student debtors, how easily our deal can be changed, and how effective we can be when we elbow our way in and claim a piece of the debate.

HOW STUDENT GROUPS DEFENDED YOUR FINANCIAL AID WHEN CONGRESS VOTED TO GUT IT

Though dozens of organizations across the country pitched in to save student aid in 1995, the student battle in Washington was led by three groups with slightly different constituencies. Since they all have services to offer you, let's take a minute to meet them:

The U.S. Student Association (USSA)

Founded in 1947, it represents 3.5 million students, mostly undergraduates. It has professional lobbyists in Washington, but its elected officers are students on campuses across the country. The group has a long-standing association with the civil rights movement, and it's still the place to be if you're particularly interested in issues facing students of color.

U.S. Public Interest Research Group

Usually called "U.S. PIRG" (to rhyme with "burg"), this consumer watchdog organization was founded by Ralph Nader. It's been working since the seventies with affiliated college offshoots called Student PIRGs. These groups are designed partly to teach you how to take part in politics. Students work with professional staffers, sometimes for college credit. As of this writing, there are more than one hundred campus chapters nationwide. Student members of U.S. PIRG have pitched in during legislative battles on recycling, pollution, and homelessness—and they run a huge youth voter registration operation, too, if you haven't yet registered.

National Association of Graduate and Professional Students

Front and center in the student-aid battle of 1995 was NAGPS (usually called "nags"). Founded in the mid-eighties, NAGPS started out trying to bring basic protections like health insurance to that perpetually broke and overlooked population, graduate students. By virtue of its powerhouse website, run by Georgetown University doctoral student Tony Rosati, NAGPS assumed perhaps the most visible role in a guerrilla war that students took to the halls of Congress—and won.

EDUCATION ON THE CHOPPING BLOCK

Here's how Rosati remembers it. "We got started right after the Republican congressional election in '94," he says. "The Republicans had pretty much told everybody what they were going to do in the Contract with America: they were going to cut education. They wanted to remove the Department of Education, cut the funding drastically in all areas."

NAGPS's membership had learned through experience, says Rosati, that "when students get hit, grad students get hit worse. So we made an agreement with USSA and U.S. PIRG to fight whatever problems were going to happen, based on whatever the Contract with America was targeting. NAGPS would be the Internet side of the deal. USSA and U.S. PIRG would be the field operatives. They'd do face-to-face kind of stuff: phone calls, phone banking, letters, postcards. They'd get people to go door to door on campuses."

During those first wild days of the 104th Congress, everything was upside down. The leadership of powerful committees suddenly fell to Republicans whose newness in their jobs may have encouraged them to consider any new ideas to make government spend less, no matter how unorthodox. Since a lack of education is not life-threatening, exactly, higher education aid programs made a juicy target—especially Clinton's favorite programs, Direct Lending and AmeriCorps. But they weren't the only programs on the chopping block. So were Pell Grants, Perkins Loans, and even college work-study.

Gingrich put his newly appointed Congressional Budget Director, Rep. John Kasich of Ohio, in charge of swinging the budget ax, and when Kasich turned his attention to how government should save on student loans, his conclusions were, well, stunning. An undeniable whiz, Kasich went to work and produced a blueprint for a brave new Republican world of shrunken education funding that gave the shivers even to some moderate Republicans.

The In-School Interest Subsidy

In this new world, student loans would become more expensive in several ways: we'd pay higher fees up front; we'd pay interest while in school, losing the in-school interest subsidy that had always been a key part of the guaranteed loan program. And when we graduated, we'd lose the traditional six-month grace period before our loans came due. In Kasich's mind, that was only fair. His "what's-the-big-deal" attitude made the situation all the scarier.

"Tell me where else you go to get free money," Kasich would say at an August press conference. "You're going to tell me students can't pay another $20 a month? Give me a break. We're talking about the price of a Big Gulp."

Kasich's figures were contested by studies estimating that the death of the in-school interest subsidy would almost certainly close college doors to many students and dig graduates anywhere from 20 to 50 percent deeper in debt. According to U.S. PIRG, cost to the average undergraduate borrower would be more than $3,000; some large-loan borrowers in graduate school would see their debt increase by $25,000. That's a very big gulp.

Hitting Students, Protecting Lenders

Moreover, Kasich and company hadn't asked for a single concession from the student loan industry. Student groups now found themselves fighting bitterly not to improve the terms of loan programs but simply to keep loans available at all.

"During the first couple of months, January and February, they were throwing out plans amongst their own colleagues," says Rosati, "and a lot of these got leaked because even though there was Republican leadership, there were people in the Republicans who were reasonably moderate and did not want to see education screwed.

"We were reacting sort of like fire people in a brush fire. Something would start up somewhere, we'd go and try to douse it," Rosati remembers. "All the higher education associations [mostly lobbying groups for colleges and universities] had also gotten together to fight the cuts in education. They called themselves the Alliance to Save Student Aid, and they created an 800 number where you could call and give your opinion. We had the website, and we developed an E-mail list to alert people to what was happening with their interest exemption.

"It was a broad frontal assault they were putting on student aid," Rosati continues, "and we responded in kind to each one of those attacks, primarily by putting out the word, asking people to call their congresspeople. We used the Alliance's 800 number—which was great, because people could call without incurring a cost—and we nailed those puppies," he remembers happily. "I was told there was one week where they got ten thousand phone calls. We were swamping the congressional switchboard. They did not know what to do with us."

Cooking the Books?

Gingrich and his troops did know that Direct Lending had to go. Not only did they disagree with the program politically, but for them it was a prime example of government waste through duplicated programs. Either FFELP or Direct Lending had to be eliminated, and it sure wasn't going to be FFELP.

The question was how to proceed. Both houses of Congress held hearings on Direct Lending, expecting to hear tales of mismanagement that would warrant cutting the new program. Instead, a series of university financial aid directors said they loved Direct Lending.

Republican opponents of Direct Lending faced another problem that was still more awkward. This was the money-saving Congress, and the Congressional Budget Office (CBO) had long ago pegged Direct Lending as a big money-saver, maybe as much as $6 billion in its first five years. If that was true, why fight to keep FFELP—the more expensive program?

The Republican leadership dealt with that question in a way that bitterly angered their opponents and has tainted the student loan debate ever since. Revising government's accounting rules for Direct Loans only, Congress simply directed the CBO to go back and refigure the costs of Direct Lending, adding in a list of expenses that made the program more expensive than FFELP.

Both sides now agree that original Direct Lending cost estimates had left out maybe a billion dollars' worth of administrative expenses. But the new Republican plan erred in the other direction, said critics, by heaping every possible future expense on Direct Loans but ignoring corresponding costs for FFELP. The result, says one observer, was that "the Republicans figured out how to make a Subaru cost more than a Jaguar."

The Subaru strategy ignited a firestorm of protest in the media. "With a simple technical amendment," writes Steven Waldman in *The Bill*, "they ordered the Congressional Budget Office to count the money a different way—a way that made Direct Lending a money loser, instead of a money saver. Without changing anything about the program. One year Congress saved money by creating this program; two years later they saved money by eliminating it."

The Republicans' next move was equally adroit. If students wanted the in-school interest subsidy so much, they'd have to give up Direct Lending.

The students were having none of it. "We were getting students to call, call, call, write letters, letters, letters," says Rosati. "We had rallies organized at the local schools. We put everything on our web page, and we even set aside a portion for Direct Lending, so that people could go directly to it and get as much information as we had." Student "snail mail" letter-writing campaigns were effective, Rosati remembers. But even better was NAGPS's special congressional E-mail relay. (You can still use it on their website today.) "We printed letters out and hand-delivered them," he says. "During the height of the '95 budget battle, we dropped about three to four thousand letters in the House and Senate."

Students also delivered their message in person, on Capitol Hill, and in the media. "USSA and U.S. PIRG would do press conferences with the Democratic leadership," Rosati remembers. "They were really pushing hard to keep Direct Lending from getting attacked. We would send in three of our elected spokespeople at once to go to congressional meetings and put the pressure on."

Harried Republicans

By spring, these gonzo tactics had Republicans feeling battered. In an April 21 editorial in the *Washington Post,* House education committee leaders Rep. William Goodling of Pennsylvania and Rep. Howard "Buck" McKeon of California defended their student-loan proposals as more than reasonable, based on what the opposition felt were suspiciously rosy forecasts about students' financial prospects.

"Regarding student loans, Republicans are attempting to do what is fair," wrote the two lawmakers. ". . . Any college-caliber student, even one from a disadvantaged background, can expect to have a future income well above the national average. According to a recent survey, graduates of four-year colleges can look forward to an average annual income of $32,600—a full $14,000 more than the average high school graduate."

Thus, they argued, making students shoulder extra expenses wouldn't put college out of reach:

> For the average student, removal of the in-school interest subsidy will amount to an extra $21 a month over the 10-year repayment period. This is about equal to the cost of basic cable television. For students borrowing the maximum amount all four years, the added cost amounts to approximately $45 per month. The only students who would face substantial increases in their monthly payments are "professional degree" students, such as doctors and lawyers. Of course, professional students will have average annual incomes of almost $75,000 and lifetime earnings in excess of $3 million.

When this editorial was published, NAGPS struck right back. "The [in-school] interest exemption is our nation's largest federal investment in graduate education," wrote NAGPS executive director Kevin Boyer in an answering *Washington Post* letter to the editor.

> The editorial conveniently mentions medical and law students as recipients of the interest exemption. What about the anthropology Ph.D. student who graduates with $68,000 in loans ($100,000 if the exemption is cut) but with a starting wage of just $28,900 . . . ? Why, in the name of cutting the budget for our children's future, do we have to cut student aid—one of the key programs designed to allow our children to take advantage of that future?

In a season of hot-headed debates, student aid proved to be one of the hottest. Sure enough, student loans in general and Direct Lending in particular were set to take an enormous hit as Congress finished the budget it would send to the President. By September, both the Senate and the House had decided to get most of their budget savings by cutting Direct Lending back to 10 percent of the volume of new loans made each year. Beneath that statement was a financial fact: at 10 percent, Direct Lending wouldn't survive long.

As a conservative Republican, Rep. Tom Petri continued to stand against his colleagues and defend Direct Lending. In a widely quoted statement, he commented at a September hearing, "If at the end of this whole process we kill off Direct Lending, President Clinton and others will tell the American people that the Congress under Republican control shut down a conservative reform effort that was good for students and schools in order to keep the gravy flowing to powerful special interests. And that argument will resonate with the American people because it will be right."

Americans Favor Choice

By November, Congress was discovering that junking Direct Lending wouldn't be all that easy. On the 16th, Senate Majority Leader Bob Dole received a letter signed by 472 university presidents opposing the idea of eliminating or even capping Direct Loans. As the letter made clear, not all these educators headed schools in the Direct Lending program. Some were in FFELP and planning to stay. What the presidents liked was competition.

"Maintaining the availability of both direct and guaranteed loans is a sound policy that should be preserved," reads the letter, "because schools' ability to join either of the two programs has improved the student loan process for all students and schools, regardless of whether they participate in direct lending." It turned out that Americans who were fed up with FFELP's high-handed ways—but didn't necessarily trust Direct Lending—really wanted to go right on choosing between the two programs.

The 104th Congress did cut education funding by roughly $10 billion, in fact. But the cuts were redistributed after those thousands of calls from students like us came pouring in to Congress. And in the end, the FFELP industry came up with a number of concessions that helped meet the goal.

"It was pretty impressive," Rosati says. "We had intensity, fact-based reasoning, logic, urgency, passion, threats of votes, everything. By the time things were heading to the '95 shutdown crisis, it was pretty clear that education was hands-off."

Christmas Goose: Why You and I Can Still Choose Between Student Loan Programs

Of course we all remember what happened over Christmas 1995. The Republican Congress cooked its own Christmas goose. As Newt Gingrich handed Bill Clinton the budget that gutted Direct Lending, he also handed Clinton a miraculous political rebirth by giving him something he could refuse to sign.

The result? The Department of Education still stands. Students have joined Direct Lending to the tune of $16 billion worth of new loans and counting. FFELP has introduced streamlined application procedures and started giving us better service. There's no mystery to how this happened. The right to choose between FFELP and Direct Lending was saved by people like us. "The student groups were unbelievable," says economist Fred Galloway. "It was a remarkable grassroots effort. I mean, they really led the charge."

PART 3

How Your Loan Works

CHAPTER 8

Smells Like Payback: Deferment, Forbearance, and Consolidation

Graduation day begins the countdown toward the time you have to start repaying your student loans.

If you can find a high-paying job and start making your payments right after graduation, you don't need any advice from a book. Your future will be mind-numbingly simple. Your lender will mail you a book full of numbered coupons listing the amount of each successive loan payment and its due date. Every month for ten years, you'll rip out the proper coupon and send it in along with your check. No drama whatever.

On the other hand, if you don't know how you're going to pay and you're privately wondering why you borrowed so much, you're no worse off than the millions of students who owe more than $100 billion in loans.

In this chapter, I'll give you a whole kit full of tools to help get your loan payments in line with how much money you make. But before we get into any of that, here's a warning: *putting off your debt is hazardous to your financial health*.

It's both cheaper and wiser to pay on time and keep paying, even if that challenges you to think small about your possessions.

When you put off repayment, your debt grows at a rate that can turn out to be pretty horrifying, because your unpaid interest keeps magically adding itself to the original sum you owed. So your problem literally gets bigger all the time. There's also another great reason to pay up fast. If you can get this section of your life behind you, you'll be free to get rich or lay back or whatever it was you wanted to do in the first place. That's when your loan will really pay off.

"I just think of it as paying two rents," said my friend Tom, when I asked him how he was managing to pay back his massive loan from Columbia University on the rock-em, sock-em ten-year schedule. Looking at Tom today, you'd have to say that paying the two rents was worth it. He's thirty-six, and he's got all the things he hoped for when we first met. A challenging job that uses his education, a great apartment, a brilliant wife, a fabulous baby. And because he's debt-free, Tom is able to put his energy into his future, not his past.

You're thinking, Shut up and get to the part where I pay less. I understand. But remember, you've been warned: every alternative that lowers your monthly student loan payments is probably going to cost you thousands of extra dollars in the end. So the very smartest advice I can give you is, Pay it now.

Having said that, let's get on and talk about all the alternative ways you can handle your debt. With this book as your guide, you'll be more comfortable negotiating on your own behalf, so think of this chapter as a jumping-off point. We'll cover everything that exists right now—the good, the bad, and the ugly. But feel free to enter into creative thinking of your own.

FIRST, THE GOOD NEWS: ALTERNATIVES IF YOU CAN'T PAY NOW

Even if you can't pay now, don't be scared. When you look calmly at your situation, what may seem like a snake pit full of worries actually boils down to a small and manageable list of possibilities. Some are more comfortable than others, but with student loan law the way it is right now, none are so awful that you have to scream and run.

First of all, if you have to delay starting your payments, you can.

Most college loans give you six months' grace period, and if you need to, you can probably wait much longer to start paying. Are you unemployed or really broke? With most loans, either situation allows you to put off paying for up to three years. If your loan is subsidized, it won't cost a thing: even your growing interest is paid by the government.

After that, if you're willing to allow your debt to grow as interest is added, you may be able to delay paying for two or three additional years, by negotiating with your lender. And if you hit a rough financial spot later on, that can be dealt with too. Understand, this doesn't mean the debt goes away. It's out there like The Blob, getting bigger and bigger. But that still doesn't mean you have to pay now or else.

Whatever you do, don't feel guilty. America is caught up in an escalating educational-debt crisis that's way beyond anybody's control. Like most of us, you went to school for the very best reasons. But you may be finding out that the education you invested in hasn't yet brought you the job you expected. What you got instead was the chance to learn humility, renew your trust in yourself, and, um, live with a great big debt.

Paying for your education with student loans was a high-stakes gamble. You have to remember that you haven't lost that gamble yet. Owing doesn't make you a loser. Your loan does not have to dominate your life and paralyze your efforts to move on.

You're Running This Show

Remember, you're the consumer. You don't necessarily have to do the first thing your lender asks. Your student loan is a valuable commodity to the professionals who are dealing with you. It may be bought and sold several times during the years as it "matures," or comes closer to repayment. You won't profit directly from those transactions, but you and your loan will be missed if you take a hike, which you can do if you feel you'll get a better deal somewhere else. During the next few years, you'll probably renegotiate your loan at least once, maybe more than that. As long as the FFELP and Direct Lending programs are in competition, you're free to keep looking for lower interest, smaller payments, and longer terms. So don't get stressed. Get comfortable.

Figure Out Your Moves

If you borrowed enough money in school to be faced now with a big chunky debt, there's no point in worrying. Your choices are really pretty simple. You can attack the debt now, which may mean learning the art of living on a lean budget. You can evade the debt, by leaving America and living somewhere else. You can pay for seven years, then discharge the loan in bankruptcy—if the current laws don't change. You can go back to school and learn a skill that will pay better. Or you can defer repayment and gamble that your financial situation will improve in the future.

Understand, this is risky. It means your debt begins to grow. And no matter what you hope, there's no guarantee you'll be able to pay later. But once you decide, stop worrying. Go live your life. Your optimism and positive energy are your most valuable tools in helping you handle your debt.

A second big factor in your personal payback strategy is the kind of loan(s) you owe. Some student loans give you more advantages than others. But you generally have the right to defer and consolidate to improve your position. (I'm talking federally guaranteed loans here; private-sector loans are another story.)

Finally, your situation depends on when you took out your first loan. As you've figured out by now, Congress revamps student loan law every five years, in a process called *reauthorization*. Every time the law changes, loan rules change, but your loan keeps operating under the same rules you started out with. Different loans have changed on different dates, but if you first borrowed before (roughly) summer 1987, you're eligible for one official list of deferments. If you borrowed between (roughly) 1987 and July 1993, you're eligible for a different, more far-reaching list. If you took out your loan after July 1993, though, you're subject to 1993's Student Loan Reform Act, which drastically narrowed the grounds for deferment. To know what's up, check your specific loan.

SEVEN HABITS OF ALL-CAUGHT-UP BORROWERS

1. Don't ignore your debt. *No matter whether you can pay or not, don't make your lenders come looking for you.* Remember this one simple guideline, and you've automatically saved yourself a ton of grief. As long as you owe, you need to make sure they've got your correct address and phone number. If your lender (or, in the case of a Perkins loan, your school) tries to contact you and you're nowhere, your loan starts its step-by-step journey to some hired collector who'll work the phones to track you down—and that's nobody's fault but yours.

If you can't pay right now, suck up your courage, call your lender, and say so. We're raised to believe that if you can't say something nice, you shouldn't say anything at all. That does not apply to your student loan. If you've got a problem, it will come as no shock to anybody, starting with your loan providers. They hear the same thing all the time. Especially in the first couple of years after you graduate, they're more than ready to work something out. So relax. Nothing too uncomfortable is likely to happen—if you do the simple things you're asked to do.

2. If there's anything you don't understand, ask. Your questions aren't stupid. If this is your first experience with finances and lenders, so what? Everybody has to start somewhere. It's not important whether some voice on the other end of the phone gets impatient with you. What's important is that you know all the facts, so you can look out for your own best interests.

3. Keep organized records. This rule absolutely can't be overestimated. *The paper trail between you and your loan provider is the only defense you've got if something goes wrong*—like, say, if your lender gets your account crossed up with somebody else's and decides you owe a few thousand dollars extra. You think your lender can't make a mistake? Get a grip.

When you're a student debtor, trouble almost always comes from a discrepancy between your records and your lender's, whether it's a notice you didn't receive or a check they didn't post to your account. Unless you've got the paperwork to prove your point, you're going to lose, and it's going to cost you money. It's that simple.

3A. Keep a file including every letter you receive from your lender and a copy of every letter you send in return—in chronological order, in one place, within arm's reach. Incidentally, *read* every letter they send. If anything doesn't make sense, get on the phone and ask why. Don't assume it's over your head. If something looks wrong to you, it very well may be, and you're more likely to catch the mistake than anybody else.

3B. In that same file, include your detailed notes on every phone conversation regarding your loan. Whether you're talking to your lender, your guaranty agency, or your school financial aid office, keep notes. If there's a problem, your own records are your only defense. Write down the date and time of every conversation, what you were promised, and how soon it was supposed to happen.

Always write down the name of the person you're talking to. To save themselves possible abuse, most customer representatives won't tell you their last name. In fact, they may give a fake first name—and because sometimes borrowers physically threaten them, that's their legal right. But does that mean they're really anonymous? Can they just treat you any way they want?

Absolutely not, says Cathy Mayes, assistant vice president of servicing policy for Sallie Mae Servicing Corp. "We record your call by your Social Security or account number," Mayes explains. "You have called on July 14 at 3 P.M. I can pull up your account by your Social Security number, and I can tell who you talked to."

But can't we tell who we talked to? "Only by asking them," responds Mayes. "You certainly can keep a record in terms of the date and time that you called. From the name they give you, we should be able to tell precisely who that person is. Our computer generates an automated record of your account. Yes, you have to trust that the computer works, but the person who answers the telephone doesn't get to choose whether or not to record your call."

So, your personal record of your telephone conversation needs to be precise about the name (real or fake), the date, and the time of your call.

4: If you ask for a service of any kind on your loan, double-check to see that it's actually been done.

The student loan industry runs on computer automation. If it's not recorded in the computer, it didn't happen. Your loan is one account number among thousands, stored in the computer files of your servicer. *You don't have the benefit of one personal account executive with a human knowledge of your situation.* Instead, your account is tossed around among numerous customer service representatives who are supposed to record the ongoing tale of you and your loan on your computer file.

"We don't assure our customers they can talk to the same person again," says Cathy Mayes. "We have a system that allows any one of our customer service representatives to review summaries of previous conversations and transactions. If you dial into one of our Loan Servicing Centers, for instance, any one of our operators can answer the phone—in fact, sometimes not even an operator at the same center where you previously called. We are able then to handle the largest number of calls with the least amount of wait time all around the country.

"I can't say we haven't heard complaints," she acknowledges, "because we have. I know the system is not perfect in all cases. But right now, at least, our view is that it's the most responsive to the largest number of people."

And if somebody treats you badly? "Generally when a customer has had problems with a particular customer service rep, we can tell on our end, and we can take appropriate training or disciplinary action," says Mayes. "We also have situations where borrowers or customers have called or written with complaints, and we have then assigned them a particular person to work through the resolution of that particular issue."

Okay, that's the reality. *This mass-production system works fine most of the time—unless you need something out of the ordinary. Or unless either you or your lender makes a mistake.* In that case, you'd be amazed at what can happen.

We'll talk about more serious loan troubles in the next chapter. (A quick preview: you can handle them!) In this chapter, let's stick to the everyday, ordinary ups and downs of living your life with student loans.

JAKE'S STORY: HE IGNORED THE COLLECTION LETTERS

Here's an example—not a real horror story, but the kind of everyday thing that could happen to you. My friend Jake got in trouble with his loan servicer when the servicer's computer started generating threatening letters claiming he was late by two payments. True, Jake hadn't made the payments, for a very good reason. He had decided to resell his loan, and a customer rep at the old servicer had offered to relieve him of any expenses accumulating during the transfer by adding them to his new account.

When he got the overdue notice, Jake did the right thing. He called both servicers to clear up the misunderstanding. Each servicer blamed the other for the delay. He explained his situation to a customer representative, who agreed that Jake didn't owe. "Don't worry," she told him. "I'll make a note on your file. You'll get a few more letters, because the computer is automatically programmed to send them out. Just ignore them. This delinquency won't be held against you."

But did that solve Jake's problem? Absolutely not, as he found out a few months later when he got an unpleasant phone call from the guarantor that had cosigned his loan years ago. (Remember, guaranty agencies are FFELP's student-loan cops.) "You're thirty-six hours away from default," he was told. "Your servicer has tried to contact you repeatedly, yet you haven't responded. Pay the money you owe, or you'll be in big trouble."

It didn't matter that Jake had only been following instructions. There was no time to go back and fix things. When he called, his old loan servicer told him there was no record of *any* of his previous requests. The default clock was ticking. He had already been reported to the guarantor. By standing on principle and insisting that the loan servicer correct its mistake, Jake would only be creating more trouble for himself. He'd be in default until the situation was solved—whenever that might be. Jake borrowed the money and paid. Jake's loan servicer raked in a couple hundred bucks extra at the end of their deal—just by being inept.

One moral of this story is, *Don't ignore the collection letters*. "We must send certain letters on certain days, or we risk financial penalties from the federal government," says Mayes. "That's the kind of thing you should establish before you get off the telephone. I should be able to tell you, 'You will get one more delinquency notice, or you will get two more delinquency notices.' We have to send two letters approximately every thirty days, and if they don't process something within thirty days, I would guess there's a problem."

And what happened to the customer representative who got Jake into this mess? Nothing. The customer rep and Jake had a classic student loan miscommunication based on mutual wrong assumptions: the rep said "Ignore the collection letters," but she assumed Jake would know better than to ignore the letter that finally placed him in danger of default. Jake said, "I have a special problem," but he falsely assumed that the customer rep's phrase "I'll make a note in your file" meant she would—or could—follow through and make sure his problem was corrected. He should have taken one more step:

5. When you make a special deal of any kind with a loan provider, write up your understanding of the agreement, send it to the provider, and check to see that it's in your file. Do not trust anybody to take care of you. Follow up.

You can't rely on customer representatives to take responsibility for seeing your problem through to its solution. Whether they're smart or stupid, courteous or rude, you can count on it that they're just as overworked as you are. And if they happen to make a mistake, the methods of protest at your disposal aren't exactly sweeping, so it's better to prevent mistakes before they happen.

So what should Jake have done? When the very first customer rep offered to tack his payments onto his new loan, he should have written his own description of the deal and sent it to the lender. After sending the letter, Jake should have called in two weeks to see whether his letter was on file, and whether his agreement was being upheld.

Time after time, you'll deal with people who say, "I'll make a note on your account." That won't cut it—unless it results in action. *Never settle for a vague answer. If the person you're dealing with can't guarantee you a specific result in a specific time, you haven't solved your problem yet.* That's especially important in light of the next rule:

6. Remember that the default clock keeps ticking against you, even if you're in a dispute with your loan providers. Even if they've made a mistake at your expense. It doesn't seem right, but that's the way it is. You can't just say, "Fine, until you figure this out, I'm not paying." That won't hurt your lender, but it will hurt you. He's going to be paid anyway, whether by you or by the federal government, so he couldn't care less about you and your little attitude. You, on the other hand, will wind up owing extra interest, and you'll eventually have to knuckle under anyway.

In light of all this, rule 7 may sound silly, but it's still important.

7. Don't start every conversation spoiling for a fight. Federal student loan regulations are hellishly, ridiculously complicated. The "rules and regs" governing you and your loan cover page after page of tiny print in a book that's an inch and a half thick. *So before you decide to go off on your lender, be sure you ask for all the facts. You might be the one who's mistaken.* "For whatever reason, there seems to be a perception that it is better for a company like Sallie Mae if the customers are unhappy," comments Mayes. "How do we communicate to our customers that we win when they are *happy*?"

If you want to live successfully with your student loan, treat it with a state of relaxed awareness. Yes, you have to watch out for yourself. But if you're too fearful, too anxious, or too angry, you're going to pay not just in money but in long-term peace of mind, and that's too expensive.

JUST THE FACTS

In the following pages, you'll get a chance to comparison shop among some of the most prominent loan programs you might get into—and hear about their benefits from people who actually administer them at the national level.

Based on what you hear, you may want to move your loan. But if you got your original loan through the FFELP program, the law won't let you change lenders unless your original provider doesn't offer a program that meets your needs. *But,* fortunately, the competition between FFELP and Direct Lending has started to tilt a few advantages your way. If you don't like the deal you're getting with FFELP, you can simply call your FFELP provider and say, "This program's not meeting my needs." That's all it takes. They have to let you go.

You can choose to do business with your original lender, a FFELP consolidator, or Direct Lending. That's not a wide choice, but it's a lot more choice than you had a few years ago.

So what do you want in a loan program? First, you want to know how your lender stands on the issue of deferment.

What is Deferment?

What exactly is deferment, and why do you care? It's the most common and often the most advantageous method for delaying repayment of your loan.

Deferment is a written agreement between you and your lender specifying that your student loan payments are suspended for a certain period of time. Grounds for deferment are mandated according to law, and according to when you received your loan. Current student loans allow you twelve three-month deferments, for a total of thirty-six months, if you can't find full-time employment or if your loan burden causes you economic hardship (there's a formula for determining this). Once you reach the end of a thirty-six-month deferment period, you don't necessarily have to cough up the money, but the terms will become less attractive if you keep delaying. The best deferments come from subsidized loans—in which the government pays your accumulating interest. Deferments for unsubsidized loans, in which the interest is charged to you and added to the principal you owe, wind up costing you a bundle.

Loans made before July 1, 1993, offer more possibilities for deferment, many of them involved with do-gooder activities like teaching or various patriotic jobs.

Will you always be granted a deferment? Yes, if you're able to say truthfully that your situation matches circumstances (such as unemployment) that are covered by law. If the deferment charts in this chapter make your eyes glaze over, a customer service representative from your lender should be able to do the calculations on the phone to see whether you qualify. And even if you don't qualify for a deferment—or if you've already taken the maximum deferments allowed for a particular reason—your options are not necessarily shot.

What is Forbearance?

Whereas you can only ask for deferment under certain circumstances, you can request a forbearance—a three-month break from paying—just because you don't have the money to make payments right now. But if you have more leeway in asking for a forbearance, your lender also has more leeway about granting it. "In general, a deferment is an entitlement, where a forbearance is not," says Mayes. "But time has adulterated those distinctions. It's very complicated." By now, some forbearances are mandatory; others are voluntary (meaning the lender doesn't have to give them to you unless you're judged to be responsible, serious, and capable of making up lost time by repaying faster later on).

Lenders often use deferment and forbearance in combination. For instance, you might have twenty-seven months' deferment for unemployment and three more months' hardship forbearance because you're still broke and just getting started in your new job. Depending on the guarantor who issued your loan, rules and limits can change slightly. But a customer representative can always tell you which one applies to you.

Since interest capitalizes during forbearance, it's expensive to you, and it will make your loan get bigger.

The Interest Time Bomb: How Interest Compounds When You Postpone Payment

Why do I keep talking about interest? Interest on your loan seems imaginary, like somebody playing a game. But it's thousands of very real dollars coming out of your pocket.

When you get into deferring a student loan, your interest starts building on itself, like this: every time you're granted a three-month deferment, the interest you're not paying is added to the principal (also called the "capital") you owe. *That's what it means to say your interest is "capitalized."* So a $10,000 debt at 9 percent interest increases by about $225 during three months. Beginning the next forbearance, the principal is then $10,225. And during that next three months, the $10,225 racks up not an additional $225 in interest, but almost $232. If you defer for another three months, your interest will be about $237, and if you defer for a whole year, your last quarter's interest will be close to $242. So the principal's now $10,936. Not a big deal? Let a little time go by. Five dollars here and five dollars there quickly becomes five thousand.

To get a realistic idea how this works, try the interactive calculator on Sallie Mae's website, *www.salliemae.com*. It will show you how interest compounds, and it will also show you how big your monthly payments will be according to how much you borrow and how you decide to pay it back.

KEISHA'S STORY: SHE MADE $10,000 GO UP IN SMOKE

My friend Keisha began with a $36,000 debt plus interest. She started out her professional life in Hollywood as an assistant to a casting director, making $350 a week. Obviously, Keisha couldn't make payments. Now, after three years of deferment, her debt is $46,000 plus interest. Just so we're clear, that extra $10,000 is interest that kept piling up and is now added to Keisha's principal—her basic debt—which continues to rack up still more interest, still faster than before. When Keisha does start paying, her payments will be much higher, because her basic debt is more than a fourth bigger—$10,000 in new debt and counting. That's a car, a trip to Europe, or a down payment on a house.

Tacking on deferred interest means increasing your base debt, causing your monthly payments to go up a lot—forever. That can mean the difference between twenty-five years of paying $200 a month, and twenty-five years of paying $300 a month.

If you possibly can, it's great to approach deferment by continuing to pay your interest while you defer payment on the principal. This may make things easier for you without bloating your loan at the end of the deferment period.

Whether you're deciding to apply for another deferment or to bite the bullet and pay, or you're shopping around for a new lender to buy your loan, it really makes a difference to get the lowest interest rate you can and never miss a chance to pay down your principal.

FFELP LOANS AND DEFERMENTS

If you're like the majority of student debtors, your loans were issued by a bank, according to rules set by your state's higher education assistance commission. Most of those loans are Stafford loans, whether subsidized or unsubsidized. (Direct Lending also originates a healthy percentage of loans, and it's scheduled to originate more in the future.) Since FFELP loans have been around longer, they're subject to more varied sets of rules.

Deferring Loans Made Before July 1, 1993

The loan world has changed, but the rules you signed up under still apply. Even if you take out a loan after July 1, 1993, you get to play by the old rules if you still have a loan outstanding from before.

So, from the politics of the bygone eighties comes a list of patriotic deferments you can still take advantage of. Notice too that in some of these situations, some or all of your loan could be canceled. (See Grounds for Loan Cancellation, page 122.)

Deferments for Loans Made Before July 1, 1993

You're eligible if . . .

1. **You're in school full-time.**
   Subsidized Stafford: You can defer principal and interest. Some banks will also defer you for half-time schooling. Unsubsidized Stafford, PLUS: Principal only. Perkins: No deferment.

2. **You're disabled and enrolled in full-time rehabilitation training.**
   Subsidized Stafford: You can defer principal and interest until six months after training ends. Unsubsidized Stafford, PLUS: Principal only. Perkins: No deferment.

3. **You're temporarily totally disabled.**
   Subsidized Stafford: You can defer principal and interest for up to three years. Unsubsidized Stafford, PLUS: Principal only. Perkins: Principal and interest. Perkins before 1987: No deferment.

4. **You're in the military.**
   Subsidized Stafford: You can defer principal and interest for up to three years. Unsubsidized Stafford: Principal only. Perkins: Principal and interest. PLUS loan before August 15, 1983: Principal and interest, for up to three years.

5. **You're a full-time volunteer in a tax-exempt organization, the Peace Corps, or an ACTION program.**
   Subsidized Stafford: You can defer principal and interest for up to three years. Unsubsidized Stafford: Principal only. Perkins: Principal and interest. PLUS loan before August 15, 1983: Principal and interest, for up to three years.

6. **You're on active duty with the National Oceanic and Atmospheric Administration Corps.**
   Subsidized Stafford: You can defer principal and interest for up to three years. Unsubsidized Stafford: Principal only. Perkins: Principal and interest, up to three years. Perkins from before fall 1987: No deferment. PLUS: No deferment.

7. **You're a full-time teacher in a government-identified teacher shortage area.**
   Subsidized Stafford: You can defer principal and interest for up to three years. Unsubsidized Stafford: Principal only, for up to three years. Perkins, PLUS: No deferment.

8. **You're completing a professional internship.**
   Subsidized Stafford: You can defer principal and interest for up to two years. Unsubsidized Stafford: Principal only. Perkins: Principal and interest, for up to two years. PLUS: No deferment.

9. **You're unemployed but looking for work.**
   Subsidized Stafford: You can defer principal and interest for up to two years. Unsubsidized Stafford, PLUS, Perkins: Principal only, for up to two years.

10. **You're the mother of preschool children, entering or reentering the work force, and earning no more than $1 an hour above the federal minimum wage.**
    Subsidized Stafford: You can defer principal and interest for up to two years. Unsubsidized Stafford, PLUS, Perkins: Principal only, for up to two years.

11. **You're on parental leave.**
    Subsidized Stafford: You can defer principal and interest for up to six months. Unsubsidized Stafford: Principal only. Perkins: Principal and interest, for up to six months. Perkins before fall 1987: No deferment. PLUS: No deferment.

The Big Five: Deferring Loans Made After July 1, 1993

If you took out your first FFELP or Perkins loan on or after July 1, 1993, or if you're in a consolidation program, things are much simpler. The same goes for Direct Loans, which became available one year later, in July 1994. Only five kinds of deferment are available. This doesn't mean you can't defer; it just means you have to state your case in a way the government will acknowledge. Remember, with subsidized Stafford loans, interest does not accumulate during deferments.

Deferments for Loans Made After July 1, 1993

You're eligible if . . .

1. **You're enrolled in school at least half time.**
   Subsidized Stafford, Perkins: You can defer principal and interest. PLUS, Unsubsidized Stafford: Principal only.

2. **You're enrolled in an approved graduate fellowship program.**
   Subsidized Stafford, Perkins: You can defer principal and interest. PLUS, Unsubsidized Stafford: Principal only.

3. **You're enrolled in an approved rehabilitation program for the disabled or chemically dependent.**
   Subsidized Stafford, Perkins: You can defer principal and interest. PLUS, Unsubsidized Stafford: Principal only.

4. **You can't find full-time employment.**
   Subsidized Stafford, Perkins: You can defer principal and interest up to three years. PLUS, Unsubsidized Stafford: Principal only.

5. **You're suffering economic hardship.**
   (Here, if you don't qualify for a deferment, you can ask for a forbearance.) Subsidized Stafford, Perkins: You can defer principal and interest, up to three years. PLUS, Unsubsidized Stafford: Principal only.

PERKINS LOANS: IN A CLASS BY THEMSELVES

If you had exceptional financial need when you entered school, you may now be dealing with a Perkins loan—a slightly different animal than FFELP or Direct loans. An outgrowth of the National Defense loans of the sixties, Perkins loans are administered through your college campus, not through the various lenders we've been talking about. These loans carry a lower interest rate than FFELP or Direct loans (5 percent as of this writing), though they bear the same requirements if you want to defer. (See Appendix 2, Sallie Mae Deferment Guide.)

Having Your Loan Canceled

Believe it or not, your loan can be canceled under certain circumstances. Unfortunately, if we're talking about FFELP or Direct loans, the circumstances have to be very serious, up to and including your death. Perkins loans, however, offer a range of amazing possibilities you won't get with the other programs: they give you a number of options to do service and have your loan discharged.

Grounds for Loan Cancellation

You're eligible if . . .

1. **You die, or you're totally and permanently disabled.**
   100% canceled. This is the only cancellation that applies to FFELP and Direct loans also.

2. **You're a full-time teacher in a designated elementary or secondary school serving students from low-income families.**
   Up to 100%. You can be deferred for this also.

3. **You're a full-time special education teacher.**
   This includes teaching children with disabilities in a public or other nonprofit elementary or secondary school. Up to 100%. You can be deferred also, if your loan was made on or after July 1, 1993. This should apply to FFELP loans too, but Congress hasn't set aside funding as of this writing.

4. **You're a full-time professional provider of early intervention services for the disabled.**
   Up to 100%, if your loan was made after July 23, 1992. You can be deferred also, if your loan was made on or after July 1, 1993.

5. **You're a full-time teacher of math, science, foreign languages, bilingual education, or in other fields designated as teacher shortage areas.**
   Up to 100%, if your loan was made after July 23, 1992. You can be deferred also, if your loan was made on or after July 1, 1993. This should apply to FFELP and Direct loans too, but Congress hasn't set aside funding.

6. **You're a full-time employee of a public or nonprofit child or family service agency providing services to high-risk children and their families from low-income communities.**
   Up to 100%, if your loan was made after July 23, 1992. You can be deferred also, if your loan was made on or after July 1, 1993.

7. **You're a full-time nurse or medical technician.**
   Up to 100%, if your loan was made after July 23, 1992. You can be deferred also, if your loan was made on or after July 1, 1993. This should apply to FFELP loans too, but Congress hasn't set aside funding.

8. **You're a full-time law enforcement or corrections officer.**
   If your loan was made on or after November 29, 1990. You can be deferred also, if your loan was made on or after July 1, 1993.

9. **You're a VISTA or Peace Corps volunteer.**
   Up to 70%. This service qualifies for deferment also. This should apply to FFELP and Direct loans, but Congress hasn't set aside funding.

10. **You're serving in the Armed Forces.**
    Up to 50%, in areas of hostilities or eminent danger. This service qualifies for deferment also.

11. **You declare bankruptcy.**
    You can take this action with a FFELP, Direct, or Perkins loans, but only if seven or more years have passed since the loan came due.

12. **Your school gives you a False Loan Certification or closes before you can complete your program of study.**
    100% for FFELP and Direct loans received on or after January 1, 1986.

HEAL LOANS: TOUGH LOANS FOR TENDER PEOPLE

Though they're specifically designed for our nurturers—doctors, chiropractors, and other health professionals—HEAL and HPSL loans are downright stingy when it comes to deferments. Not only that, you can consolidate HEAL loans with each other, but not with Stafford loans. Is this the kind of angst you want cluttering up your doctor's mind?

Deferring HPSL Loans, and HEAL Loans Made Before Oct. 13, 1992

You're eligible if . . .

1. **You're in school full-time.**
   HEAL: Yes. HPSL: Only for loans made after November 4, 1988, and then only if you attend a health professions school. Want to go to school half time? Tough.

2. **You're unemployed.**
   HEAL: No. HPSL: Yes, but employment and disability periods are treated like forbearances, so interest may capitalize on your account.

3. **You're serving in the Armed Forces, Public Health Service, Peace Corps, or VISTA.**
   HEAL: You can defer up to three years in each: Armed Forces, National Health Service, or Peace Corps. HPSL: Up to three years, but serving in VISTA is not eligible.

4. **You're on active duty with the National Oceanic and Atmospheric Administration Corps.**
HEAL: No. HPSL: Up to three years.

5. **You're serving an internship that's needed to receive professional recognition and begin a professional practice.**
HEAL: This deferment is actually unlimited if your loans were disbursed before October 22, 1985. If your loans were disbursed on or after that, you get up to four years, but the internship must be in a field related to health education. HPSL: Up to five years.

6. **You're serving in an internship or residency program leading to a degree or certificate awarded by a school, hospital, or health care facility.**
HEAL: Unlimited, if your loans were disbursed before October 22, 1985. Disbursed on or after that date, up to four years. HPSL: Yes, if you're participating in advanced professional health training.

7. **You're participating in a fellowship training program or full-time educational activity related to the health profession you're preparing for.**
HEAL: You can defer up to two years for loans made after October 21, 1985. HPSL: You can defer up to two years—if your loan was disbursed after October 21, 1985, and if you're doing this fellowship within the first year after you complete advanced professional training.

8. **You're temporarily or totally disabled, or you can't work while caring for a disabled spouse (or dependent for Subsidized Stafford, Unsubsidized Stafford, or PLUS borrowers, effective 10/17/86).**
HEAL: No. HPSL: Yes, but employment/disability periods are treated like forbearances, so interest may capitalize on your account.

9. **You're a full-time volunteer for a tax-exempt organization.**
HEAL: You can defer up to three years if you volunteer under Title I of the Domestic Volunteer Service Act of 1973. HPLS: No.

Deferring HEAL Loans Made on or After Oct. 13, 1992

You're eligible if . . .

1. **You're a chiropractic school graduate.**
   You can defer up to one year.

2. **You're practicing primary care after completing your internship/residency in osteopathic general practice, family medicine, general internal medicine, preventive medicine, or general pediatrics.**
   You can defer up to three years.

UNEMPLOYMENT AND HARDSHIP: THE TWO MOST COMMON DEFERMENTS

Since they're the ones you'll most likely be dealing with, you'll want to know more about what qualifies you for unemployment and hardship deferments. Knowing how to phrase your request can have a lot to do with getting the answer you want.

Unemployment

Unemployment is a deferment where even the length of time available depends on the date you got your loan. If you borrowed before July 1, 1993, you can get up to twenty-four months; from 1993 to the present, you can get up to thirty-six months.

To get an unemployment deferment, you'll have to prove that you're "conscientiously seeking, but unable to find, full-time employment in the United States." This means you fill out a form outlining your efforts to find work—which is defined as a job of at least thirty hours a week, expected to last at least three months.

You'll have to list the name of the employment agency you're signed up with. (Legally, if there's an agency within fifty miles of you, you're required to get yourself there.) You don't have to be completely without resources to get an unemployment deferment: if you're in school and looking for work, or if you're working less than thirty hours and looking for more work, you may qualify. Also, you won't be disqualified if you're unemployed because you were fired. On the other hand, you will be disqualified if you refuse to consider a job, a salary, or a level of responsibility that you feel is beneath you.

You'll also be asked to write down names, addresses, contact names, and phone numbers of businesses where you applied for a job in the past six months. (You need to give at least six examples.)

Whenever you ask for an extension of your first unemployment deferment (remember, the limit is three years), you'll have to do the paperwork again. Please keep a photocopy of each application so you always know how you described your situation the last time.

I can hear you weasels thinking, Do they check up? Can I just write down six company names from the phone book?

Actually, they don't check up, says Mayes. "Sallie Mae does not do any oversight except what we would call a reasonableness test," she frankly states. "If the student lives in New York City and says there isn't an employment agency within fifty miles of his address, we'd probably say that's unreasonable. But if somebody literally makes up contacts and applications, then we probably would not catch it."

But don't whip out your Yellow Pages yet.

"If the student falsified his unemployment deferment and then resumed repayment and it never went into default, probably he's going to get away with it," says Mayes. "He has, however, committed a felony. If his loan goes back to the guaranty agency [because it's delinquent and headed for default], they might catch it. They're more likely to investigate than we are. What would they do then? That's up to them."

Hardship

Your eligibility for an economic hardship deferment is determined by law, and you qualify if you can show that you fit any one of several measures.

You'll get a hardship deferment on your FFELP loan if you already have one on your Perkins or Direct loan. You'll also get one if you're receiving payment under a state or federal public assistance program. You'll qualify if you earn less than minimum wage, or if your debt outweighs your income according to a legally defined formula.

How is Hardship Legally Defined?

This gets a little technical, but hold on: you'll get a hardship deferment if you're working full time and earning a total monthly gross income (i.e., before taxes) that doesn't exceed the bigger of these numbers: the legal minimum wage, or the legally defined poverty level for a family of two.

You'll also get a hardship deferment if your debt burden is more than 20 percent of your income. (That condition holds true for a lot of us, but here's the fine print: your monthly income after you subtract your loan debt can't be more than 220 percent of the minimum wage/poverty level number you came up with in the last answer.)

Finally, one more formula: you'll also get a hardship deferment if you're not working full time, and your monthly gross income is no bigger than two times that minimum wage/poverty level number— and then, after you subtract your debt, your income is no bigger than the same minimum wage/poverty number.

In other words, don't expect to get this deferment unless you're having a really hard time. (But remember, you might still be considered for an economic hardship forbearance.)

THE WORLD OF FORBEARANCES

If the world of deferments seems complicated, forbearances are more complicated still. Broadly, they're designed to fill in the common-sense gaps where you have a need, but the need doesn't qualify for a deferment. And remember, some of these are given at the discretion of your loan holder. Lenders take forbearances on a case-by-case basis—another reason you should learn as much as you can about their guidelines.

Administrative forbearance is basically used to keep you out of delinquency and away from default while some bureaucratic issue is being worked out. For instance, when my friend Jake finally made it from his old lender to his new lender, he was put on administrative forbearance until a missing piece of his paperwork arrived. In this case, his interest was paid by the government.

Mandatory forbearance covers internships and residencies after med students have used up all their deferments. It also applies for Defense Department loan payment reduction, and for work you do as an AmeriCorps volunteer. This is also the forbearance you'll get if you're burdened by excess student loan debt.

Mandatory administrative forbearance covers more intricate bureaucratic holdups: you'll get one of these if you're caught up in a designated disaster area or a military mobilization—or if you're temporarily making monthly payments that are lower than your interest. By the way, "mandatory" means your lender has to give it to you.

Voluntary forbearance is what you get when you plead financial hardship. Notice, this is different from the excess student-loan debt forbearance listed above, which is figured according to a set formula. This is the time when you've got illness in your family and you need to take time off from work, or when you've been hit with a big expense. You may ask for either reduced payments or no payments, for no more than sixty months at a time.

If you feel dizzy from looking at all these choices, that proves you're pretty normal. It's not because they're plotting to withhold information from you that student loan pros say, "Just let me figure it out." Experience has taught them that to you, the rules probably sound like gibberish. Unless you persistently ask questions, they'll probably assume you don't want the details. So they'll do the thinking for you.

But with your student loan, as with every financial transaction of your life, you'll be sorry if you let yourself stay in that position.

To get deferred with no hassles, remember to describe your case so it fits the government definition of the deferment you want. Also, give the system time to work. (Don't apply on June 1 to renew a deferment that ended April 15.) Here are some easy rules of deferment.

How to Apply for a Deferment or Forbearance

1. Have your lender send you a deferment or forbearance request form.

2. Return it along with a detailed letter outlining your income versus your expenses. Naturally, your expenses should be almost as high as your income. If you're applying for an unemployment deferment, give accurate information on the places you've looked for work. (You weasels: don't lie. Be sure you've at least had a conversation with somebody at this place.)

3. Be polite, whether you want to or not.

4. Always specify that you plan to pay.

5. When you have a problem or a question, contact a customer representative promptly by phone. (When you call, it's recorded as a mark in your favor.)

6. Always write down the representative's name, the date, the time, and the main points of your conversation.

7. File the papers they ask for, and do it promptly.

8. Keep a copy of every piece of mail you send—and every piece they send you.

9. When you get a letter saying your deferment is about to end, repeat from step 1.

LOAN CONSOLIDATION

So you've taken every deferment you can. Your thirty-six months are ending. Expensive and uncertain forbearances are next, and you haven't got the job of your dreams. In fact, maybe you don't have a job at all.

Don't sweat. That just means it's time to consolidate your loan—with your current FFELP lender, with another FFELP lender (if your current lender doesn't have a consolidation program), or with Direct Lending.

Consolidation is really refinancing: reworking the terms of an old debt, or debts, and making them more satisfying to you. Consolidation means instant good news: instead of a ten-year term, you'll have much longer to pay.

The bigger your debt, the longer the repayment term you're allowed:

$7,500 to $10,000	12 years
$10,000 to $20,000	15 years
$20,000 to $40,000	25 years
$40,000 to $60,000	30 years

Like every other fact in the student loan maze, these terms are a starting point. They can be stretched, under FFELP, by something called "Income Sensitive Repayment." (We'll talk about that in a minute.)

There's also bad news. After you consolidate, your payments will be lower, and you can choose from several repayment schedules that will ease your monthly payments either a little or a lot. But you'll owe thousands of extra dollars in interest. Taking an example in rough, rounded-off figures, if you consolidate a $50,000 loan at 8 percent interest, you'll wind up paying back more than $75,000—and $25,000 of that money is interest. And that's assuming that in thirty years you never ask for a forbearance, during which accumulating unpaid interest would make your original debt grow bigger.

If you're paying 9 percent interest on that same loan, your total cost goes up to almost $79,500, of which $29,500 is interest.

This is . . . shocking. Right?

Did you realize what you were really getting into when you signed for your loans? If you're like most of us, you didn't. You saw numbers, but they didn't sink in. In order to get yourself to go through with signing that paper, you probably did the same thing we did. You told yourself, I'm about to get the education that will make it possible to pay this back. I'm an honest person. I'll do it somehow.

Even now, you may have trouble thinking of this debt as real.

Well, maybe that's not so bad. You'd never hear this from any lender, but my classmates and I have found that our sense of unreality is actually a big help. We've all discovered that it's very demoralizing to sit down and meditate on how big our debt really is and how long we're going to be paying.

Instead, we've learned to take a lesson from our friends in twelve-step programs. We don't look at the whole debt. We look at how much we can pay today. This does not mean we don't pay. It just means we focus on what we can do, not on what we can't.

If you have to consolidate, look at it realistically. You're making your debt a lot bigger. You're accepting that it may be with you through a lot of your adult life. You're also doing the best you can, today.

How Competition Between FFELP and Direct Lending Helps You

By now you understand that FFELP and Direct Lending are feuding, and that in the next few years, one system or the other may win. Whatever the outcome, it will have its drawbacks, because for the last couple of years, competition has forced both loan programs to ask what you want—and try to give it to you. As long as there's competition, you're the winner.

Legally, if you got your original loan through Direct Lending, that's also where you have to consolidate. If you got your original loan through FFELP, you get to comparison shop among consolidators including Direct Lending—a privilege students have never had before, and one we should certainly try to hold on to. As things stand right now, you can actually mix and match, taking the best of all the advantages offered under various plans.

My classmates and I call this "loan surfing." But before we talk about how to catch this particular wave, let's look at the strengths and weaknesses you'll encounter under Direct Lending and FFELP consolidation.

DIRECT LENDING: WHAT YOU PAY, WHAT YOU GET

Even FFELP professionals who think Direct Lending is a tool of the devil admit that since it came into existence, students have been better served.

Direct Lending has wildly improved the student loan landscape for two very practical reasons. First, it's, well, direct. Like a big student-loan supermarket, Direct Lending offers one-stop shopping—making new loans, buying and consolidating old loans, and giving you an easier job of keeping track of where your loan is.

That doesn't mean it's perfect. Direct Lending is growing more complicated as it expands. As more and more students join the system, we need to pay attention to how we're being treated in Direct Lending and hold the program to its original promises of courtesy and efficiency.

The second reason Direct Lending has ushered in a whole new era for students is, of course, its killer special ingredient: Income Contingent Repayment (ICR), which lets you pay a portion of your income for up to twenty-five years. After that, anything you still owe is forgiven. (You'll be taxed on whatever's left of the debt, which could turn out to be plenty.)

As of this writing, ICR is an option FFELP lenders are not legally allowed to offer. You can only get ICR from Direct Lending, and students have been switching in droves. FFELP lenders have been demanding the right to offer a bank-based income-contingent plan too. Meanwhile, they've been calling ICR destructive, and advising students to shun it.

The truth is, there are valid concerns about Income Contingent Repayment. But if you owe a massive debt—and you know in your heart that the career you've found won't ever pay the bill—ICR will make your life practical and livable again.

Does this promise sound too good to be true? Will you be turned away? It isn't, and you won't.

If you're a parent who has defaulted on a PLUS loan, Direct Lending may deny you another. But if you're applying for a loan as an independent student, you won't be denied. Direct Lending will do business with you whether you're consolidating for the first time or you've already consolidated with another lender. Even if you're turned down initially because you've defaulted on a previous loan, you can rehabilitate your loan and reapply to Direct Lending.

Here's the list of repayment options students have fought to keep.

Direct Lending Repayment Plans

1. **Standard Repayment Plan:**

   This means fixed monthly payments of at least $50, paid over a set period up to ten years (not counting deferments and forbearances). This plan is the cheapest, because it involves the least interest.

   Direct Lending interest rates are variable, recalculated each July, but capped at 8.25% (except for PLUS loans, which are capped at 9%).

2. **Extended Repayment Plan:**

   This option lets you extend loan repayment from twelve to thirty years, depending on how much you borrowed. You'll still pay a fixed amount each month (at least $50), but your monthly payment will usually be less than if you chose the Standard Repayment Plan. The longer term means a big jump in interest paid. Interest rates: variable, capped at 8.25%, or 9% for PLUS loans.

3. **Graduated Repayment Plan:**

   Under this plan, your payments are lower at first and increase every two years. Your monthly payment must be at least half of what you would pay under Standard Repayment. Your repayment term varies from twelve to thirty years, depending on how much you borrowed.

The amount you pay at the beginning will be the larger of two numbers: the monthly interest on your loan, or 50 percent of what you'd pay each month under Standard Repayment. This loan will probably cost you more, interest-wise, than the first two. And in later years your payments will be high, though they're not allowed to climb past 150 percent of what you'd pay under Standard Repayment. Interest rates: variable, capped at 8.25%, or 9% for PLUS loans.

4. Income Contingent Repayment Plan:

Direct Lending's most popular option. More than 50 percent of student borrowers chose it in 1995–96. *This option bases annual repayment amounts on your IRS Adjusted Gross Income and the total amount of your Direct Loans.* As your income rises (or falls) each year, your repayment amounts will be adjusted.

Your payment will be the smaller of two math formulas: your monthly payment if you were repaying in twelve years, multiplied by a percentage number based on your income, or 20 percent of your discretionary income (figured as your Adjusted Gross Income minus a number based on the U.S. poverty level for a family the size of yours).

If this math makes you dizzy, call a Direct Lending representative and let her do the figuring for you. In fact, call anyway, because many people want Direct Lending's current ICR plan to be modified. By the time you apply, things may be slightly different.

Income Contingent Repayment: How it Works

After you pay under ICR for twenty-five years, whatever you still owe turns into taxable income. You'll owe tax on your loan, but you won't owe the whole loan anymore. Say you're taxed at 15 percent. If you still owe $10,000 after twenty-five years, your loan will be written off by the government—but you'll owe the IRS $1,500 in taxes. It ain't perfect, but it's a big improvement on the old till-death-do-we-pay routine.

Of course in order to do this, Income Contingent Repayment has to be designed to deal with any income, all the way down to no income. Can the plan deal with you no matter what? No problem. If your monthly payment is figured to be between $0 and $5, you'll be asked to pay the $5. But if your income is lower than the poverty level for your size of family, your payment will be $0. No matter how rotten things are, you're covered.

Remember, this does have a downside. If you're not paying, your loan is growing. But you won't have the added credit problems that come with being declared in default.

The ICR plan also contains a compassionate provision to help defuse the interest time bomb. Yes, when your payments are lower than your monthly interest, you'll encounter *negative amortization,* meaning that your loan will keep getting bigger. The interest you're not paying will be added to your original loan once a year, but only until your principal balance is 10 percent higher than the original. After that, interest will keep being added, but not to your principal—it won't compound. So your loan will keep growing, but not at quite so crazy a rate.

I'm not trying to kid you here—it's very depressing to think how much interest you'll pay by the time you've sawed away at your student loan for twenty-five years. But as crazy as this sounds . . . it could be worse.

How Do I Prove My Income for Income Contingent Repayment?

In order to be approved for Income Contingent Repayment, you're required to submit proof of how much money you're making. The first year of repayment, you'll have to provide documentation of current income, and maybe the second year as well.

You'll also sign a form that gives permission for the Internal Revenue Service to give income information (about you and your husband or wife) to the U.S. Department of Education. Your Adjusted Gross Income from your annual income tax returns will be used to figure your future monthly loan payments.

If you're married, your income is figured as the total of yours and your spouse's, no matter whether you file tax returns separately or together.

Can I Change Repayment Plans?

Yes, but the plan you choose has to have a repayment period that's longer than your loans have already been in repayment. So, for instance, you can change from the Extended Plan to the Standard Plan only if you've been in the Extended Plan for less than ten years. When you change to a new plan, you'll still be allowed the maximum repayment period for that plan. The years you've spent in another plan won't count against you.

Other than that, you can change plans as many times as you want.

If you're in Income Contingent Repayment because you've had a past default, you have to make three consecutive on-time payments before you can switch. Otherwise, you can switch back and forth between plans anytime, as many times as you want. No penalties, no delays. If you suddenly inherit a gazillion bucks, you can pay the whole loan off and they'll forget about the thousands of dollars in interest you would have paid in the next twenty-five years.

Unfortunately, Income Contingent Repayment is not available to PLUS loan borrowers. Your mom and dad have to stick to one of the other repayment options.

Where Can I Find Out More?

For information on Direct Lending, call the Servicing Center's toll-free number at 1-800-848-0979. (The TDD toll-free number for the hearing-impaired is 1-800-848-0983.) The Center is open from 8:00 A.M. to 8:30 P.M., EST, Monday through Friday. The Servicing Center's address for correspondence is:

U.S. Department of Education
Borrower Services Department
Direct Loan Servicing Center
P. O. Box 4609
Utica, NY 13504-4609

Your loan papers will give you clear instructions, but as of this writing, send loan payments to the following address:

Direct Loan Payment Center
P. O. Box 746000
Atlanta, GA 30374-6000

FFELP: WHAT YOU PAY, WHAT YOU GET

Direct Lending may be the newest consolidation lender in the business, but it's far from the only one. As you've seen, student loans are a booming industry, and the turf is crowded with companies that want to make money by lending you money. They can only be so creative in this; the choices they can offer you are strictly regulated by law. Within their limitations, they have worked hard to make their loans more attractive to you.

In the FFELP industry, the most recognizable leader—holding a third of all student loans, $36 billion and counting—is the blue-chip corporate powerhouse Sallie Mae. To keep this book as simple as possible for you, this chapter will explain the details on Sallie Mae's repayment options as an example of FFELP repayment plans in general. But remember, with FFELP and Direct Lending slugging it out, your lender could conceivably invent a repayment plan that suits you better than any you see listed here. As always with your student loan, you should call and aggressively ask what's the newest and best deal for you.

Sallie Mae: She Rules

The most visible secret of Sallie Mae's success is its Smart Loan consolidation plan, the first and most famous of its kind. The perky design of this program, combined with Sallie Mae's aggressive salesmanship to lenders and college financial aid departments across the country, is a big reason why your loan is so often sold to Sallie Mae when you graduate.

Like Direct Lending, Sallie Mae gives you four basic repayment choices. Its newest option, Income Sensitive Repayment, was developed under the Student Loan Reform Act of 1993. It's designed to give relief to overextended borrowers, and to come as close as possible to matching Direct Lending's income-contingent plan. But, partly because FFELP lenders are governed by different federal "rules and regs," the two plans don't get you nearly the same results. As you might expect, Sallie Mae's officers like to say their income-sensitive plan is better. What this turns out to mean is that, like eating sprouts, it's better for you. Won't you really feel like a better human being if you pay back every cent of what you borrowed, no matter what?

If you feel confident you'll earn enough money to pay your loan, Sallie Mae does offer more appealing discounts, interest breaks, and variations on the repayment theme than anybody else. *Please note that among the following plans, several options are designed to get you through repayment in ten years. Only when you start with Smart Loans are you talking about the much longer terms that come with consolidation.*

Sallie Mae Repayment Plans

1. Standard Repayment Account:

With a Standard Repayment Account, *you make principal and interest payments each month throughout your loan term, which has to be ten years or less.* This means you'll pay the least amount of total interest over the life of your loan. If you can swing it, this is the one you want. Interest rate is the same as your original promissory note (the paper you signed when you first got your loan). Eligible loans: subsidized and unsubsidized Stafford loans, PLUS loans.

2. Graduated Repayment Plans:

Sallie Mae offers the Select Step Account, which lets *you make reduced payments in the early years and still pay off your loans within the standard ten-year repayment plan.*

The Select Step Account comes in two flavors. *You can choose two years of interest-only payments;* after that, your payment amount increases once and then stays the same through the end of your ten-year term. *Or you can go for four years of interest-only payments,* which will then give you higher, but still equal, payments for the remaining six years of your term. Interest is the same as your original promissory notes. Eligible loans: subsidized and unsubsidized Stafford and PLUS loans.

3. Income Sensitive Repayment:

Available for standard ten-year loans as well as consolidation loans, *this plan figures your payment as a percentage of your gross (before taxes) monthly income. Payments must at least cover your monthly interest.* Since taking this option will slow down your repayment a lot, you get five extra years on your ten-year repayment term, for a total of fifteen years.

FFELP Loan Consolidation:

1. Sallie Mae's Smart Loan Account:

The original and still the winnah! America's most famous student loan consolidation plan offers various combinations to give you *lower monthly payments for longer periods.* You can start with interest-only payments that might be more than 40 percent lower than Standard Repayment. The payment term begins at twelve years and climbs to a maximum thirty years, depending on how much you owe. (If you can't afford interest-only payments, you should streak like a lightning bolt to Direct Lending.) Aside from its relatively low monthly payments, the Smart Loan program's big appeal is its simplicity. It lets you combine all your eligible loans into a single loan with a single monthly payment.

You can pick *two years of interest-only payments,* followed by principal-and-interest payments; or *four years of interest-only payments,* followed by principal-and-interest payments for the whole term. Figuring a $10,000 debt, the two-year plan adds about $5,350 interest; the four-year plan, about $6,000. Eligible loans: subsidized and unsubsidized Stafford loans, Perkins, HPSL (Health Professional Student Loans), PLUS, and Federal consolidation loans.

2. Income Sensitive Repayment for Consolidation Loans:

You've already seen how this plan works during a ten-year repayment. Naturally, it's also available for consolidation loans. If you choose the income-sensitive option, *you add five years to the repayment term of your loan*, so if your loan term is thirty years, you now have thirty-five years. (This extra five years is an example of "mandatory administrative forbearance.")

You can't get five years all at once, though. You're required to resubmit proof of your income every twelve months and be reapproved. You can choose monthly payments anywhere between 4 percent and 25 percent of your gross monthly income—as long as you're paying at least your monthly interest. Eligible loans: subsidized and unsubsidized Stafford loans, and consolidation loans.

So how does FFELP's income-sensitive option stack up against Direct Lending's income-contingent plan? Well, not so great, if you're really overwhelmed with debt. And if you're not really overwhelmed, why ask for payments based on how much money you make?

Direct Lending really does figure your payment as a percentage of your income, even if that means you pay less than the monthly interest on your loan. But despite all the talk about income-sensitive payments being a low, low percentage of your income, you still have to pay at least your monthly interest. If you owe a really big debt, that may just be too much.

And under Income Sensitive Repayment, there's no such thing as taking a rest after twenty-five years. You pay until you're all paid up, and you have to do that in thirty-five years or less.

Sense and Income-Sensitivity: FFELP's Income-Sensitive Repayment

Still, Sallie Mae's executives are willing to fight to prove that Income Sensitive Repayment is almost as comfortable as Direct Lending's plan. Barbara Jackson Ash, the product development director who helped to design Sallie Mae's Income Sensitive Repayment option, took me through a grueling list of "what-ifs" in order to show how user-friendly the plan could really be.

"With Income Sensitive Repayment, it has to be very flexible," explains Ash. "A borrower conceivably could have used five years of income-sensitive repayments, and is now at a point where we would require them to make at least standard principal-and-interest payments." (A standard principal-and-interest payment on a $50,000 consolidation loan is around $600 per month.) "They could ask for graduated repayment at that point. We'd put them in a graduated plan for the remainder of their loan, which could be ten years. That would allow them an additional two to four years of lowered payments."

Could a borrower later ask for another round of income-sensitive payments? "Absolutely," Ash states, although this second five years doesn't also give you another five years extra to repay—and Sallie Mae is not obliged to grant it.

Whatever the problem you're having, notes Ash, don't assume your lender will turn a deaf ear. "We do have the ability to establish repayment schedules directly with the borrower, if we feel that he is in a situation that's critical."

Having said that, Ash returns to a favorite Sallie Mae theme: in struggling to lower your payments, you're only hurting yourself. "I understand and empathize with the desire to accommodate borrowers' needs," she observes, "but I would ask you to question: Is it a service to them to allow them to make payments for an extended time and end up increasing their total loan cost? We do want people to pay back their loans, so that they're not doubling and tripling the cost of the loan."

The End of the Road Can Still Mean Default

All this sensitivity will come as a shock to borrowers who left school before 1993. Many of us have vivid memories of asking for reduced payments or additional forbearance, only to be told, "Sorry. Nothing we can do." Since then, more flexible laws—and relentless competition from that sexy new Direct Lending—have encouraged FFELP to go the extra mile in negotiating to keep us, the customers, happy.

But as current law stands, unless you can pay at least the monthly interest on your FFELP loan, there still comes a day where you have to cough up or else go into default.

"There is a point where the customer service reps run out of tools to help," admits Cathy Mayes. "Generally it's most difficult to deal with people who have chronically low income. People who have periodic income and are able to make payments from time to time, I think we can work with for an extended period—years. But we can't keep working with students or recent graduates who don't have income, because they keep losing ground."

And what happens to such borrowers? "We file a claim, and it goes to the guaranty agency," Mayes confirms. "The guaranty agency has more tools and more flexibility than we have in terms of negotiating payment arrangements. They can take income tax refunds, they can do wage garnishments, they can turn the loan over to the Department of Education for litigation, they can take assets, or they can make a decision to write the loan off. As a lender, we don't have that kind of flexibility."

But aren't these "tools" all punitive? "Well, the student didn't pay his loan back," Mayes answers. "They probably are viewed as punitive by the student, I think that's right."

War of the Worlds (Your Lender's Ideas Versus Yours)

Conversations like the ones I just quoted can teach you a tremendous amount about the lenders we all have to deal with. They aren't monsters, but many see one bottom line, and it's a fair one: they lent you the money, you accepted it, and now it's only right for you to pay it back.

In the research for this book, financial pros have told me over and over again that it doesn't matter how much people owe. Some debtors will find a way to pay it back, and some will duck their responsibilities. Consequently, many lenders have come to see repayment as a matter of personal integrity.

The educational lenders I've spoken to are very committed to serving students. But some seem to feel that service means simply delivering the money efficiently. When it's suggested that America's current levels of student debt may be damaging our generation, some loan professionals are concerned and aware. Some are actively seeking change. Others, sadly and surprisingly, tune right out.

Do the Right Thing . . . for You

The lesson here is about your own self-esteem. If you're worried that you're in over your head with your student loan, don't expect a FFELP financial officer to say, "Totally! This is a disaster! You can't even pay your interest! Bail out however you can!" They're not going to do that. Income Contingent Repayment does have pitfalls, and besides, lenders know things would get better for you eventually, if they could just convince you to make big enough loan payments to reduce your debt.

So please notice: whatever you do to negotiate your student loan, you're liable to irritate somebody. That's why you have to read, listen, learn, and then do what you have to do—what you think is best.

How Is My Income Figured For Income Sensitive Repayment?

"Since the law requires proof of your current income, we ask for your current pay stub," says Ash. "We also have ways of dealing with people who are self-employed. We require them to submit some form of documentation. We'll accept a letter from the borrower's employer stating their income. We'll also accept a tax form, if that's what they choose to send us. If you're self-employed, we'll accept a letter from a borrower, signed by the borrower, saying, 'This is my income, and this is a true and complete statement.' These options are simple and easy for the borrower, and also much more private, I think."

A Few Words of Interest

Smart Loan consolidation interest rates are not capped at 8.25 percent but are calculated at "a weighted average of the interest rates on the loans being consolidated, rounded up to the nearest whole percent," according to Sallie Mae's description. (Direct Lending may offer you a lower consolidation interest rate.) Since all federal loans are variable-interest, make yourself keep track. It won't be hard, since they only change once a year.

Aside from its various repayment options, Sallie Mae also offers interesting and potentially quite profitable incentives to borrowers who pay on time.

Sallie Mae Incentive Programs

1. **Great Rewards Program:**

    This incentive enables Stafford loan borrowers who make their first forty-eight scheduled monthly payments on time to receive an interest rate reduction of two percentage points for the remaining term of the loan. At current rates, if you owe $60,000, you'll save $3,467 in interest.

2. **Smart Rewards Program:**

    This is a similar program for Smart Loan (consolidation) borrowers. Make your first forty-eight payments on time, and you'll get a one-point interest reduction.

3. **Direct Repay Plan:**

    This plan rewards you for authorizing Sallie Mae to electronically deduct your monthly payments from your checking or savings account. Give 'em the code, and you'll save ¼ percent in interest. If you're a Stafford borrower, this will ensure that you'll also be eligible for Great Rewards. Interest savings on a $60,000 debt: $1,450.

4. **Great Returns Program:**

    Available only for Stafford loans disbursed after January 1995, this is a new perk aimed right at those of us who borrowed way too much, and it's definitely worth looking into. If you can swing your first scheduled twenty-four payments on time, you get a credit equivalent to the 3 percent origination fee you paid when you first took out your loan (less $250). Savings on a $60,000 loan: $2,961.

The Grand Total (Savings with Loan Discounts)

If the circumstances are just right, *you can take advantage of all Sallie Mae's financial rebates and interest breaks at the same time*. If you qualify for Great Returns and Great Rewards (or Smart Rewards) and then authorize Sallie Mae to put you into Direct Repay, you can save a total of $7,216 on a $60,000 debt.

Note: The examples are calculated based on current interest rates and a ten-year repayment schedule. So don't count on seeing these perks if you're in the thirty-five-year repayment crowd.

Where Can I Find Out More?

For more information on Sallie Mae and its programs, write:

Sallie Mae
1050 Thomas Jefferson St., NW
Washington, DC 20007–3871

Or call:

Borrower Hotline:
(800) 292-6868
Mon.–Thurs., 8:30 A.M. to 6:45 P.M.;
Fri., 8:30 A.M. to 5:15 P.M., EST

Smart Loan Account:
(800) 524-9100

Available twenty-four hours a day, seven days a week (to give information, send applications, and help students complete worksheets showing their potential payments).
Information about your existing account is available only:
Mon.–Fri., 8:00 a.m. to 9:00 p.m., EST

HEAL Relief Account:
(800) 643-0040
Mon.–Fri., 9:00 A.M. to 9:00 P.M., EST

IT'S A SIN TO TELL A LIE

Whether you're working with Sallie Mae, Nellie Mae, USA Funds, PHEAA, Great Lakes, ASA, Direct Lending, or another loan holder, here's a word of advice. *If you want Income Contingent Repayment or Income Sensitive Repayment, you have to give your lender honest documentation that proves the size of your income.* Whether it's a copy of your current paycheck, or a copy of your latest income tax return, lenders are going to be rooting through your private records.

Examining your tax return has never been a student loan lender's privilege before, and it can't happen if you don't authorize it. But repayment plans that involve your private, personal financial records are clearly the next big thing in student lending. So that's all the more reason to tell the truth on the deferments you ask for, or at least stick pretty close to it. If you've been getting an unemployment deferment and at the same time getting a paycheck and a W2 form, Income Contingent Repayment is not gonna be for you.

But It's Smart to Give the Best Interpretation of the Truth

You'll notice that FFELP lenders and Direct Lending have slightly different policies about how you're asked to prove your income. In their continuing business rivalry, it's a big issue that FFELP lenders can't ask the IRS for your federal tax return, whereas Direct Lending can.

But privacy issues aside, if you want to present the lowest honest representation of your income, thereby getting yourself the lowest possible monthly payments, you should always choose to send your income tax form. Remember, this shows your Adjusted Gross Income, the total amount of money you haul in, minus any and all deductions you claim on your taxes. If you use your current pay stub, you'll be assessed according to your gross monthly income—the whole enchilada.

The art of documenting deductions and filing taxes as advantageously as possible has filled many books already, and it's one of your rights as a citizen. It means keeping records of what you spend during the year, but you're doing that anyway, right?

If you have a job, and it offers any kind of pretax withholding benefit, like a 401K plan or a pretax medical account, sign on right now. Whatever amount you authorize will be taken automatically out of your paycheck before your tax is calculated. If you make $25,000 a year, and you put just 2 percent of that in a 401K, you'll be taxed on only $24,500 of income. Even your built-in personal tax deduction is a help. Once you learn what you can legally do to lower your own income, you'll soon see how much your efforts help in lowering your Direct Lending Income-Contingent monthly student loan payments.

Let's admit it. There are big and potentially ugly privacy issues here. There's a good reason the IRS has never let anybody look at your tax returns. Your taxes contain information that could be used against you if the wrong people got hold of it. The choice is yours. You have to decide what's most important to you.

PRIVATE LOANS PLUS GOVERNMENT LOANS

Although this book limits its discussion to federally guaranteed student loans, I know a lot of you out there have a whole other deal to worry about. You're attending school on a combination of government loans and private loans.

Particularly in the debt-ridden nineties, private loan programs have sprung up all over the country. Most of these loans are more like traditional bank loans than those guaranteed by the federal government. Lenders take more risk, interest is higher, and you have to pass a bank-style credit check before they'll fork over the money. (As TERI's CEO, Ted Freeman, wryly points out, "The government's Stafford loan program is the only one I know where in order to get the loan, you have to prove you can't pay it back.")

The more specialized and complex the area of training, the more often private loans enter the picture. Among these few examples from a rapidly growing industry, maybe you'll find your loan:

Private Loans (A Brief Listing)

• Law Access, Bar Examination, Medical Access, Medical Residency, Dental Access, and Business Access loans are offered by The Access Group, often administered through TERI (The Education Resources Institute).

- GradAssist, MBAAssist, MedicalAssist, EngAssist (for engineers), and Nursing Loans are offered through Citibank.

- ChiroLoans (for chiropractors), OpLoans (for optometrists), and VLoans (for veterinarians) are available from EFS (Education Funding Services) in conjunction with TERI.

- GradEXCEL, LawEXCEL, MBA-EXCEL, and MedDent-EXCEL loans are offered from Nellie Mae, New England's student loan marketing association.

- P.L.A.T.O. Loans, from University Support Services, Inc., let you borrow to cover leftover expenses from last year, as well as expenses for the year to come; you can also borrow $3,000 for a computer.

- LAWLOANS, MEDLOANS, and MBALOANS come from Sallie Mae, through its affiliation with private loan programs offered by several private banks.

- TERI Continuing Ed and TERI Alternative Loans offer extra graduate and undergraduate money beyond federal loans or for people who can't qualify for federal loans. (For instance, you can get a TERI loan if you want to take classes less than half-time, which is the cut-off point for Stafford loans.)

- TERI PEP (Professional Educational Program) Loans offer loans for Medicine, Osteopathic Medicine, Law, Pharmacy, Business, Dentistry, Engineering, Physical Sciences, and general graduate study.

The toughest thing about combining private and government loans is that you owe them all at the same time, and they're like apples and oranges: you can't consolidate them together to get the relief of lower payments.

Still, because there's an obvious need for progress in this area, change is sure to come. *Lenders are now working on various private-plus-government loan repayment plans.* Though these may not give you true consolidation, where all your interest rates are recalculated and your repayment term is extended, you still should be able to get all your loans corralled in one place, so you make only one monthly payment.

To find out the latest news on government-plus-private repayment, try calling either Sallie Mae's Consumer Service Center at (800) 643-0040; or The Education Resources Institute at (800) 255-TERI.

LOAN SURFING: TRANSFERRING BETWEEN PROGRAMS

Now that you know the practically limitless repayment options you can ask for from FFELP and Direct Lending, you're ready to think how you might benefit by combining both programs. It may not always be so, but for now, if you use up your thirty-six months' deferment in one program and then move your loan to a new program, you can actually start fresh with another thirty-six months' deferment.

For example: between hardship and unemployment, you might conceivably defer your FFELP loan for sixty-four months. After that, you could probably qualify for various forbearances, though at some point your loan will start to grow.

And once you're all out of deferments and forbearances at, say, Sallie Mae, you can transfer your loan to Direct Lending, where you could possibly defer for hardship and unemployment for another sixty-four months. (Your interest might be paid during these deferments, but might not, depending on what loans you consolidated.) After deferments would still come forbearances, and you might also qualify for those.

My friends call this strategy "loan surfing." It's quite legal, and you'll be able to try it as long as we're dealing with two loan programs in competition. Loan surfing does have a couple of downsides. First, it means your papers will be transferred between two bureaucracies that have so far shown little interest in teamwork. This may take weeks or months, and you'll have to watch over the transaction to make sure nothing goes astray. Loan surfing also has obvious drawbacks in terms of the interest time bomb.

But if paying is out of the question, at least there's something you can do. You don't have to worry that you'll run out of alternatives. So time your moves the way you want, and remember, surf's up!

TIPS FOR WEASELS: RUNNING AND HIDING

At the beginning of this chapter, I promised you the good, the bad, and the ugly when it comes to student loan alternatives. So let's take a moment to answer a question we've all pondered some sleepless night or other: if we wanted to act like total weasels, could we just run away?

Before you read further, I warn you: *this is not legal advice. Don't act on it.* The people interviewed here were kind enough to share their opinions, but those opinions aren't legally valid, nor are they meant to be. Besides, as you well know, this stuff may be fun to hear about, but you'd be a total fool to try it.

That said, if we wanted to get lost, could we?

"It's done all the time," answers financial counselor Jeni Tambash. "The hardest debtor to find is a female, because she can get married and change her name."

How Skip-Tracers Find Us

An expert skip-tracer (someone who finds people who don't want to be found), Tambash has done her tracking for collection agencies. She and her husband, Tony Tambash, a former student loan debt collector, now offer a brief guide to getting out of default through their home page, JENITAM@aol.com. Tambash offers us weasels a few tips to make her own job more challenging in the future. "Did you know that all the magazines sell their mailing lists to a central company?" she says. "If I can't find you, but I want to find a relative, I'll go to the database and enter your last name, and the approximate area I think you're in. It'll give me all the instances of your last name in that area, according to the subscription list. If you subscribe to a magazine, you can be found."

As an authorized collector, Tambash is allowed to see your credit bureau report, and she sometimes searches indexes to check whether your name was ever in the newspaper. But one of her favorite stories concerns pizza.

"At one point I got an unlisted phone number, but no address," she says. "So I called the local pizza company, gave my 'name' [the name of the person she wanted to find], and said, 'I want a pizza delivered, but I'm not sure if you have my current address or my old one. What address do you have me at?'" Tambash got the address in just under two minutes.

"Any service you subscribe to is good that way," she adds. "Cable TV companies are good. They're so free with what they'll tell you." The secret, concludes Tambash, is never to do business under your own name. "If you don't want to be found," she stresses, "subscribe to everything under a different name, order everything under a different name."

One cautionary note from the skip-tracer: you can't open a checking account under an assumed name, since you would be illegally changing your name for fraudulent purposes. Still, there is a solution, though it's cumbersome. "You can pay by money order," says Tambash, "under a different name."

Sallie Mae also has a skip-tracing unit, Cathy Mayes confirms. But at the corporate level, actions are somewhat more orthodox. "We look at a big database that holds the equivalent of all the phone books in the country," she explains. "We might not find you the first week because you haven't applied for a telephone. But if you move from New York to California, it won't be long before you're out looking for a phone, and we find you. If we can't find you that way, we have the references on your application. We know where you went to school, who your bank was. Eventually, if we can't find you, we contact the government. If you're paying taxes, they know where you are."

Naturally, skip-tracing is something of an art form in the student loan industry, and legends have sprung up around certain characters. One is Ken Reeher, retired CEO of PHEAA (the Pennsylvania Higher Education Assistance Authority), one of the nation's largest state-run guaranty agencies.

Younger colleagues recall fondly that Reeher never let a single student get away. A pet tactic: Reeher would place an advertisement in the missing borrower's hometown newspaper, reading *Urgent! We must locate Jane Doe!* Thinking Jane had won an inheritance or contracted a rare disease, friends and relatives would obligingly call and give Reeher the lead he wanted.

Asked for this book if a student ever outsmarted him, a now-elderly Reeher commented mildly, "I don't recall it."

In the end, Mayes stresses, hiding from your lender just makes things worse. "We find most people," she says. "But the harder we have to work and the longer it takes, the more interest is accruing on your account."

Weasels Abroad

That takes care of living in America. The other big weasel question, though, is more global. Could we move to a foreign country for seven years and then try to discharge our student loans in bankruptcy when we return?

"I would think that's a more onerous penalty than paying," comments Mayes.

Right, but if we did it, would we face lawsuits or criminal charges when we returned? "The year you came back, you'd file your bankruptcy action," Mayes says, "just the same as if you'd skipped on any other debt. I don't think it's a criminal penalty not to pay a debt. It's a civil matter, a breach of contract."

In other words, weasels, whether you skip the country or stay right here and burrow your way underground, it's at least as much work to evade your debt as to face it and deal with it.

TIPS FOR HEROES: STEPPING UP TO YOUR DEBT

You've spent this whole chapter bracing yourself for a lifetime of debt. But wouldn't it be great if you could get free sooner? You can work toward that if you're willing to consider taking the occasional chunks of money that come your way, and throwing them into your student loan. The first opportunity that comes to mind is *your annual tax refund*, if you happen to have a salaried job where taxes are withheld. If you get a refund of as much as $1,500, you can apply it to the principal—not the interest—of your student loan. This means the lender can recalculate your loan payments to be lower, which is better than fifteen hundred bucks in your hand. Really.

I realize that in order to give up cash of this magnitude, you would probably have to sedate yourself. But if you could manage it, maybe even a few times, you might start to feel that choking debt collar loosening around your neck.

On the other hand, if you get a check for a hundred bucks from Aunt Sheila, it won't make a dent in what you owe. So, hey, go out and do something fun. You can't think about your loan every minute of your life.

CHAPTER 9

Troubleshooting and Delinquency

If you've read very much of this book, you already know that daily life with your student loan doesn't have to be as scary as you thought. Of course, as some joker said, Life is what happens after we make other plans. This chapter is here to show you how to defend yourself when something goes wrong with your student loan.

I hope you'll read this chapter and the next as two halves of one whole, because *delinquency and default are really one continuous process.* They share a lot of the same characteristics: the same sequence of steps the lender must take against you; the same sequence of opportunities you're given to reply. The difference is that, as the process goes on, the consequences get more serious. Which means, in turn, that you have to guard against getting more frightened and concentrate on getting more focused.

In researching this book, the complaint I've heard over and over from FFELP borrowers is that, when one mistake happened on their account, nobody seemed to be able to correct it. So the mistake snowballed and finally went out of control, doing real damage to the student's academic and financial future. This seems unlikely, until you think how student loan law is set up. Every event associated with collecting your loan happens on a rigid time schedule dictated by law, and that schedule must be maintained whether or not some big, dumb mistake has been made.

Remember the animated movie *Fantasia,* where Mickey Mouse played the sorcerer's apprentice? Mickey didn't want to mop the floor, so he swiped his master's magic wand and put a spell on the mop to do its own job. But Mickey made a terrible mistake, because he didn't know how to lift the spell. Before long, Mickey was overrun with hundreds of demented mops, carrying thousands of buckets of water, flooding the castle, and completely unable to hear Mickey begging them to stop.

If your student loan happens to get out of hand, the next two chapters will teach you to say "Stop." Even if you're in default, the law gives you lots of ways to put things right. But why go there, when you don't have to? In the next pages, we'll look at how you can avoid the various pitfalls that can lead to default—which is a genuine, long-lasting, and completely unnecessary ordeal. Whatever problem comes your way, student loan law gives you time to make things right. Taking advantage of that time is the best weapon at your disposal.

Nobody can throw you into default just because they don't like you. There's a very complicated ritual that has to be performed first. So don't get hysterical at the first piece of bad news. You've got 180 days—six months—until your loan defaults. On the other hand, don't sit around and do nothing. Get moving now, because it may take six months or more to get the just outcome you deserve. Whatever the problem, don't duck it. Confront what's going on. Ask questions, especially dumb ones. If something seems wrong to you, it probably is.

RICHARD'S STORY: HE DIDN'T ASK QUESTIONS

Like so many students who get into big loan trouble, Richard is an artist.

A jazz musician with a bachelor's degree from the New England Conservatory, Richard reapplied for graduate study when he fell in love with musicology and realized that he wanted to earn the Ph.D. he'd need to teach at the university level. Richard says that having accepted him for its master's program, "The Conservatory gave me a small scholarship and arranged for me to take out all of these student loans. I worked to pay rent and living expenses, but I took out loans of about ten grand a year to pay tuition."

Already $20,000 in debt, Richard was accepted into Columbia University's doctoral program in musicology. There, he says, student loans anchored a policy that he compared to an academic variant of the old "bait and switch" game, in which a store lures you with a half-price sale—but once you're there, only full-price items are in stock.

"Columbia sent me a note saying that for my first year they would not have any scholarship money, but that for my second year there'd be a very good chance that I would be fully funded," Richard explains. "This was in the award letter, the acceptance letter." He paraphrases its message from memory: "So why don't you get some more student loans and pay your way for your first year at Columbia? And then we'll most likely have money for you for your subsequent years."

Richard took out $15,000 in new loans and headed for New York City. But when he got to Columbia, he says, "I realized that it was like a trap. They had given the same award letter to maybe thirteen other people. We were pitted against each other to see who would win the money for the following years. Unfortunately, I was not one of the winners. It wasn't like I flunked out. It was just that I didn't want to, nor could I afford to, take out any more loans."

Flat broke, Richard went home to Kentucky, got an assistantship at the University of Louisville, and happily swore off taking out more loans.

But part two of his story was just beginning. "As a full-time student," he continues, "I could defer my loans. But I had three different types of loans from two different banks taken out in three years—and, I guess, one of my loans was sold. I'm not sure how the process works, but I'd get statements in the mail saying this loan was now the property of another bank. Before I knew it, the paperwork was flying around, and I had lost track of which companies were supposed to get which deferment bills.

"In the winter of '95, I was deep in taking exams when I was notified that I had about three weeks to get a deferment form in, or I would be found in default.

"I took the form to the registrar's office, which insisted on handling the paperwork themselves. Two and a half weeks later, my deferment form came back to me as having not been delivered—the registrar's office had sent it to the wrong company.

"Consequently I defaulted on that loan," says Richard, "and now I'm in big trouble.

"This company, American Student Assistance, located in Boston—knows where I live. They've been calling me constantly. This lady from ASA has been on my case for several months, saying things like, 'This will be the ruination of your credit.'" Asked what kind of company this is, Richard has no idea. "A student management company of some kind?" he ventures.

Now that you've read this book, you know why Richard is confused. ASA is the guaranty agency for Massachusetts—just your basic guarantor-servicer FFELP mutant cop. Hard to explain that to a student who's stressed out, scared—and alone.

"We have a legal consultant here at the University," says Richard. "I've talked to him, but he could only refer me to a lawyer." Unable to afford that option, Richard took action on his own. "I sent them a note saying that I could pay maybe $50 a month," he says. "They agreed to consider reducing my payments, but I had to send them three months' worth of income payment checks, my lease, my credit card bills, car payments, my insurance payments. Then they turned me down.

"I got a letter saying that I was going to arbitration. That lady started calling me again. Then they sicced their lawyers on me. I sent them another letter with a $50 payment. I'm waiting to hear whether they'll accept that."

Today, Richard owes $40,000 in Stafford and Perkins loans, and another $2,800 in credit card debt. His credit rating is shot, he's still trying for his Ph.D., and by now he's come to grips with the fact that jobs for musicologists don't exactly grow on trees. If you dial his number in Louisville, you'll hear Richard's Southern drawl saying, "Hi. If you're a friend, leave a message. If you were stupid enough to lend me money for any reason—the check's in the mail."

YOU'RE THE BUYER, SO BEWARE

At this point in his career, Richard doesn't need a lecture. But it's not hard to see what went wrong for him. From beginning to end, Richard suffered because he didn't quite understand what was going on with his student loans, and he didn't insist on finding out. He was trying to focus on his dream of an education. Unfortunately, that was too expensive.

If you have a student loan or loans, you have to keep on top of your records. As Richard found out, this is not optional. This is called surviving. The art of defending yourself during any financial disagreement begins with your ability to present your side of the story and back it up with proof. With your student loan, this is especially important. Because you're young, you face an uphill fight in convincing lenders that you know what you're talking about—even when you do.

FFELP FOLLIES: WHY YOUR LOAN CAN BE MISLAID

Whether or not FFELP lenders want to hear this, the kind of problem Richard had—where one technical error, not his fault, somehow ballooned into an ongoing credit nightmare—is a hallmark of the traditional FFELP program. Until 1992, FFELP loan holders were not legally required to notify you in writing if your loan was sold to some other holder. "As an industry practice, it was done," says Sheila Ryan, director of policy and planning for Nellie Mae. "I don't know of a player that didn't do it." Yet thousands of borrowers call the Department of Education each month because they're confused about where their loans are. Obviously, something hasn't been working.

Sallie Mae's Lawrence A. Hough indignantly insists that "this kind of bouncing around doesn't happen with Sallie Mae, and hasn't for years." But there's no denying that FFELP borrowers are saddled with a certain number of sensitive moments in the life of their loan, when, during a transition, some mistake could easily be made. And like Richard, if such a problem happens with your loan, you may find yourself trying to wade through details you don't understand, sorting through trouble you didn't cause, attempting to communicate with lenders you don't trust.

"I think the biggest problem students have had with FFELP is, 'Who's got my loan?'" says Diane Voigt, who helped untangle many a bureaucratic knot during her service as Chair of the Direct Lending Task Force. "That, and the number of technical defaults we ran into because students got lost in the system. The number of students who contacted us and said, 'I've been in school, and I kept sending in in-school deferment forms, but they never processed them, and now I'm in default. What do I do?' That," says Voigt, "is an unacceptable problem."

HOW TO COMPLAIN ABOUT LENDERS AND SERVICERS: CALL 1-800-4 FEDAID FOR HELP

Of all the unpleasant angles of Richard's student loan experience, maybe the most frustrating is that, under current federal policy, it didn't have to be this way. Down in Louisville, dodging intimidating calls from collection agents, *Richard had nobody to tell him that he could report his problem, ask for advice, and get his case investigated, just by making one phone call.*

The number is the Department of Education's direct line to you and your needs: 1-800-4 FEDAID.

If you call with a problem, you will be heard. But, as you might guess, results may vary, depending on whether your loan is with FFELP or Direct Lending.

"We receive about fifty thousand calls a month, on all kinds of issues," says David Longanecker, the U.S. Assistant Secretary of Education. "The bulk of those are students who are calling concerning their student debt. [When the students are FFELP borrowers], we turn those concerns over to the guaranty agencies, because that's one of their jobs."

But doesn't that sometimes leave the student in the hands of the same organization that caused his problem?

"I think that's one of the fundamental dilemmas we have in the program," Longanecker admits. "It's particularly a problem if in fact the guarantee agency is sort of quasi-related to the secondary market that's holding the loan. How are the guaranty agencies ever going to find the servicers in arrears, given that [the servicers] are themselves?"

Despite the problematic setup, the law does try to assure you fair treatment by stating that *when your delinquent FFELP loan reverts to your guaranty agency, you must get a chance to tell your side of the story*—to an official who's not connected with the agency's debt collection arm and who therefore wouldn't profit from sending your debt to collection. *And if you suspect you haven't had a fair hearing, you can still complain to the Department of Education.*

Your Case Will Be Investigated

"Students can call 1-800-4 FEDAID with any kind of problem they're having," says U.S. Deputy Assistant Secretary for Student Financial Assistance Betsy Hicks. Formerly head of financial aid at Harvard, Hicks now directly oversees the operations of both FFELP and Direct Lending.

"The 1-800-4 FEDAID number is answered by our Public Information Contractor," Hicks explains. "And that's also where written correspondence that comes to the Department is sent for response. Say a borrower writes in and says, 'I'm having trouble; USA Funds is billing me for a loan, and I'm still in school; I should have a deferment.' We will, through our contractor, take the responsibility to go out and contact USA Funds, find out their side of the story—because there are always two sides of the story—and then write the borrower back."

This investigative service does a roaring business, Hicks acknowledges. Of course, the same factors that make FFELP confusing for students also affect examiners. "The borrowers aren't completely out there on their own," says Hicks, "but it's a lot more difficult for us, as opposed to when they have a Direct Loan, when we can simply call up one servicer and go into those files and see what's going on. We're there to help all borrowers, but we believe the Direct Lending program gives us much better control and ability to resolve customer complaints."

"The lenders and the guaranty agencies basically control [the FFELP] program. We don't," says the Department's Longanecker. "Unless that loan defaults, and is subrogated to us for our debt collection service, we don't have any ownership of that loan. It's very different in Direct Lending. If that student is having a problem in Direct Lending, then we are culpable. We're responsible, and the student ought to be as concerned with us as with anybody else, because we should be working on their behalf to try and find out the truth."

Of course, in Direct Lending, your loan is also in the hands of a contracted loan servicer, just as with FFELP. Neither program is foolproof. No matter how committed and how efficient the system, nobody is going to watch over your loan as closely as you do.

Note: If all this talk of mistakes and defaults is making you really paranoid, stop a minute. Nobody's saying this stuff is going to happen to you. The information I'm sharing with you here is designed to relax you, not stress you out. Knowing what can go wrong with your student loan debt is truly your best assurance that nothing will go wrong.

HOT TIMES IN THE LIFE OF YOUR LOAN

The fact is, you can go for months at a stretch without having to expend any psychic energy on your loan, if you're willing to tune in and concentrate every so often. Here's a list of times when you should check to see that you and your loan are being treated correctly:

1. **When you first get your coupon book or a payment invoice.** Are your name and address correct? Especially important: is your Social Security number correct? Open your eyes and look, because a digit off can convince a lender's computer that you never made all those payments. You'll clear it up eventually. But on the other hand, my research turned up some pretty horrifying instances of students who were dunned and pursued because of computer error. Convincing lenders the mistake is theirs is an uphill battle, especially if you've let the error persist a while. Who needs the hassle?

2. **When you request a deferment or forbearance.** When you apply for either of these, your loan provider sends you an application to fill out. Make a photocopy of the application before you send it back, and record the date on your copy. Now jump three weeks forward in your calendar and mark that date as follow-up day. If you don't have a written response in three weeks saying that your deferment has been granted, call your loan provider and ask what's up. It takes five minutes, and it will guarantee that you have plenty of time to correct whatever the problem is.

3. **When you consolidate or reconsolidate with a new lender.** This is a transaction to watch over, because your account keeps accumulating interest during the time it takes to process your loan's transfer. The faster it all goes, the less expensive for you. So call your old lender every week or so just to check on their progress.

   Note: If you're making this transition, don't decide to yourself that you'll never have to pay another cent on your old loan. You will probably have to make at least one more interest payment. Don't put your head in the sand. Call the week before your old loan payment is usually due, and ask how much money you ought to send in.

4. **When your income-contingent or income-sensitive payment is calculated.** Your lender will send you a letter every year telling you how your new payment has been calculated. Take a minute and sit down with the letter. Make sure they've got your information right. Check everything out. If there's anything you don't recognize, call your lender right now.

5. **If you decide to drop to half-time attendance,** it's a good idea to call and make sure you're still getting an in-school deferment on your loan.

   Also, if you decide to reduce your hours, call your lenders first and ask whether they grant deferments for half-time attendance, so you won't get any nasty surprises.

If you happen to be a little bit afraid of this whole student-loan business, there's nothing more empowering than asking questions. Once you know how they figured your payments for this year, you won't feel so worried about next year. You think this doesn't work? Try it, and get ready to sleep better tonight.

WHEN YOU HAVE A DISPUTE WITH YOUR LENDER

If a mistake is made at your expense, you can definitely take action to get things fixed. Of course it's a little like a good-news, bad-news joke. The good news: you can vent your temper by legal means. The bad news: you may have a tough time proving your case. (*That's why you must keep records*.) As you've just heard its top officials say, the U.S. government does want to help. But with your call plus 49,999 others on the line every month, you won't get your answer in a day. To protest an action that's been taken on your student loan, you have to be willing to write letters, keep copies of documents, tackle bureaucrats, and wait as long as a couple of months for your answer.

You may also be facing default, because if your dispute is not resolved quickly, you can fall into technical default and stay there until your inquiry comes to a conclusion. To clean it up, you'll then have to ask for the help of the lender you've just been fighting with.

Once again, none of this is likely to happen to you, okay? But just in case, here's how to handle a persistent difference of opinion.

Let's say you get a bill from your loan holder, Huge Mutant Loan Corporation (HMLC), even though you're in school and your loan is supposed to be deferred.

Don't wait a single day to start dealing with this.

1. **Call HMLC and report the problem.** Specify the date when you started this semester, and ask what went wrong. Do they not have the correct paperwork from your school? If not, who will they contact, when should they receive the information, and when can you expect to have written notice in your hand that everything is right again?

   If the customer rep says, "Sorry, but our records show you left school in 1995, so you owe the bill," you should:

2. **Call and present your case to an HMLC supervisor.** Once you've presented your case, let's say the supervisor promises, "Okay, I'll look into it." After this conversation you should send a letter, marked to the supervisor's attention, that outlines your understanding of what the supervisor promised to do, and when. By now, your account will be on its way to sixty days delinquent, so be sure you mark your calendar and make your three-week follow-up call.

   If the supervisor gets on the phone and says, "Our investigation shows you're delinquent, and in fact you're three payments late," then something's very wrong, and it's time to get other people involved.

3. **Call 1-800-4 FEDAID.** Report your problem on the phone; also submit it in writing. The investigation will take a few weeks, and you'll have to keep paying in the meantime. But just the fact that you've taken this step will help get action from your lender. And now that you've involved the Department of Education,

4. **Write a letter to the lender's CEO.** This time, you'll take your case directly to the Chief Executive Officer of Huge Mutant Loan Corporation, asking for an investigation of your problem. (To double-check who that is, make a phone call and ask the CEO's name. And make sure you ask how to spell it. If you want someone's help, don't start off by misspelling their name.)

   In your letter, you'll send a copy of your previous complaint letters, so the CEO can see that you stated your case the customary way, and got no results. You'll also mention the Department of Education. And to finish it off, you'll do something more dramatic.

5. **Send a copy to your U.S. congressperson.** The CEO will read your letter and know you've done this, because below your signature, he'll read a little line that says:

   cc: The Hon. Your Representative's Name, D-NY

   Believe it or not, your congressperson works for you, and she's around to help with stuff like your student loan problem. She may not be able to solve everything, but writing to her gives you the crucial advantage of visibility and credibility.

Look at it from the CEO's point of view. You're angry enough to complain to the national student loan hotline, and to ask a national lawmaker to intervene, because his company was just too shoddy to take care of your problem? That CEO will give your problem serious attention.

By handling your situation assertively—by taking the fight to your lenders, instead of letting them bring it to you—you show them that you're serious, that you know how to complain and who to complain to, and that you're not going away until you get some results.

When you get down to it, student loan self-defense is really just a dance with four simple steps.

Call,
Keep a record,
Write,
Keep a copy.

Repeat.

PREVENTING DEFAULT IS IN EVERYBODY'S INTEREST . . . ESPECIALLY YOURS

Once your loan is officially delinquent, both you and your loan holder go into an elaborate ritual. First, your lender has to try to warn you several times, by phone and by mail, that trouble is coming. If they neglect to give you one of those warnings, and you don't eventually pay, the lender won't be fully reimbursed by the government for the cost of your loan.

The name of the game at this point is preventing default—and it seems every lender, collector, and civil servant in the business believes his or her organization leads the rest in its efforts at default prevention.

According to Earl Esterly, vice president of the Van Ru collection agency—which processes a mere $1.8 billion in loan accounts each year—profits are not uppermost in his colleagues' minds. In fact, he says, the collection business pushed for laws that required more emphasis on preventing defaults, not on collecting loans already defaulted. "At any level," says Esterly, "getting students on the telephone and sitting down and talking to them—75 percent of the accounts we get here, we stop them from defaulting."

"It's a cost to a bank every time somebody defaults," agrees Patricia Scherschel, vice president of communications for USA Group, the nation's largest nonprofit guarantor. "The name of the game for us is to prevent the default. We work very hard on this."

Just remember, when you get those scary phone calls and letters, *answer them*: you will not be forced to pay more than you can, and it'll never be as easy as it is today. If you wait and let your loan fall into default, you'll still have to pay, but collection fees will be added to your debt.

Finally, as of this writing, there's no statute of limitations on your student loan. So unless you deal with this now, you'll be running forever.

DON'T THROW OUT COLLECTION LETTERS ADDRESSED TO YOUR ROOMMATES!

It is not helpful to dispose of warning letters addressed to your friend who used to live with you and now moved. This will not get their debt erased. Those collection letters are a gift to them, an opportunity for them to take command of their own situation, get in touch with their loan holder, and square things away before default kicks in.

You're costing your friends money, probably thousands of dollars. Their debt is getting bigger, whether they're dealing with it or not. Interest accrues with every passing day. And once their loan goes into default, they face the same tacked-on collection fees you would, if you hid from your loan.

"Often the student doesn't really know about it," says David Longanecker, "until they go to buy a car and somebody says, 'You can't, your credit record's got a negative notation.' We get an awful lot of calls every week with people saying, 'I'm trying to buy a house, and I just discovered I've had a student loan in default from such-and-such university ever since the seventies.'"

Conversely, if you haven't heard anything about your loan in a long time—and you think maybe they just lost track of you—snap out of it. They didn't. "My advice to people would be to stay very current on their loans and to know that we have quite a sophisticated system," says Longanecker. "If they haven't heard from us, we're still looking for them. They'll pay us sooner or later."

It takes courage to seek your lender out, but you'll be much happier, and it will cost you much less, if you just take a deep breath and get started.

TIMETABLE: HOW DOES DELINQUENCY BECOME DEFAULT?

Before you read any further, let me gently remind you that if you've got a real student loan situation, you should close this book right now, get on the phone, and start negotiating with your lender or guarantor. If your case is serious enough—if you're being harassed by collectors, say—hire an attorney who's specifically experienced in the student loan field. Having said that, let's look at the steps on the long road from delinquency to default.

When do you become delinquent? Here's what the law says. "Delinquency on a loan begins on the first day after the due date of the first missed payment which is not later made." In other words, if your payment was due on May 12, you're delinquent on May 13—unless your payment later arrives to clear things up.

That date, May 13, becomes the basis of a whole universe full of legal calculations that will dictate what happens to you and your loan. It's all figured by formula, like so much else dictated by student loan law.

Have you ever hung up on a FFELP customer rep and said to yourself, "Don't these people have a heart?" Well, actually, the law that governs their actions is so rigid, it wouldn't matter if they had angels' wings. The law is all laid out by chunks of time. And incidentally, it's not all one-sided. True, the law requires the lender to keep moving things along toward default. But the lender also has to make the best effort possible to tell you what's happening, on the phone and in writing, and give you repeated chances to make things right. Here's how it goes:

- **Days 1–15:** Unless you're hitting this period because a deferment or forbearance expired, the lender must send you at least *one written notice or collection letter*, informing you of the delinquency and urging you to pay up. Please note, you weasels. This first fifteen days is *not* a grace period. Your loan payment is *due* on the written *due date*. You're supposed to mail it beforehand.

- **Days 16–180:** The lender has to make at least *four diligent efforts to contact you by phone* and send at least *four collection letters* urging you to pay. At least one phone effort must be made before ninety days, and at least one must be made after ninety days. At least two of the collection letters have to warn you that if you don't pay, your loan is going to be assigned to the guaranty agency (FFELP's student loan cops). The letter must explain that if this happens, the guarantor will in turn report the default to all national credit bureaus, and the agency may start proceedings to offset (confiscate) your state and federal income tax refunds; to garnish (seize a percentage of) your wages; or to assign your loan to the federal government, which will then sue you. *Lenders can report you to the credit bureaus during this time, but many don't.*

- **On or after Day 151:** The lender must send a *final demand letter* requiring that you pay the loan in full—and notifying you that a default will be reported to a national credit bureau. The lender must also allow you at least thirty days after the date the letter is mailed, to "bring the loan out of default before filing a default claim on the loan."

    If you don't happen to have shared your current address, this is the point where the law says the lender has to start *skip-tracing* to find you.

    There's a bit of leeway here. But at some point between 190 and 270 days, your lender turns your loan back over to the guarantor, which pays the lender's default claim. Now the lender has washed its hands of you. You're dealing with the guarantor.

WHEN YOUR LOAN GOES BACK TO THE GUARANTY AGENCY

If your loan goes back to the guaranty agency that originally okayed you, that first phone call from them is probably going to feel like a plunge in ice water. But you're not necessarily going to freeze and sink. The very first thing that happens, by law, is an opportunity for you to state your case, and you'll probably have a chance to square things before they put you in default.

If you don't negotiate some settlement within 60 days, your guarantor reports your loan to the national credit bureaus. This report must contain your loan balance, the balance remaining, the date of default, and any collection information. This looks very bad on your credit rating. But you can stop it from happening. Before the guaranty agency is allowed either to report you to the credit bureau or charge you any collection fees, you get three chances to make things right.

Three Wishes: Getting an Administrative Review Before You Go Into Default

1. You get to see—and make copies of—your own records.
2. You have the right to an administrative review, at which the guarantor gets to hear your side of the story. What's surprisingly okay about this is that by law, this review can't be conducted by somebody who stands to make money on your collection fees.
3. Of course, you can "enter into a repayment agreement on terms satisfactory to the agency." As you can see, this used to be a discouraging definition. But now the law has changed in your favor. The Higher Education Amendments of 1992 gave you the right to *consolidate your loan, making payments that are "reasonable and affordable" to you.*

The downside of being turned over to the guarantor is that your rights get narrower. For instance, in the usual course of repayment, Congress says you must be given a forbearance if your monthly payment is more than 20 percent of your income and you submit a written request to your lender. Once you've gone back to the guarantor, you don't have to be given that right.

But they must give you a chance to tell your story, and they also have to help you understand theirs. You should be trying to prevent that official declaration up to the very last minute. Even on day 179, you should be calling, offering to send what you can or work out a deal on paper. If you let yourself slide into default, the government will send collectors after you, or even sue you, and you will pay your loan *plus* litigation costs and collection fees.

I DID EVERYTHING AND NOTHING WORKED

It's only natural. Sometimes luck just doesn't seem to be with you. Maybe you were out of the country. Maybe every tactic you came up with so far went mysteriously wrong. Or maybe you're feuding with your lender, and you're determined not to pay until you get a written apology and a dozen roses. Whatever.

Life's not over. Read on, and prepare to learn about the adventure of default.

CHAPTER 10

Default (You'll Live)

Okay. You're here, where you never wanted to be. It's called default, and you're going to live through it.

We've all been told that default is miserable. But it's not quite as scary as it used to be. A few years ago, default was much harder to repair. Once it happened to you, it was tough to find the way back. Now that's changed.

Even if you've been in default for months or years, new laws exist to help you get through it, get over it, and even, in some cases, erase it.

Nasty as this situation is, it can be fixed, and you can do the fixing. It will hurt, maybe for a long time. Your ability to get credit may be severely hampered, not for a few weeks but for seven years. But you're not powerless. So don't be scared.

The key *is understanding how to negotiate a payment plan that works for you*. Fear, intimidation, and your own confusion are big weapons for the professionals who get hired to collect unpaid loan money. That's why it's especially important to get a good grip on the facts about what really happens when your loan defaults.

This chapter will give you the facts you need to start separating the scary old default stories from the reality you're actually facing. But please take note: the more complicated your loan problems get, the more important it is to speak personally with one or more experts who can advise you on your specific case. *(If your problems are serious, please consult an attorney.)* The pages that follow will show you where to turn for help, and what to ask when you get there.

WHO REALLY DEFAULTS?

Like so many other statistics tangled up in America's vast student loan mess, the facts about default are very different than you might imagine. Legislators who don't know much about the subject tend to believe that defaulters are spoiled kids who never grew up and don't plan to. America paid for their education, goes the theory. Don't they care to pay it back?

We can't blame people for thinking this way, because there's been plenty of student loan fraud and abuse to give them that impression. Back when a kid could just sign his check at the bursar's office and run off with a few thousand bucks in his pocket, loans were definitely used for any number of fun things that had nothing to do with college. Having ripped off the government that far, some students had no ethical problem with the idea of going one step further and declaring bankruptcy before repaying a nickel. Nobody knows how many motorcycles, stereo speakers, and ski trips to Colorado the U.S. government financed before the loan delivery system was finally tightened up.

Even now, TV news sometimes tracks down stories of wealthy doctors and lawyers who manage to get out of paying their student loans at all. How do they do it? By realizing that any system with this many complexities is bound to have a loophole somewhere. (You will probably never find such a loophole, unless you're one of those genius computer hackers in movies where they break into the CIA.)

Still, the vast majority of defaulters aren't the students with the most advanced degrees and the biggest debts. They're the students who started out poor and tried to reach for something better.

They're men and women, sometimes without high school degrees, who went to beauty school or truckdriving school, only to find that the instruction they got wasn't worth a dime, much less the $2,000 they borrowed. Or they're poor students who decided midway through their first year of college that it was just too risky to borrow the extra thousands of dollars they'd need to get a four-year degree. Having dropped out, they might owe just $3,000. But on a high-school graduate's wages, that $3,000 might be more than they can ever pay.

Student Loans Divide Us By Class

Default statistics dramatically show how loan-based education divides us by class. *Compared to middle-class kids, one-fourth as many poor kids who started college used to graduate. Now it's down to one-tenth.* You could argue that these students lack persistence and belief in themselves. You could also argue that, having grown up in a harsher reality, they're just savvier than a middle-class student who borrows thousands of dollars in loans to study for a career that won't pay the bill.

Looking at the numbers on default, most FFELP lenders reason that student loans are still under control. Otherwise, they figure, defaults would start showing up across the board.

On the other hand, many observers inside the FFELP business and out are uncomfortably aware that with the huge new loan levels allowed since 1992, our biggest problems could be yet to come.

Attorney Elizabeth Imholz is one such observer. During her years as the consumer law coordinator of legal services in New York City, Imholz personally defended many low-income students who had been defrauded by trade schools. Now, with the number of enormous loans made in the nineties and not yet due for repayment, she's concerned about borrowers as a whole.

"From my perspective, representing the folks that I have over the years, we've been in crisis for a very long time," Imholz says. "We're not going to see the fallout [of these new loans] tomorrow, maybe. It's going to take a little while to see the full effect of what's going on. But there's a whole other cross section of people who I'm afraid may be facing trouble—the traditional college students who are building up these huge debts. And when these loans are unsubsidized [where interest starts accruing the moment you sign]," says Imholz, "God help us. That's really frightening."

For the moment, though, default has become more manageable even if loan balances have not, partly thanks to the ongoing efforts of Attorney Imholz.

NEW LAWS GIVE YOU A SECOND CHANCE

A leader in the battle to keep student loans equitable for students, Imholz personally helped to write several amendments to the 1992 Reauthorization of the Higher Education Act that emphasize helping you get back on your feet instead of making you miserable.

No matter why you're in default, you get a chance to pull yourself out of the hole, consolidate your defaulted loan, and get back into repayment, at a price you can afford. (You'll see how to do that in the next few pages.) Even better, if you want to buy a car or qualify for a home mortgage in the next few years, you can "rehabilitate" your loan by making twelve consecutive on-time monthly payments. Do that, and your default will be dropped from your record.

"What we got written into the 1992 amendments," explains Imholz, "is that defaulters are entitled to a reasonable and affordable repayment plan—on the principle that it's better to make some payment than no payment."

Having Your Debt Forgiven

If you were defrauded by a trade school, you can even be declared free of your obligation. *If your school was falsely certified (fraudulent), or if it closed its doors before giving you the training you were promised, your student loan debt can be totally forgiven.*

If you're in this situation, you're in good company. According to Department estimates, about seventy thousand loans are probably eligible to be discharged in this way. (Because the mechanics can be complicated, though, please get an attorney to take you through the process.)

"It doesn't help anybody to have a debt they will never be able to repay," says Imholz. "It ruins their lives."

WHAT IS DEFAULT?

What exactly is default? This word, like all the other terms in student loan lore, has a specific, legal definition.

Here's how default is defined in *Unfair and Deceptive Acts and Practices,* the terrific and readable handbook published by the National Consumer Law Center (NCLC). "Default occurs 'where the Secretary [of Education] or guaranty agency finds it reasonable to conclude that the borrower no longer intends to honor the obligation to repay' and when the failure to pay persists for 180 days."

If you haven't paid in 180 days—and after all, that's six months, folks—common practice, as well as common sense, allows your loan holder to conclude you don't intend to pay. But right up to the last ten minutes of your 180 days, you can argue that you do intend to repay your loan. Therefore, you should still be eligible for a deferment or forbearance—and like a time-out in football, deferment stops the default clock from ticking.

Deferments can even be retroactive, meaning they can go back in time and correct your record before your deferment application was received and processed. Is this confusing? Say you're sixty days delinquent, halfway down the trail to a default. You've been unemployed and just too depressed to deal, but now you steel yourself to take care of business. You apply to your lender for an unemployment deferment on March 1. When your deferment is granted, it can possibly go into effect as much as sixty days before you applied—so your delinquency is effectively wiped out.

Even at 180 days, there's a chance you may not be reported in default. According to Earl Esterly of the Van Ru Collection Agency, his agents work to prevent default all the way to day 270, "which is when lenders have to file claims. There's quite an effort made to contact people," he says.

A Choice of Solutions

If you do end up in default, you can now choose from several strategies in order to get out. As of this writing, the quickest and easiest way you can take care of your default is to consolidate your defaulted loan with Direct Lending. You can do this free, if you agree to accept Direct Lending's Income Contingent Repayment (ICR) plan.

If you'd rather not do Income Contingent Repayment, you can consolidate into either Direct Lending or FFELP by making three reasonable and affordable payments agreed on by you and your loan holder.

None of this will happen without unpleasantness. But if you stick with it and don't just ignore the situation, you'll get through it. Before you make your final decision, call both Direct Lending and your FFELP lender. To get the best deal possible, you'll want to know about any updates or changes in the law.

YOUR BORROWER RIGHTS AND RESPONSIBILITIES

If you want a whirlwind tour through the basic consequences of default, take a second look at a notice called "Borrower Rights and Responsibilities," which your loan holder sent you when you signed for your original loan. Since the document contains a few sort of threatening statements, you may have had an allergic reaction and pitched it in the trash.

It might be good to get another copy. Remember, with the law as it is, none of these bad things have to happen to you.

Your Rights As a Borrower

1. Your FFELP lender (the Department of Education, if you're in Direct Lending) must give you written information on your loan obligations, including information on loan consolidation and refinancing. You must also be given this written list of rights and responsibilities.

2. Your FFELP lender (or ED) must give you a copy of your promissory note, when your loan is made, and give you proof of cancellation when your loan is paid in full.

3. Before you start repaying, your FFELP lender (or ED) must give you a repayment schedule, and a detailed explanation about the interest rates and fees you're being charged, the total amount you owe, and the different repayment options you can choose.

4. Your lender must notify you if your loan is sold or transferred to a loan servicer. (Just a reminder: if you've got a FFELP loan, and

you get some odd letter saying, Attention, your loan has been bought by the Extremely Powerful Student Loan Secondary Market, keep that letter. It may prevent you from having to act like a private detective to trace down your loan later on.)

5. (FFELP only) You have a right to federal interest benefits, if you qualify. This means stuff like the Great Rewards program, where they swoosh the money out of your checking account by electronic magic, and reward you by giving you a lower interest rate.

6. You have a right to a grace period, if your loan comes with one, and an explanation of what that means. It'll probably be six months until you have to start paying. Maybe even nine months. Call your loan holder and find out.

7. You have a right to defer repayment for certain defined periods after the grace period, if you qualify.

8. You have a right to an explanation of default and its consequences.

9. You have a right to a forbearance, if you meet the lender's (or ED's) criteria.

10. You can prepay your loan, either the whole loan or part of it, anytime, without penalty. This may just seem like common sense, but it isn't. If you pay early, the bank will miss out on some of the interest income it expected to make over the term of your loan. So the right to prepayment is really very generous.

Your Responsibilities

1. You must attend an exit interview before you leave school. This is to remind you that the loan is out there, and you're going to pay it.

2. You still have to pay, no matter whether you drop out before you get a degree, you can't find a job after graduation, or you feel your education was a rip-off.

3. You can't try to vanish. You have to inform your FFELP lender (or ED) before you move, graduate, transfer to another school, withdraw from school, or drop down below half time (usually six academic hours). Incidentally, you weasels: if you think there's some way to keep your loan money—and not actually attend school that semester, forget it.

   The "don't vanish" rule also applies to your name. If you change your name, you have to let your FFELP lender (or ED) know.

4. For all loans, you must pay at least $600 a year—that's $50 a month—unless you're in deferment or forbearance, or your lender gives you permission to pay less.

5. You have to notify your FFELP lender (or ED) if anything happens to change your deferment or forbearance. If you're on a hardship forbearance and Uncle Hezekiah dies and leaves you $400,000, it's not only bad taste to hoard the money, it also violates your loan agreement.

Consequences of Delinquency and Default

1. If you don't make timely payments on your loan, your delinquency and/or default will be reported to the credit bureaus, which will seriously mess up your credit rating. Almost certainly, this means you won't be able to borrow money for things like cars in the future.

2. Your lender can tell you, "Pay us the whole balance of your loan plus the interest you owe—now." This would be inconvenient, and very bad for any gastrointestinal problems you may have.

3. Your college transcripts can be held by the school. (You may not think this matters, but it'll be a pain if you ever decide to go back to school.)

4. You can be denied any more federal aid money. This seems only fair, you have to admit.

5. Your FFELP account can be assigned to a guaranty agency, which will continue to collect from you. In this process, you'll lose some of the repayment privileges you've had.

6. Your federal income tax returns may be seized. Now we're getting into some seriously negative life experience, although people do survive this.

7. Your wages may be garnished. This means that the agency in charge of getting the government's money back can whisk away 10 percent of the disposable income in your salary each month.

8. You may be assigned reasonable attorney's fees and other costs of collecting your debt. This is in its way the most worrisome provision here, because it's so vague. Considering that the Department of Education has capped collection fees at 43 percent, "reasonable fees" may mean one thing to you, and something very different to the guarantor.

9. In Massachusetts and other states, you may be denied a state professional license.

These are all very unpleasant possibilities, but they can't happen right away. Like the delinquency process that got you here, default is another highly regulated, ritualistic process with lots of predetermined steps along the way, all defined according to time.

The idea is that for every period of time that you don't fork over, the agency will turn up the heat on you a little more. You can expect more phone calls and collection letters. You can also expect to pay extra money, sometimes a lot of extra money, in collection fees.

Once you're in default, there's a big shift in how your loan holder views you, and you definitely won't like it. If you're in FFELP, your loan is now with the guarantor, who has almost certainly tried to get hold of you several times. If you hide out and refuse to answer, you only make yourself look rotten.

Face it. You've blown their trust. You may be able to earn it back, but only with a committed effort to change your behavior.

DEFAULT: INFORMING YOU OF YOUR RIGHTS

Here's what the FFELP guarantor is required by law to do if they're holding your defaulted loan.

   Promptly after it pays the lender's default claim on your loan, but before it starts charging you collection fees or even reporting you to the credit bureaus, the guaranty agency must give you, in writing, every speck of information that might help you solve your problem before it gets any worse. The agency's written notice to you must:

1. Tell you that the agency has paid a default claim filed by your lender, and has now taken assignment of your loan.

2. Give the name of the lender who made your loan, and the school you attended.

3. List the sums that add up to the total you owe: your outstanding principal (original debt); your accrued (accumulated) interest; and any other charges you've added up along the way.

4. Demand that you immediately begin repayment.

5. Explain the rate of interest that will accrue on your loan; show how the interest will be calculated; inform you that all costs of collecting the loan will be charged to you; and state where the agency gets its authority to take all these actions.

6. Notify you that the agency will report your default to all the national credit bureaus, and that this will harm your credit rating.

7. Specifically describe the various steps, like tax refund offset and wage garnishment, that will be taken if you don't start paying. This description of the bad stuff has to include an explanation of the actions you can take to keep the bad stuff from happening. *That means giving the same three wishes you got during the delinquency process*. You must get:

   7A. A chance to inspect and copy the agency's records about your loan.

7B. A chance for an administrative review to see whether the past-due status of the loan obligation is legally enforceable. In other words, a chance for you to question whether they've really got a case against you.

7C. A chance to enter into a repayment agreement on terms that are satisfactory to the agency.

8. Describe the grounds on which you might object that the loan obligation isn't a legally enforceable debt you owe.

9. Describe how you can go about appealing a negative decision from the agency's administrative review.

10. Describe any right to a judicial review of an adverse decision by the agency on the past-due status of your loan obligation.

11. Describe the collection actions that may be taken in the future, if the ones already mentioned don't work. These include turning over your loan to the Secretary of Education so that the government can file a lawsuit against you.

Demand Your Administrative Review

When you get this letter full of threatening possibilities from your guaranty agency, you'll probably have a moment where you picture yourself destitute and roaming the streets in a blizzard.

Cut that out. You're a long way from real trouble, if you take action now. In fact, you have two alternatives. You can *tell the guarantor you want a reasonable and affordable payment plan*, and they have to give it to you. Or you can *move to consolidate with Direct Lending right away.*

If you've been in a dispute with your lender and you'll be damned if you'll pay, this is your golden opportunity to explain your case and get some justice. Since you have the right to see your file, make sure you do. Call your guarantor immediately to set up your review—the sooner, the better.

It's great if you can go in person, but this conference will often take place on the phone, since your guarantor may be far away. The important thing is, have your records ready. It's good to write down all the points you want to make. Also, don't yell. Bad idea.

You may doubt that you'll get an objective hearing, but the law does try to arrange things so that you'll be dealing with someone who's impartial. Federal rules and regs specifically forbid a guaranty agency to put anyone in charge of your hearing who is either employed by the collection branch of the agency, or who makes money based on collecting loans.

In fact, says Cathy Mayes of Sallie Mae Servicing, these reviews can result in real unpleasantness for lenders. "This is one very significant check in the system," she says. "If the AG [U.S. Auditor General] finds that the loan servicing has been poorly handled, not only do we have to buy the loan back, but we pay penalties up the kazoo."

REPORTING YOU TO THE CREDIT BUREAUS

Once the procedures designed to inform you have been carried out, the guaranty agency is required by law to report you within sixty days to the national credit bureaus. You can prevent this if you respond before the agency's deadline passes. When's the deadline? It varies, so read the papers you receive thoroughly.

The contents of the guarantor's credit report on you are also explicitly spelled out in the federal rules and regs. It must contain:

1. The total amount of the loans made to you.
2. The balance you still owe.
3. The date of your default.
4. The repayment status of your loan, and what's being done to collect it.
5. Any updates that change your situation as time goes on.

"But haven't they reported me already?" I hear you saying. Not necessarily. Different lenders handle this differently. Some lenders reported you delinquent long before this point, back when your account hit sixty or ninety days overdue. Some reported you in default at 180 days, when they turned your loan over to the guarantor.

But some lenders try harder to give you a break. So it's at least possible that if you hop right on the situation, get in touch with your guarantor, and work out a payment plan, you can avoid getting a rap sheet with the credit bureaus, which saves you the totally irritating labor of getting yourself unlisted with them later.

Honestly, at this point it would be surprising if you and your loan holder couldn't find some way to get along. But let's say you have some strange psychological need to keep being punished. In that case, it's time for the fireworks—time for the guaranty agency's collection efforts to go into high gear.

TIMETABLE: WHAT THE GUARANTOR MUST DO TO COLLECT

The guaranty agency can come at you in two ways, either acting on its own or hiring an outside collection agency to do its legwork. In both cases, collection procedures are outlined step by step in the federal rules and regs.

Here's the schedule for an agency that acts on its own:

- **Days 1–45:** The guaranty agency must send you *the written notice* outlined above, and a written notice stating that if you don't pay, the agency will either start procedures to administratively garnish your wages, or turn your loan over to the federal government, which will garnish your wages through the courts or institute a civil lawsuit to compel you to pay what you owe, plus collection costs.

  The agency must also diligently attempt to contact you by phone.

- **Days 46–180:** The agency must send you at least *three written notices* forcefully demanding that you immediately start repaying, and telling you you've been reported to the credit bureaus (if you have), and that your credit rating may have been damaged.

  The last of these three notices must tell you that it's the *final notice* you will receive before the agency takes more forceful action by starting proceedings to take your tax returns, garnish your wages, or turn you over to the federal government, which will sue you for your debt plus collection costs.

During this period the agency must diligently attempt to contact you by phone at least twice.

- **Days 181–545:** Thirty days after that last letter goes out, it's time for the guarantor to start initiating the proceedings to offset (take) your federal and state income tax returns.

- **By day 225:** The agency must initiate wage garnishment; or

- **By day 545:** The agency must turn you over to the federal government, which will institute a civil lawsuit against you.

What If I'm Too Poor to Sue?

Being broke may actually save you from being sued. If the agency looks over your income and realizes that the cost of suing you would probably exceed the amount of money they could recover, you're off the hook—for a while. But every six months thereafter, the agency is required to conduct a "diligent semi-annual review" to see whether your circumstances have improved and it's now worthwhile to sue you. Sixty days after finding out you have the money, or even a significant part of it, the agency has to start proceedings to sue you again.

Can they ever stop? According to the law, "only in accordance with criteria and procedures approved by the Secretary [of Education]." Considering that there is no statute of limitations on student loans, this means that they will be on your case forever.

What If They Sue Me and Win, but I'm Too Broke to Pay?

As of this writing, it's not clear exactly how the government intends to go about the business of suing you in the future. The federal rules and regs are in the midst of change. But here's what we know so far.

The legal powers of guarantors have been diminished on this issue. Guarantors once had the power to pursue you through the courts, whether by instituting a civil suit against you or by initiating a judicial garnishment of your wages (in other words, getting a judge's okay to confiscate a portion of your wages). Now, guarantors have to turn you over to the Department of Education, which then files the lawsuit or initiates the garnishment.

Guarantors can still do administrative garnishments (in which it's not necessary to go through the courts). But this power varies from agency to agency, and from state to state.

At this point, if the government sues you and wins, the current rules and regs aren't exactly clear on what happens next. What follows is the law as it stands now, but you'll want to check out the latest developments with your attorney or some other expert.

Once there's a judgment against you, the guaranty agency is then required to "attempt diligently to enforce" it. That includes getting the judgment renewed if you don't have "sufficient assets or income attachable under applicable law" to settle it when it's first issued.

Wait a minute! Did you catch that phrase "sufficient assets . . . attachable"?

That, my friends, means that *the guarantor can "attach"—that's legalese for confiscate—whatever valuable things you own, like your house or your car.* Can they actually take our house or car? "They have," says Jerry Davis, Director of Education and Student Loan Research for Sallie Mae. "But typically they wouldn't."

Still, believe it: the guarantor will collect. "I used to work for PHEAA [the Pennsylvania Higher Education Assistance Agency]," says Davis, "and we had all kinds of means of getting the money back from people. It was just awful. I felt really sorry for them."

So if you've actually had a court judgment issued against you, then the guaranty agency is going to be conducting a semi-annual review of your finances *forever*, to keep checking whether you've acquired enough money or assets to satisfy the rest of the judgment.

If you do come into any money, they'll ask you to pay in full. Can you negotiate monthly payments? You can try, but if you have the whole sum and you've been avoiding your debt this long, don't expect a lot of sympathy. And if you don't pay satisfactorily, then within thirty days, the agency has to start enforcement efforts again.

Considering all this, it's much less work to pay what you can, even if you don't have the minimum payment. For one thing, advises Sheila Ryan of Nellie Mae, it's a way to slow your mounting interest charges. "Even minimal payments, ten dollars a month or whatever, will help to stop the loan from growing, so that when students do get in circumstances where they can pay, the loan won't be so astronomical." She offers this example: "The average loan default—I think this is still a valid statistic—is about $3,200. At an interest rate of eight percent, that's $256 a year in interest. Divided by twelve, that's $21 a month." So just ten dollars a month can cut the problem practically in half. "I would want to do that," says Ryan, "if there was any way I could."

What If I Run?

Either ten days after they get word that they can't locate you—or sixty days after they sign the lender's default note, whichever comes later—the agency must "attempt diligently" to track you down by contacting your school, and by using skip-tracing techniques "including, but not limited to, any skip-tracing assistance available from the IRS, credit bureaus, and state motor vehicle departments."

These are government agencies, and being chased by them is a big deal. It's just one more argument for facing your loan problem early. Maybe you can manage to duck everybody, but the effort will turn into your life's work. Is that how you want to use your education?

What If I Send a Payment?

Good for you. Send another. Otherwise, you get a sixty-day rest before collection efforts start up again.

TIMETABLE: WHEN THE GUARANTOR USES AN OUTSIDE COLLECTION AGENCY

- **Days 1–30:** During this period, the guaranty agency must send you a *written notice* that describes all the details of your situation: how much you owe, how to defend yourself, and what bad things can happen if you don't pay.

- **Days 31–180:** The guaranty agency must send *at least two "forceful collection letters,"* make two diligent attempts to contact you by phone. Over and above these requirements, the agency has to ferret away at you, using "such collection tools and activities as it deems appropriate."

- **By day 181:** Your loan is farmed out to a collection contractor (a collection agency hired by the guarantor).

This collection method also leads eventually to your being sued, assuming that the collection agency either can't find you or can't "persuade" you to pay. As we've said, this is an area where the law is in transition. But whoever does the suing, the schedule will go something like this: you'll be sued on whichever is earlier—the ninetieth day after the collection contractor gives up and returns your loan to the guarantor, or the 365th day after the agency referred your loan to the contractor, or the 365th day after the contractor last received a payment from you.

Revolving Collection Agencies (Your Loan Is Passed from One to Another)

Because there's no statute of limitations on your loan, keep in mind that the collection actions above are like those crazy, bewitched bucket-toting mops in the Mickey Mouse cartoon. Until you break the spell, they'll never stop. If one bunch of collectors can't recover your loan, another bunch will be set on your account. And so it goes, down the years, until you pay or until you die.

WHAT IF THEY GARNISH MY WAGES?

As the guaranty agency and/or its collection contractor turn up the heat on you, the next step after phone calls and collection letters is *administrative garnishment* of your wages. The procedure is called "administrative" because, depending on its structure, the guarantor may not have to get a court order to take action against you. (Other kinds of creditors have to go to court for the right to touch your salary.)

Still, the law says you will get some warning: *at least thirty days before the initiation of garnishment proceedings, the agency must mail to your last known address a written notice of what's about to happen.*

Once again, you must be given the basics of the situation: the nature and amount of your debt, an explanation of your rights, and notice that the agency plans to start collecting the debt by taking a part of your wages.

Again, you're offered the chance to look through your records, as well as a chance for a hearing with an independent official inside the agency.

Again, you're invited to enter into a written repayment plan that's agreeable to the agency. Though the repayment amount doesn't have to be explicitly tailored to your ability to repay, the guarantor is urged by the Department of Education to accommodate your needs if you can show special hardship.

If none of this works, then get ready to see your paycheck shrink. But it may not be as bad as you think.

How Much Money Can They Take?

Whether it's the Secretary of Education or a state guaranty agency, your loan holder is authorized to garnish only up to 10 percent of your "disposable pay." So what's "disposable"? According to the federal rules and regs, it's

> "any amount of the borrower's income from an employer, other income from any source that remains after deductions required by law to be withheld, or any child support or alimony that are made under a court order or legally enforced from a written agreement. Amounts required by law include, but are not limited to, federal and state tax, Social Security contributions, and wage garnishment payments."

From a more specific dollar angle, *disposable income* is defined as the lesser of 10 percent of your pay (once taxes and other necessary deductions are subtracted), or a legally determined amount that (as of this writing) basically exempts your first $127.50 of after-tax income per week.

In other words, you are not going to be left without money for toothpaste.

Even if your wages are being garnished by other creditors as well as your student loan holders, *the total garnishment can't exceed 25 percent of your disposable income.*

And check this out: *if you've been involuntarily separated from employment, your wages can't be garnished until you've been continuously employed again for twelve months.* In other words, if you left that last job because you were fired, you're still protected. However, the guarantor is not required to know this about you. You have to tell them. If you're wrongly garnished, make a stink.

You're also protected in another crucial way. *By law, your employer is forbidden to fire you, or even to penalize or discipline you, just because your wages are being garnished.* (Although if you're being garnished by two separate creditors, you can be fired. But remember, you still have to be warned. If you're threatened with a second garnishment, try reminding creditor number two that without a job you can't pay anything.)

What Part Does the Collection Agency Play?

The law limits what collection agencies can do regarding garnishment—sort of. They're not allowed to issue withholding orders to your employer, for instance. On the other hand, they're allowed to send out the notice of garnishment, recommend that orders be issued, prepare orders for review, and mail them out once they've been okayed by the guarantor. To sort out whether a particular collection agency is exceeding its legal authority with you, you may need the help of an attorney.

Those Rotten, Misleading Collection Letters

For all its supposed enlightenment, the Department of Education (through its hired collectors) has been known to mail out misleading collection letters that threaten to garnish your wages without letting you know your rights in the matter. These letters suggest that you could just wake up one morning with your paycheck sliced and diced, without any warning or recourse. They may also imply that being garnished will get you fired. As you've seen here, these suggestions are bogus.

When you think about it, garnishment is not so bad, at least in terms of the portion of your income you're giving up. In truth, 10 percent of your check probably ought to be going to your student loan anyway. So . . . could there be a good side to garnishment? Well, according to the Department of Education, a surprising number of student debtors have sort of lodged themselves in garnishment and settled on that as their repayment method. Weird, huh? But, hey, whatever works.

WHAT IF THEY INTERCEPT MY TAX REFUND?

If you can't or won't respond to the guarantor's in-house collection efforts, get ready to learn all about *tax refund interception* (or *offset*, as it's often called). According to Internal Revenue Service rules, only the federal government is allowed to touch your taxes. So if a guaranty agency is holding your loan, it temporarily assigns the loan to the Department of Education, which has the power to put the offset into action.

Your guarantor and the Department of Education may work together, tossing you and your loan between them, like so: the guarantor assigns your note to the Department. Some months before tax time, the Department sends you a notice that it intends to intercept your tax refund. Then, after taking your refund, the Department sends the note back to the guarantor for more collection efforts. What makes this all harder to understand is that the Department often hires the guaranty agency to do all the actual paperwork. It's another reason why documents may be confusing, and why you may want to ask for help from an attorney, or your school's financial office, or your congressperson.

Fighting Off an Intercept

One of the first tactics you can use to keep the government's paws off your tax refund is *bankruptcy.* In general, bankruptcy has limited usefulness in terms of your student loan debt. But bankruptcy does work for you here, whether you want to stave off a tax intercept before it happens or recover your tax refund after the government's already made off with it.

If you file a bankruptcy petition before the tax intercept happens, then you've activated something called the *U.S. Bankruptcy Code automatic stay provision.* This shields you from just about every poke and grab anybody can make at you and your property, including an attempt to take your tax refund before it reaches you. *If the intercept just happened, you can also get your money back.*

Does Your Spouse Owe, But Not You?

If you and your husband or wife file a joint tax return that's intercepted—and you don't owe, though your spouse does—the IRS will give you a partial refund if you file the proper paperwork with them. (Next time, file separately.)

Fighting Back Before the Intercept

In a practice you're now familiar with, the Department of Education has to mail you a *written notice* that your tax return is about to be referred to the Secretary of the Treasury for offset. *You're invited to examine your records, and you get the chance for a review* within the Department regarding the existence, amount, enforceability, or past-due status of your debt.

Deadlines for Requesting a Hearing

To take advantage of any of this, though, you have to act fast. If you want to see your file, you must make that request in writing no more than twenty days after the date of the notice. If you want a Department review, you must request it by whichever date is later: either sixty-five days after the date of the notice, or fifteen days after the Department provides your file, if you've asked for it.

Even then, what you may get is a review with the guaranty agency. If that happens and you don't like the outcome, you can ask for a second review with the Department, but you have to ask within seven days after the guaranty agency makes its first decision.

In doing all this, you have to file documentation—your Social Security number, name of your loan program, and so on. You must write down why you're contesting this debt. And if you insist on a personal hearing, rather than just letting the Department look over your paperwork, you must submit a list of witnesses you intend to call, what the witnesses will say, and why their testimony would change anything. (When we say "personal hearing," please note: a phone hearing is probably what you'll get.)

You definitely have the right to this review. But this is a good place to watch out for yourself. Since the Department of Education thinks of the guaranty agency as its natural go-between, read the fine print on all notices you receive, to make sure they affirm your right to a Department hearing.

Getting Your Refund Back

After your tax refund has been intercepted, the IRS will notify you of what's happened. In the process, the IRS also makes it very plain that it won't discuss this anymore. *If you want your refund back, and you haven't filed for bankruptcy, you'll have to sue the Department of Education*. Which means in turn that you'd better have a good case, a good lawyer, and a will to win.

All in all, according to the National Consumer Law Center, having your tax refund taken is likely to be more uncomfortable than having your wages garnished. Why? Because the guarantor can only garnish 10 percent of your disposable income. By law, you have to be left with at least $127.50 a week. But when your tax return goes, it all goes. Courts have ruled that not even your personal exemption is safe. Of course, just as with wage garnishment, a surprising number of student debtors allow their tax returns to be confiscated every year. Would it be easier just to mail in your refund voluntarily—and keep your credit rating?

CAN THE GUARANTY AGENCY NEGOTIATE A PARTIAL PAYMENT?

This is an area where the law is changing—unfortunately, not to our advantage. In the past, if you could get together a substantial lump sum, guaranty agencies were allowed to negotiate with you for partial payment, under a set of rules called *Standardized Compromise and Write-Off Procedures*.

This meant that the guarantor could usually waive your added-on collection fees, and in some cases even up to 30 percent of your principal and interest. But now, says Sheila Ryan of Nellie Mae, new rules have taken away some of the guarantors' bargaining chips. "In the past," she says, "guaranty agencies had flexibility on how to apply payments from the borrower after a default." Guarantors typically applied your payments to your original loan first, and left your collection costs for last. With the loan money recovered, it wasn't such a big deal to forget about the tacked-on collection costs.

But as of January 1998, guarantors are required to apply your *first* payments to your collection costs. Interest comes second; principal, last. The effect, says Ryan, is that "when you're getting down to the end [of repayment], you still have the principal balance remaining, which is more difficult for the agency to write off and compromise on."

As of now, federal rules and regs still give guarantors permission to compromise. But exactly how they're supposed to go about it . . . that's still up in the air. What should you do? Take your best shot at getting an agreement anyway. Maybe your case will involve some special circumstance. Or maybe by the time you start your negotiation, the rules will have been clarified in your favor again.

Assigning You to the Feds

This is when the guaranty agency throws up its hands and says, "You. Out of my life." At that point, the guarantor gives up and assigns your loan to the U.S. government for a tougher round of collection efforts. You don't want this outcome. The feds will charge you much stiffer collection fees, and you're poor enough already. The smartest thing you can do is deal with your loan business long before you get to this stage. Besides, even if you do engineer yourself a compromise or a write-off, keep in mind that if you ever want to borrow more money and go back to school, you'll have to reaffirm (acknowledge that you owe) the whole debt after all.

It doesn't have to be the guarantor who turns you over. If the government decides the guarantor isn't working hard enough to collect from you, then the Department of Education can demand to take over your loan. This is called *subrogating* the loan. The distinction depends on who's acting. If the guarantor turns you over voluntarily, you're *assigned*. If the feds demand your loan from the guarantor, you're *subrogated*.

THREE WAYS TO CLIMB OUT OF DEFAULT

Under current law, you can actually choose one of three ways to get your loan out of default and get yourself back on track.

1. **Reinstatement.** You can reinstate your loan by making six consecutive, on-time payments to your loan holder. They're generally $50 each, but you can also negotiate a "reasonable and affordable payment" that's lower. After six months of payments, you're still in default. But you become eligible to apply for additional aid once again. This is the legal milestone that's changed the entire student-loan landscape, because it gives you a chance—just one, but still a chance—to correct your mistakes and get your loan and your life back on track. But remember, the law specifically states that *you can only reinstate your loan once*. If you blow this, too bad for you. A word of advice: whatever you do, mail your payment checks early, so they arrive by the due date.

2. **Rehabilitation.** It requires the most persistence, but it's also the most desirable. After six on-time payments, your loan is reinstated. Make six *more* on-time payments for a total of twelve and you can apply to have your loan rehabilitated. This means your loan holder tries to sell your defaulted loan to a lender. If your

loan is bought, you'll be eligible again for civilized niceties like deferment and forbearance. Even better, your default will be erased from your credit record. It's a real fresh start.

3. **Consolidation.** It's the fastest way to get out of default, and you can pursue it either through FFELP or through Direct Lending. (We'll talk about details later.) Under FFELP's rules, you have to make three consecutive, on-time reasonable and affordable payments before you can apply to consolidate. As the law stands now, Direct Lending's method is cheaper and faster. If you're willing to go into Income Contingent Repayment, you don't have to put up a cent, and you'll wait only as long as it takes them to process the paperwork.

Once you've consolidated, you'll be eligible again for deferment and forbearance. You'll also be able to apply for new loans and grants, so that you can supplement that extremely useful degree in medieval French literature with a few courses in computer programming.

Clear Up Your Old Defaulted Loan

It may even be that you've long wanted to go back to school, but you've been afraid to alert anybody about that $5,000 loan you took out back in 1978—the one you figure maybe they forgot, because nobody's ever come after you. If you've got a long-standing default like this, the Higher Education Amendments of 1992 give you a chance to come in out of the cold and get the rest of the education you've been wishing for. Whether you want to rehabilitate or consolidate, the steps are simple, and the burden on you won't be too great.

To begin the process, all you need to do is find out where your loan is now. This may be a bit of a challenge, but you're up to it.

Finding Your Defaulted Loan

If your loan has been in default for a long time, like more than six years, it's probably in the hands of some collection agency hired by the Department of Education. *You can find out by calling 1-800-621-3115.* There you'll speak to a Department contractor who has computer access to all the facts about you, including your loan type, your account number, and the name and address of the collection agency servicing your loan.

If a guaranty agency is holding your loan, you'll have to get the same set of facts: name and address of guarantor, type of loan, account number, and current balance. You can estimate all that if you just want to get a consolidation application from Direct Lending. But *without the correct information, your consolidation won't go through,* so when you're tracking down your loan, don't take no for an answer.

If for some reason you're not getting anywhere with the guarantor you remember dealing with, you can also write Experian (formerly TRW), Equifax, or Trans-Union for a copy of your credit report. (You'll find their addresses in "Gimme Credit.") Your credit report should list what's up with your loan and who's holding it.

Your Legal Right: Reasonable and Affordable Repayment

Once you've found your loan, your next step is to call the loan holder and ask them to set up a reasonable and affordable repayment plan.

That phrase, *reasonable and affordable*, is the heart of the 1992 Higher Education Amendments designed to help you climb out of default. What's meant by reasonable and affordable? The law doesn't say, exactly, besides the fact that you have the right to a payment that's determined to be reasonable and affordable based on your total financial circumstances. The usual payment is $50 or more. But if you can't afford $50, you're not out of the running. You'll probably have to submit documentation of your income and expenses, though—maybe a pay stub or proof of public assistance, as well as a detailed list of your monthly expenses.

Just as in a wage garnishment, your guarantor (or the Department, if it's the holder) must consider your disposable income as well as your spouse's—whatever's left after taxes, child support or alimony, and even other garnishments. Your family expenses have to be figured in, too: housing, utilities, food, medical costs, dependent-care costs, work-related expenses, and of course, other student loan debt. (A word to the wise, you weasels: if one of your expenses is a $300 monthly car payment, you're not going to meet with a lot of sympathy.)

You may run into some collector or lender who insists the law requires you to pay a $50 minimum. Not true. If your expenses add up to more than your income, then "reasonable and affordable" payments for you might be as low as $5. According to the National Consumer Law Center, payments as low as $1 have been set.

Under the $50 line, creditors do have to keep a file listing your financial information. But if your documented expenses don't allow you to pay $50, they have to deal with it.

Standing Up for a Payment You Can Afford

Under the law, guarantors and collectors do have the right to base a normal repayment plan on the size of your loan. It's up to you to tell them you want something different, says attorney Elizabeth Imholz. As one of the crafters of the 1992 legislation, Imholz warns that *you probably won't hear about reasonable and affordable repayment unless you demand it.*

"Unfortunately, people have to use those talismanic words 'reasonable and affordable payment' in order to get through to a bill collector sometimes," says Imholz. "Often we have borrowers call and say, 'I told them I just couldn't afford it.' If you just try and argue with a collector, the reality is, unless you use the words, they're not going to click into this. Use the words 'reasonable and affordable repayment. I know I am entitled to this by law.'

"It shouldn't just be a free-flowing discussion," Imholz cautions. "You should do it all in writing. They should have some kind of income and expense form to be filled out. Make sure you've gotten your agreement correctly in writing, because otherwise, you can end up with what you thought was an agreement, but they had a different understanding."

Getting Out of Default: A One-Shot Deal

When dealing with a guarantor, Imholz adds, *don't let yourself be intimidated into an impossible position.* "Fill out an income and expense statement to the guarantor, and they will probably come back with a proposal," she says. "If you think their proposal is reasonable and fair, and you can do it, that's fine. You should confirm it in writing and ask them to confirm it in writing. But *don't agree to anything that's clearly more than you can do, because if you default, you have lost your opportunity to ever get one of these consolidation agreements again*. It's a one-shot deal."

WHERE SHOULD I CONSOLIDATE, FFELP OR DIRECT LENDING?

If you defaulted on a Direct Loan, you have to consolidate into Direct Lending. But if you originally had a FFELP loan, you have a couple of choices about how to consolidate. Partly you'll choose based on how much money you have. You'll also want to think about how much you value the future strength of your credit rating. (Remember that you can actually erase the record of your default, if you're able to bypass consolidation for the more difficult process of loan rehabilitation.)

Consolidating into FFELP means you'll have to come up with your three consecutive reasonable and affordable payments. After that, you can resume making regular payments. Of course, if you defaulted in the first place because you couldn't afford your payments, FFELP's lowest-priced repayment option, Income Sensitive Repayment, may still not be low enough for you.

Fortunately, Direct Lending is in your price range, even if your price is zero. (As of this writing, that's the designated Direct loan monthly payment if your family income is $900 or less per year above the poverty line.) You can consolidate right away with Direct Lending and make no payments, affordable or otherwise, if you're willing to accept Income Contingent Repayment.

There's one bit of fancy footwork here. If you started with a FFELP loan, you're supposed to consolidate with your FFELP lender. In fact, your Direct Lending application contains a certification that you couldn't obtain a FFELP consolidation plan that was satisfactory to you. Considering that FFELP offers nothing lower than interest-only payments, though, you'll find it easy to make that statement.

Don't let a guarantor or collector scare you into thinking you have to consolidate with FFELP. You can do what you want. In fact, applying for a FFELP consolidation first may slow your process with Direct Lending. If you say FFELP can't offer a plan that satisfies you, then that's all there is to it.

How Long Does the Process Take?

About two months after you send in all your application papers, assuming you've done your footwork correctly, you'll get a notice that you're now the proud owner of a Direct Lending consolidation loan. You'll also get something you probably never thought you'd see: a letter from your old loan holder saying "Paid In Full."

The Downside of Consolidating

If bankruptcy is on your mind, remember that you have to have been in repayment seven years in order to file and have any hope of winning—and consolidating will start the seven-year period running all over again. Moreover, according to the National Consumer Law Center, you may lose your right to protest various problems that existed at your school under your original loan agreement.

The Bruising Subject of Collection Fees

Aside from all the other hassles, here's one of the biggest reasons you want to avoid default: *once your loan has to go to collectors, you pay their fee.*

As of this writing, the Department of Education sets collection fees at 27 cents for every dollar collected. But that's not necessarily the limit. The Department has okayed fees as high as 43 percent, and with that ammunition, some collectors may try to stick you for 43 percent all the time.

This is serious money, of course. It means that if you owe $10,000 and you have to be herded into paying by a collector, your loan principal will suddenly jump up to at least $12,700—maybe even

$14,300. That's why you should always check with a third party to make sure you're not being gouged.

No matter what kind of deal you negotiate on collection fees, the fact remains, if you waited this long to clear up your loan business, you'll pay a lot extra. If you're consolidating your loan, an 18.5 percent collection fee from the old loan will be added to the principal of your new consolidation loan. That's the best you can do, take it or leave it.

Depending on who you're dealing with—a private collection agency, a guarantor, a lender, or the Department of Education—you may run into several methods of calculating the collection fee that's slapped onto your loan. Whatever the number, make somebody tell you how it was figured, because in some cases it may be really bogus, and it may be worth your while to get a lawyer.

No matter where you are in the student loan repayment process— and that includes default—you have to stand up for the good deal you deserve. That's especially true with the lovely folks we'll talk about next: collection agents.

DEALING WITH COLLECTORS: ANOTHER FORM OF EDUCATION

Whether you've defaulted on a FFELP loan or a Direct loan, you'll be dealing with collectors. This won't be pleasant, because it's their job to be unpleasant. But learning a little about the tactics they use will help you get through the experience a lot more calmly.

As we've said before, collectors make a living by trying to scare you into paying debts. They do this by threatening you. If you think about it for just a minute, you'll see that they rarely have as much power as they claim to. Otherwise, why would they waste time on threats? In its very readable book *Surviving Debt,* The National Consumer Law Center gives some prime advice: when collectors bark at you, bark right back.

Remember, your student loan is unsecured. You got the education; it's in your head; you can't return it. So really, if you can't pay your loan, there's only so much your loan holder can do. Take your tax refund, yes. Garnish your wages, yes. Have people harass you? I don't think so.

Collectors are allowed to use a certain number of tactics in "persuading" you to pay a certain debt. But there are a lot of things they can't do, because they're bound by a law called the Fair Debt Collection Practices Act. A few samples:

- They can't call your relatives or friends, or your neighbors, or your boss—unless they're just trying to locate you. If they give any hint that they're calling because you owe money, they're out of bounds. They also can't call you at work or at friends' houses, or call you obscene names or insult you.
- They can't call you at inconvenient times, say, before 8 A.M. or after 9 P.M.—which means they can't call you at work if you say they can't. They can't keep telephoning over and over; if you're represented by a lawyer, they can't call you at all. They'll have to stick to calling him.
- Collectors can't pretend to be lawyers, or threaten you with things like investigating around your neighborhood. They can't pretend you owe more than you do, or that your situation is more serious than it is. They can't publish your name as someone who owes money. Even if they talk you into sending them a postdated check (don't do it!), they're not allowed to cash it.

When it comes down to it, you have a lot of rights against collectors. For yourself and your student loan, you can take several actions to get them off your back:

1. **You can settle the matter by arranging to make three reasonable and affordable payments** to consolidate your loan, or six reasonable and affordable payments to reinstate your loan. (In the case of Direct Lending, you can simply apply to consolidate.) Remember to hold out for a plan you can afford. Collection agencies usually start by insisting that you pay the whole bill, but when you stand your ground, usually they'll start to negotiate.

2. **You can write a "cease" letter.** The law says a creditor collecting a debt for a third party must stop dunning you when you write a letter telling him to stop. (If he's collecting for himself, he doesn't have to stop, but many collectors will.) In your letter, explain why you can't pay, and what you are doing to work yourself back into a position where you can make payments again. Also mention that you know your rights under the Fair Debt Collection Practices Act.

3. **You can send a lawyer's letter.** If your cease letter doesn't get results, a lawyer's usually will. But try your own letter first.

4. **You can hire a lawyer.** Let him take the calls—and the heat. By law, collectors have to stop contacting you and call your lawyer instead.

5. **You can complain to the Department of Education.** Call 1-800-4 FEDAID and state your case. Tell them also that you want to make a complaint to the Inspector General's office. If you've been harassed by an agency or individual regarding your student loan, they could be in big trouble. Good.

6. **You can sue the collector for misconduct** and win up to $1,000 in damages against the collector, who will also have to pay your attorney fees.

7. **You can file for bankruptcy.** Once your papers are signed, collectors have to obey the automatic stay provision that the law provides to protect you from harassment. Although this may not solve all your problems in the long run, declaring bankruptcy will shut the collection agents up, at least for a while.

These student loan self-defense techniques will also work with collectors who are dunning you for other kinds of debt. Why do I mention that? Because if you're in default on your student loan, you may be having some very interesting adventures with other debts too. If so, you'd be in good company. A few million Americans who are older and more experienced than you have been having a wild ride with the topic of our next chapter: credit.

Part 4

How to Live with Your Loans

CHAPTER 11

Gimme Credit: Consumer Credit Is the Other Half of Your Finances

Why did I put a chapter on credit in a book on student loans? I bet you already know. This is where student loan trouble strikes—your ability to get credit.

If all your extra money is tied up in student loan payments, you're probably buying the things you want and need on credit. Or maybe your student loan doesn't cover your campus living expenses, and you're buying your books with credit cards. You're telling yourself you'll pay it all off. You'll get a fabulous job. Your great aunt will die and leave you a fortune. It'll come out of your tax refund.

Right.

No offense. By now, you know this book is not about lectures. The point is, if you don't understand how credit works—and how to work credit—you need to learn. Just about everybody who has student loan debt has consumer debt too, and how you handle the one always affects the other. Your loan payment by itself might be tough but do-able. What can spin it all out of control is the bills for things you buy on credit.

To put it another way, you have to pay your student loan, but you can choose your relationship with credit. You can go through life getting lousy deals and paying too much for everything, which in turn makes your student loan harder to handle. Or you can learn your way around, cut good deals, come out on top—and then throw some extra money at your student loan.

There's another reason you need to be smart about credit. When you owe a big student loan—especially if you're in default—a good credit history is *the* thing that will help you get financial conveniences you need later, like a car loan. When a lender sizes you up, your student loan can look like one small problem in your sensational young life. Or it can look like disaster as usual for a loser like you.

Naturally you weren't born knowing how to manage all this. So for all you nonbusiness majors, this chapter will go right through and briefly tell you the basics on credit—why you need it, what happens when you lose it, how to clean it up.

If you're one of those geeks who could balance a checkbook at age ten, hush up and skip forward. The rest of you, let's start from scratch.

CREDIT DEFINES WHAT WE BUY AND WHO WE ARE

So okay, what is credit? First of all, credit is not evil. It's beyond good or bad. It's a fact of the way we live now. In the nineties, credit comes into play almost every time we transact business. For openers, it defines what we buy. Credit lets us purchase things over time, and we depend on that in a big way. Most of us could never swing expensive items like houses and cars without it.

Second—and really more important—credit defines *who we are*. In the age of information, your credit record is like your shadow. You can't get rid of it. It establishes your identity and your credibility in the world. If you've got a student loan, believe me, you've got a credit record. When you make a business move, good or bad, your credit record shows it. People use it to measure you, in more situations than you dream of.

You know a landlord checks your credit record before he'll lease you an apartment. But did you know potential employers may check your credit too? Especially if you're going to deal with money, they figure if you can't handle your own, maybe you can't handle theirs either. Bankers, storeowners, marketers, real estate agents, and all kinds of other people may size you up by peeking into your financial past. It's quite legal. And if your credit report plays a negative part in their decision, you'll be notified in writing. If they don't like your history, they just won't deal with you. There's a positive side, too: if your credit is good, it's a powerful advertisement for you, your character, and your grasp of how to do business.

Third—and most important of all—credit does not exist just to make your life more convenient. It's also about making money for the guy who's issuing the credit.

You're a student or recent graduate, right? Notice how you get all those preapproved applications for credit cards, even though you may have no job and no salary? This is not sympathy. Credit card issuers see you as a new source of profit, pure and simple. Everybody has a right to make a living, including creditors. But credit is about business, not friendship, and when you're young, it's easy to forget that.

Interest: A Rental Fee for Money

Credit means you're renting a lender's money. In return, you pay a rental fee. That fee is called *interest*, and it's in his interest, not yours. How much interest? That depends on how much it costs him to keep track of the loan, how long you want the money, and whether there's a significant risk that you won't pay him back. A lender makes a profit when you use his money to buy something you really couldn't pay for yourself. That's when the bucks start to roll his way, in the form of interest.

The crucial source of profit for a creditor is *the element of time*. It doesn't feel like you're shucking out money when you buy on credit. It's practically impossible to feel your outlay for what it is. You may be paying just a few dollars interest every month. You may forget all about it. But that VCR you bought may be obsolete by the time you finish paying your lender back. And counting his interest money, it may cost you $375 or more, not the $250 you should have paid.

Meanwhile, you'll definitely want something else before you've paid off the VCR. But now you have less money to spend on it, because of your ongoing credit bill. So you rent more money, and you owe more interest, and you have even less cash to spend on the next thing you need. You know where this ends? It doesn't.

Practically every store you go into has a sign on the wall that says, Easy Credit. But credit only *looks* easy. If you misuse it, it makes your whole life harder. It drains you of all your extra money, and that takes away your freedom to make any positive plans of your own. Am I saying you have to swear off credit entirely? That might be incredibly smart, but it would mean behaving differently than a lot of your friends, and you may not be ready to do that. Still, you can be smart about picking the credit deals you make. There are good deals out there, and really shabby, lousy ones, too. If you choose well, you'll pay less for the money you rent, and you'll have more money to use for yourself. Which means you'll be that much closer to freedom.

THE ART OF MONEY (TERMS YOU'LL WANT TO KNOW)

Okay, so your eyes glaze over when those boring people talk about money on TV. They may be dull, but money isn't. Money is the most fascinating game that ever was or ever will be. The whole planet plays, and whether you know it or not, you're already in. The global money game is affecting you and your student loan right this minute. By the time you're finished paying it off, your loan's value will be nothing like it is today.

Rules of the Game

You hear all the time about the global economy, about how we have to be competitive with the rest of the world. There's truth in this, because money is always for sale and for rent, and the highest bidder gets it. When the U.S. economy is doing well, when our unemployment rate is low and when we're producing at a high rate, a good part of the world's money comes here, and we keep it circulating here by paying good rental fees—in other words, healthy interest rates. Who decides on these rates? A bunch of educated guessers looking at all the signs and predicting what will come next: America's Federal Reserve Board, commonly called the Fed. The Fed is terribly powerful. It alone is responsible for setting and resetting American interest rates, thereby controlling how much money costs us to rent.

The Prime Rate, set by the Fed, is the *national interest rate*, used by law as the basis for calculating the expense of all our transactions that involve borrowing money. When the Fed announces a change, computers all over America buzz.

These factors, and lots of others, keep the true cost of all your debts shifting all the time. One thing you can count on, though, thanks to Congress. In terms of interest, *your student loan will always be much cheaper than your consumer debts*. So although you have to keep making your student loan payments (or your loan will grow), *you should work to pay off your consumer debt first*.

THE CREDIT EXPLOSION

Your grandparents never had to shop for credit, because basically they had no choices. For them, it was either the local savings and loan association (for the house), the local bank (for the car), or the local credit union (for the big vacation).

Borrowing money will never be that simple again. Now we bank at massive conglomerates with names like First Interstate Bancshares of CitiChaseCorp PartnersTrust NorthAmerica, where doing a financial transaction rarely involves speaking to another person, let alone forming a personal relationship. The money business has been reborn, and its new face is plastic.

As the financial giants of the nineties compete for profit, the sheer volume of credit they offer has exploded—especially in the area of credit cards. As a nation, we've responded by plunging into more debt than our country has ever known.

For you, this credit jungle is a good-news, bad-news situation. The bad news is, if you already have a hefty student debt, you may be turned down for a loan by the most exacting institutions. The good news—sort of—is that as long as you've got a breath in your body, some enterprising soul will probably cut you a deal.

WHERE DO YOU SHOP FOR CREDIT?

In today's banking business, all kinds of institutions that used to be rigidly separate now dip into each other's business territory, and you can get a credit card from practically any of them. A few of the most common:

Commercial banks: Aside from sponsoring major charge cards like Visa and MasterCard, commercial banks make personal and real estate loans. Could you get a loan from a place like this? Not likely, unless you inherit something, like land, that you can offer as collateral (so the bank can take it if you don't pay up). But would a commercial bank send you a credit card? Probably a walletful.

Credit unions: Usually you join these organizations through your job. For a young borrower like you who's already got a student loan, they're a more forgiving lender than a bank. Here's a good place to apply for a car loan, for instance. And yes, they'll also issue you a credit card.

Sales finance companies: These lenders are formed by companies that sell an expensive product, in order to help you borrow money to buy it. All three major American automakers have their own sales finance companies. General Motors has GMAC, Ford has Ford Credit, and Chrysler has Chrysler Financial Corporation. *If you've got student loan trouble on your credit record, will these guys lend you money to buy a car? At least one representative told me they might, if everything else about you looks good* (job, prompt payment of bills, and so on).

Finance companies: Not to be confused with sales finance companies, these lenders are often associated with, say, appliance stores. When you buy a big-screen TV and pay for it over time, the store might sell your loan paper to a finance company. Other finance companies specialize in making installment loans to people with bad credit—the worse your credit, the higher the interest. If you can avoid it, don't deal with one of these. It can be seen as a negative on your credit report, because it suggests that you were too bad a risk to get credit anywhere else.

SECURED DEBT VERSUS UNSECURED DEBT

The different institutions dishing out money also dish it out in different kinds of loans. Some of these are easier to keep under control than others, because they're designed with a definite end in sight:

Secured loans: You buy a specific item, like a car, and agree to make a certain number of equal monthly payments till you own it outright. This is a secured debt, because the lender has the security of knowing he can repossess the car if you stop paying.

Unsecured loans: Here's the financial freeway where most of the really gory credit wrecks happen. There are no speed limits, no helpful barricades to keep you from flying out of control. With unsecured debt, if you borrow more than you can repay, the lender can't get his money back unless he sues you and wins. (That's why credit card interest is so high. It includes a big cushion for the lender in case you stiff him.)

MASSIVE UNSECURITY: TYPES OF UNSECURED DEBT

Unsecured debt comes in all kinds of attractive packages—as it certainly should, because market researchers are being paid right now to sit down with your credit record and figure what loan product might tempt you.

Charge accounts

From J. C. Penney and Sears to Circuit City and Macy's, these accounts may be convenient, but their interest rates are huge.

Charge Cards: American Express and Diners Club are the most popular of these cards, which have traditionally been marketed as status symbols for established businesspeople. But they'll also be delighted to hear from you. American Express even has a separate youth marketing division. The real advantage of using charge cards is that they're *not* credit cards. You have to pay them off each month, so you can't build up big debts. In this category, too, are charge cards from Mobil, Exxon, and so on.

Credit card accounts

Visa, MasterCard, Discover, and Optima are the most popular open-end credit card accounts. They come in so many varieties, it's useless to list them here. But in a card-eat-card world, here are a couple of interesting twists.

Affinity cards: These Visas and MasterCards attract you by tying your credit card to some strong interest, or affinity, of yours. If you like Greenpeace (or the National Rifle Association), you can get a credit card that gives that organization a percentage of each purchase. Another card may give you points toward frequent flyer miles.

Gold Cards: Okay, I admit it. Gold cards are sexy. They offer fun benefits and credit limits that may start around $5,000 and climb from there. Your income has to be at a certain level before you can get a gold card—which is good, because gold card annual fees are probably twice what you're accustomed to.

A STORY OF INTEREST

To get a good credit deal, you have to understand how the lender is figuring the interest you have to pay. Some methods are better for him; some are better for you. It's all in the fine print on your credit agreement, and it's easy to understand if you know a few simple terms.

Principal: The amount you actually borrow when you take out a loan. If I borrow $2,000 from you at 10 percent interest, the principal I owe you is $2,000. The interest—the rental fee—is 10 percent of $2,000, or $200. When I pay you back, you get your rental fee first. So my first few payments are interest-only.

Variable-rate interest: If you're like most of us, you have a variable-rate credit card. Your credit card interest is pegged to a certain number of percentage points above the Prime Rate, set by the Fed. If the Prime Rate rises sharply enough, your interest rises too. Some cards refigure their rates every month; some, every three months.

Variable-rate interest can work in your favor. Every few months, you can and should demand a lower interest rate. ("I'm paying too much. I need a better deal.") If you're a good customer—one who uses your card often but pays promptly—you'll be shocked how often a credit card issuer will agree. On the other hand, if you don't pay promptly or your credit profile shows increasing risk, the company may *raise* your interest rate.

Fixed-rate interest: With a fixed rate, the interest stays the same no matter whether the mountains explode or aliens attack. On credit cards, you'll see fixed rates mostly as limited-time offers. ("Introductory rate of 5.9% APR for first six months.") Lenders want you to transfer balances from other cards. Six months later, the interest jumps up to a much higher variable rate.

Term: This means how long you want to keep the money before you pay it back. The longer you need the money, the more interest— rental fee—you have to pay. Remember, time is the crucial factor that makes credit profitable to a lender. The longer he lets you keep the money, the more profit he makes.

CREDIT CARD INTEREST: HOW DO I FIGURE WHAT I'M PAYING?

Annual Percentage Rate (APR): This is the one method American lenders must use by law in order to calculate the interest rate they're charging you. Under the Truth in Lending Act, credit cards must state the APR interest you're being charged. But that number can be misleading, because it doesn't include fees, or monthly or daily compounding of finance charges.

Periodic Rate: According to the credit-card consumer-protection group Bankcard Holders of America (BHA), here's the magic number that really determines your interest tab each month. If your credit card bill lists a Monthly Periodic Rate, that means your interest is compounded every month, which raises your cost of credit to a higher rate than the APR. More expensive still is the Daily Periodic Rate, which means interest is compounded every day. How do lenders compound interest? They charge interest on interest. In addition to charging interest on the amount you borrow (the principal), they also charge interest on the interest expense you've incurred.

Minimum Payment: The amount you have to come up with to keep your account in good shape. More and more cards are lowering their minimum payments to 2 percent of the "new balance" amount listed on your credit card bill. That may seem great, but actually you could die paying the loan off at that rate. Here's a horrifying example from BHA: Say you owe $2,500 at 18.5 percent interest, and you make only your minimum payments: 2 percent of that debt each month. It'll take you more than thirty years to pay it off. And you'll have paid $6,650 in interest!

Average Daily Balance, Excluding New Purchases: Your average daily balance is the total unpaid credit card debt you owe each day during the billing period, divided by the number of days in the billing period. This calculation method does not add anything new that you bought. According to Bankcard Holders of America, this is the method of interest calculation that's most advantageous for you—but few banks use it.

Two-cycle Average Daily Balance, Excluding New Purchases: Now we're adding together your average daily balances for two month-long billing cycles. BHA ranks this method second best.

Average Daily Balance, Including New Purchases: Since we're now adding your new purchases, your average daily balance is higher. Thus, you owe more interest. Third best, says BHA.

Two-cycle Average Daily Balance, Including New Purchases: This method is most profitable for lenders, because even if you bought nothing in the first month's cycle, they can "backcharge" interest on your purchases for the second cycle. Unless you always carry a balance from month to month, choose a card that uses this method last, advises BHA.

Annual fee: Many credit cards charge an annual fee of between $15 and $75. Most gold cards charge more. Credit cards that don't charge an annual fee will stress that savings when they advertise to you. But remember they usually make their profit elsewhere—on interest. If you pay your balance in full each month (great habit!), choose a card with no annual fee even if the interest rate is high. If you "revolve"—carry a balance from month to month—choose a card with lower interest rates.

PENALTY FEES

Any time some mistake of yours causes extra difficulty in servicing your account, your bank charges you for its trouble, usually somewhere between $15 and $20. Does it actually cost the bank that much to take care of you? Forget it! But partly because they're competing to offer low-interest credit cards, banks have quietly begun to charge extra for other services they once considered part of the cost of doing business.

Late fees are probably the penalties you'll get most often, and a particular credit card's policy on late fees should definitely be one of your shopping considerations. Some cards wait thirty days (or one billing period). Others wait fifteen days. But more and more issuers slap you with a late fee if you're as little as a day late. For them, it's another chance to make money.

There's also more to it than that. Many, many Americans are overextended right now in terms of credit. The card companies are starting to see your late payments as a sign that you're not their type. It's becoming more common for card companies to penalize you for being late by jacking your interest rates up into the nosebleed range.

Overlimit Fee: Some banks will charge you $5 to $25 if you exceed your credit limit. Since you're already forking over interest on a big credit debt, you'd think they wouldn't do this, but you're wrong.

Cash Advance Fee: The interest here can really be outrageous. Lenders often charge higher interest on a cash advance, starting the minute you get it. Then they add this interest to your balance and compound it. In addition, many banks add a 2.5 percent fee. All told, it can add up to 33 percent interest. Don't sign on.

How to Shop for the Credit Cards You Want

1. Call Bankcard Holders of America at (540) 389-5445 (or visit their website at http://www.epn.com/bha) and get hold of their list of the cheapest credit cards in the country. (There's a small fee for this service, but it's worth it.) Most of the banks on BHA's list have 1-800 numbers, so you can get your application rolling in one call.

2. Look for a card with the good traits we've talked about:
   A. No annual fee (or low annual fee);
   B. A wildly low introductory interest rate (preferably for a year, not six months), followed by a variable interest rate of 12 percent or under;
   C. Interest computed to your advantage;
   D. A monthly minimum payment that's 2 percent of your monthly new balance;
   E. A twenty-five-day grace period if you're late with a payment; and
   F. A friendly and obliging support staff.

3. Don't apply for more than two credit cards in six months, cautions BHA. You're liable to be turned down because you seem desperate. Potential creditors will assume you have a cash flow problem, and you're trying to live on credit.

4. Don't have too many cards. It reflects badly on your credit report—again, because it makes you seem desperate. Three is about the most you should have. Two is better.

5. If you like to run up smaller balances on several cards rather than having a larger balance on one or two cards, get over it. First, you're paying more interest that way. Second, you're showing potential lenders that you have a certain scatterbrained quality about money.

6. Take advantage of those "low introductory interest" offers from cards that invite you to transfer balances from your existing, higher-interest accounts. But do it so that you won't hurt your credit rating by seeming unstable. First, when you transfer a balance to a new card, close the old account. Second, wait six months before you do this maneuver again. This won't cost you, since your low introductory interest rate is probably good for six months.

7. Ignore all those "special offers" enclosed in your credit card bill every month. This includes "inexpensive" life insurance plans as well as "credit guard" features that make your minimum payments if you're fired. By the time you need one of these "benefits"—if you ever do—you will probably have paid more than it's worth in fees.

YOUR CREDIT RATING: HOW DOES IT WORK, AND WHO CARES?

Everywhere you turn, somebody's shaking a finger in your face about your credit rating. Your friends are shrieking, "Protect it." Your enemies are shouting, "I'll wreck it."

Are these people just trying to scare you?

What is your credit rating, anyway? Do you even have one? If so, who compiled it? Where is it? And most important, why should you care?

Your credit rating is a code that can be used to assess your financial attractiveness, stability, and behavior. A good rating makes people want to do business with you. A bad rating tells them to stay away.

Do you have a credit rating? Yes, if you've ever bought anything and paid for it over time; yes again, if you have a student loan.

Who decides on your credit rating? This is a bit complex, but for the moment let's say America's three biggest credit bureaus.

And what are credit bureaus? They're private companies that collect and store millions of financial facts about you, and about all Americans. These facts are used to assess, or rate, you. The three largest credit bureaus are Experian (formerly TRW), Trans Union, and Equifax, and there's a file on you at each right now. Credit bureaus make a living by selling information about you to all kinds of subscribers—people who have a business reason to ask.

What's in your credit file? Basically, your credit file is an ongoing financial portrait of you. Every financial move you make throughout the years is recorded and zapped in. When potential business connections want to size you up, a reporting agency sends a credit report—often instantly, by computer. For the creditor, this is called "pulling your file."

Why should you care about your credit rating? As human relationships become less and less important to the way we do business, people judge you more and more by your credit rating. You can't win them over with your devastating charm. They've never met you and don't want to. They judge you on your numbers.

In the wired world of information, you'll never get away from your credit rating, no matter how much you want to. On the other hand, if you've already shot your credit rating to hell and back, that doesn't mean it's all over. You can live without a good credit rating, and you can repair your credit.

If you're feeling frightened about your situation right now, remember this: there's no credit disaster you can't repair with the help of time. No matter what scary thing happens right now, it won't ruin your whole life. Don't run away. If you're willing to learn how, you can take charge of your situation and win.

What's in Your Credit Report?

A pro in the credit business can describe you down to the last freckle by looking over your credit report. It shows where you live, where you've worked, where you shop, how much money you spend, how much you charge, whether you pay your bills on time.

Credit files contain these general categories of information:

Personal Information: Your name, address, previous addresses for the last five to ten years, your date of birth, your Social Security number and that of your spouse, your present and past employers, and maybe your income. This is used primarily to identify you and make sure the credit information belongs to you.

Tradelines: That's industry slang for the accounts section of a credit report. Tradelines list your credit accounts, their opening dates, payment history, applicable balance, and any action taken against you regarding payment or nonpayment.

Public Record Information: Bankruptcies, judgments, and liens (meaning a creditor exercised the legal right to confiscate some property of yours)—in other words, any and all financial legal proceedings, whether you start them or you're on the receiving end. There's a limit to how many years these problems of yours can be on display. If you're applying for a big enough loan, the law says your whole history can be dragged up again. But "in practice," says Experian's vice-president for consumer education Maxine Sweet, "no company looks beyond the period covered in the credit report—to my knowledge."

Requests for Access: When you ask a credit bureau to show you your credit report, the law says the report must list the name of anybody else who asked to look in the last two years.

It's not the credit report itself, but how it's interpreted that determines how you're judged. *A credit report lists the facts only*—individual events in your life, and the dates when they happened. *Potential creditors then use these events to "score" you according to a predetermined list of criteria.*

Still, here's a start. Creditors might rate you on your monthly income, length of time at your job, type of occupation (professionals and managers rate high; unskilled laborers rate low), whether you own or rent your home, how long you've lived at your address, whether you have a phone in your name, the number of bank cards you carry (more than three is considered too needy), your monthly payment on debts other than a mortgage, and payment history, meaning how long it takes you to pay what you owe.

How Do You Score?

In the credit business, you're judged on the three Cs: Character, Capacity, and Collateral. Does this sound like first grade?

Character: When creditors use this word, they're referring to whether you care about paying back money you borrow. This trait of yours, or your lack of it, is easy to see from your payment record.

Capacity: This means your ability to live according to your income and not overextend yourself, even though you could buy thousands of dollars' worth of stuff on credit for just a few dollars a month.

Collateral: Anything of value that creditors could seize to recoup their money if you can't make your payments—the car you bought with a loan, a house you financed through a mortgage, the computer you charged on a store credit card. It could also be your savings account or other assets.

How do they get that information? Each month, your creditors report to the credit bureaus the exact status of your accounts. Did you pay them on time, or were you late? This record on you typically goes backward in time as long as seven years ago. In describing your paying habits for its own record-keeping, the credit industry uses number codes that are easily recognized by computers. Generally, the numbers go from one through nine: a code of one means that you paid one month late. A nine code indicates that you went bankrupt on a debt. In between are a multitude of shadings too complicated to go into here. But you won't have to worry about that, because when you ask to see your credit report, it comes to you in plain English, not the number codes used by the industry. And if there's anything you don't understand, you can call the credit bureau's toll-free 1-800 number. Every major credit bureau has one.

Just the Facts

But the credit bureau only collects information about you. It doesn't evaluate or judge your experiences with credit. The evaluation step, the part that asks whether you've got the three Cs, takes place when your credit file is "pulled" by a potential creditor—a business that might consider lending you money. With file in hand, this potential creditor goes over the facts about your payment history and assigns you a credit score.

Credit scoring is the basic tool for sizing you up in the nineties. Different creditors have different scoring systems, so the numbers described may be slightly different in your situation. But basically, if you have a fabulous score, you'll get a loan at the lowest interest and the best terms. In other words, you're trusted. With a rotten score, you may get a loan, but the interest will probably be punishing, and you might have to cough up a big down payment. In other words, you're a weasel.

If you want to score high with creditors, your credit history has to be attractive, and to make sure that it is, you have to learn to read and correct your credit report. But there's a more far-reaching reason too. More and more, business is using your credit file not just to record what you have done, but to predict what you will do.

Predictive Scoring: Tell Me the Future

With personal bankruptcies in America at an all-time high, lenders and creditors are sick of being stiffed by customers. They've fired up the computers, and they're fighting back. The basic information in your credit file may be the same as always. But your history is now being put through analyses that go past simple math and into psychology, probability theory, and advanced statistical analysis.

Predictive scoring is designed to eliminate you as a risk before you can burn a lender. While this practice defends lenders, it also defends you, observes Experian's Maxine Sweet: "It protects the good consumer by keeping credit affordable," she says. If you're deep in credit card debt and staggering your payments as a result, you might well figure your credit score is basically okay. You've never been late enough to be reported as delinquent. But with predictive scoring, your pattern of late payments will be quickly identified. In response, your credit card company may freeze you at a certain dollar limit— or refuse to back purchases over your credit limit.

Bad Marks on Your Credit

Late payments: These "dings" have two parts: how late was the payment, and how big was the amount? Creditors look for a history of late payments. Most will let a late payment or two slide. Some don't even get excited over a number of late payments, as long as the lateness doesn't last a long time and the payments don't get months behind. They're often more concerned with your recent payment pattern. Have you paid on time in the last one to two years?

It's better to be late with small amounts than large amounts. An overdue large payment attracts the evil eye very quickly in the credit business, because it's often a signal that you're having problems.

Collection accounts, charged-off accounts (repossessions), tax liens, judgments, or lawsuits: You may have had a bad credit spell in the past, and you may have cleaned it up already. Some creditors and lenders still won't take a chance on you. For them, you just have to wait out the years (from seven to ten) until your past mishaps fall off your credit report.

Income-to-debt ratio: Just a glance at your credit file shows a lender whether you already have more debts than you can manage. If you're in trouble now, why should he lend you more and risk being stiffed? A poor income-to-debt ratio will definitely get you turned down for some loans. It's one bad mark you can't really change—not today, anyway.

How Long Will These Markers Stay in Your Credit File?

Chapter 7 bankruptcy stays on your credit report for ten years. This includes a bankruptcy that involves your student loan. (More about this later.) Other negative information about you stays in your file for seven years.

A word to the wise: when your time is up and your record is supposed to be clean again, don't count on the credit bureaus to make the proper changes. *You* take action. Get a copy of your credit report and check it yourself, just to make sure the bad stuff is gone.

Errors in Your Credit Report

If you're having credit problems and you don't understand why, there's probably a mistake in your file. It could be a mix-up involving your name—the credit bureau has you confused with some career criminal whose name is the same as yours.

In order to help solve problems of mistaken identity, Experian has now introduced a new computer system in which every person entering the system is issued a PIN (personal identification number) just like that secret number that makes your ATM card work. This should cut down on confusion, and to say the least, that's a good thing. With information on nearly 200 million Americans flying through the credit bureaus, plenty of facts have gone astray. According to their own trade association, credit bureaus handle about half a million disputes every month from people who've found mistakes in their files.

When such a mistake is made about you, it can have tough consequences. Until you track down the problem on your credit file and get it fixed, you'll be denied mortgages, employment, and insurance. That's why *you should examine your credit file once a year, every year.* This may sound like a big hassle, but actually it's easy. And it's definitely worth it. If you have a student loan—which could always go sour and harm your credit rating—it's especially smart to keep the rest of your credit in great shape.

HOW TO GET YOUR CREDIT REPORT

The first step is finding your file. This is much easier than it used to be. Two of the big three credit bureaus don't even make you write your request in a letter anymore. Though you must still write to Experian, you can request your report by phone from Trans Union via an interactive voice setup. Equifax will also let you order by phone, if you pay with a credit card and place your order between 6 A.M. and 11 P.M. Eastern time.

To request your file in writing, make sure your letter includes the following information:

Full name, including any Jr.'s, III's, etc.
Date of birth
Social Security number
Husband or wife's name
Phone number
Current address
Previous address (if you've lived at your present address less than two
    years) Note: Experian wants all addresses for the past five years.
Present employer
Photocopy of your driver's license or a credit card bill that shows
    your correct current address.

You can see your file for free if you request it within sixty days after you've been turned down for credit. If a lender refuses you credit, he's required to send you a letter of refusal naming the credit reporting agency whose report led to the decision. Otherwise, you'll be charged a fee of between $8 and $15 to order a copy of your file. Call to find out exactly how much, and include a check or money order for the correct amount.

Here are the essential names and addresses you'll need:

Experian
National Consumer Assistance Center
P. O. Box 2104
Allen, TX 75013-2104
(800) 682-7654

Trans Union
P. O. Box 390
Springfield, PA 19064
(601) 933-1200

Equifax
P. O. Box 105873
Atlanta, GA 30348
(800) 685-1111

If you're willing to pay about $30, a company called Confidential Credit will get all three of your credit bureau files and compile them into one big, glorious report—with notations telling you which credit bureau says what. Cheap at the price, wouldn't you say? Contact them at:

Confidential Credit
5930 Priestly Dr., Suite 200
Carlsbad, CA 92008-9656
(800) 443-9342

Other companies are joining this game too. For a look at who's who, check out www.consumerinfo.com.

By the way, if there's something on your credit report you don't understand, call the credit bureau's 1-800 number and get somebody to help you read it, or ask your parents, or a banker, or that accounting major who used to live in your dorm. If your credit file confuses you, that does not mean you're stupid. It only means you're exactly like most of us. Here's what not to do. Don't sit and stare at the thing and get defeated, and shove it in a drawer.

HOW TO CORRECT ERRORS IN YOUR CREDIT REPORT

First, check the status of your student loan

Is your loan listed in default, when you're actually in deferment?
Are you accused of making late payments you really made on time?
If you've consolidated, have your original loans been closed out? (Or
   are they still open, so it looks like you have twice as many loans?)
Is your loan where you thought it was? What institution is holding it?

A great student loan tip: If you're in default, your loan or loans may
have been resold or passed to one or more collection agencies. In this
situation, requesting your credit report is the best way to track your
loan down, so you can begin to rehabilitate it.

Next, check for consumer credit mistakes

Inaccuracies in your name, address, telephone, and Social Security
   number
Wrong or old information about your job
Negative information from more than seven years ago
Bankruptcy information from more than ten years ago
Kind of bankruptcy (Chapter 7, Chapter 13) not specified
Account numbers that don't belong to you
Any financial lawsuits or legal hassles mistakenly pinned on you
Accounts you closed that are listed as still open
Accounts *you* closed, listed as though the lender closed out on *you*
Late payments you actually made on time

Now, Contact the Credit Bureau

When you find a problem, call or write the credit bureau and ask
them to reinvestigate your file. If you write, keep a copy of your letter. Include proof that you're telling the truth. If it's a late payment,
send a photocopy of your dated check to the creditor who's disputing

your word. That way, when the credit bureau investigates again, they'll find an accurate record. (Copies only, please! Never send original documents!) Make sure to say specifically what the error is. "This purchase is not mine" is good. "This bill is wrong" is bad. If it's an error in an account number, include a copy of a bill with the correct number.

Probably this will do the trick. But it's also possible the credit bureau may investigate and find that the creditor's record still doesn't match yours. If this happens, you can request a second reinvestigation by following the dispute instructions at each credit bureau's 1-800 number. Also, call the *creditor* to find out why the problem is persisting.

If you don't get satisfactory action after that, complain to:

Federal Trade Commission
Sixth and Pennsylvania Ave. NW
Washington, DC 20580
(202) 326-2222

Incidentally, one good thing about the age of computers: as a rule, if they do find a problem in your file, creditors automatically correct the mistake with all the credit bureaus. So you don't have to notify them all separately.

Accept right now that it will probably take time to fix your difficulty. And don't expect anybody to apologize or hold your hand. It's frustrating, but what can you do? Don't get nasty, and do be persistent. If none of that works, consider legal action.

THEY CAN'T JUST ABUSE YOU: YOUR RIGHTS UNDER THE LAW

You do have rights in all of this. You're protected under several broad and sweeping laws regulating the credit business: the Fair Credit Reporting Act, the Fair Credit Billing Act, and the Fair Debt Collection Act.

If you don't get satisfaction from either a creditor or a credit bureau, you can definitely sue. Creditors are forbidden to discriminate against you because of your race, religion, national origin, sex, or age; or because your income includes alimony, child support, public assistance, or part-time work. Also, they have to be able to show a practical reason why they decide against you. If they deny you credit because you've worked at your job less than two years, they have to be able to show that people at a job less than two years are less likely to pay than people who've been employed longer. It's worthwhile to look at the law on these issues, because it's more on your side than you might think.

REBUILDING YOUR CREDIT: IT CAN BE DONE

So congratulations! Now you know enough about credit to be able to ask good questions and begin to take charge of your situation. But what if you've already fallen behind on your cards or car payments or whatever?

That just means you have to rebuild your credit. It takes time, but you can do it. Considering how much there is to know about handling credit in the first place, rebuilding credit is extremely simple. The steps are straightforward. But since the main thing that heals your credit is time, the challenge is being consistent with your financial moves—and being patient.

Deal Me Another Card

If you've just blown your credit rating by overspending on credit cards, you won't get another card right away. But you can still have a card—just a different kind.

Secured Credit Cards: This is a credit card, but with a huge difference: the funds you're drawing from are your own, not the bank's. In other words, to get a secured card with a credit line of $1,000, you start by sending the bank your own $1,000. It's called a secured card, of course, because the lender has the security of knowing you're backing up your debt with your own money. He's not risking a cent. With most secured cards, he's also getting the consolation of very high interest.

If you've had a credit meltdown, getting a secured card is one of the first steps you'll take toward rehabilitating your credit—in other words, paying bills on time, consistently, so that those payments will be recorded on your credit report. After a while, card companies will see that "good" behavior on your credit record and decide it's time to target you for unsecured debt again. To speed that day along—and escape secured-card interest rates—look for a secured card with a *conversion* feature. After a certain number of months, it becomes a regular, unsecured credit card, with lower interest to match.

Debit Cards: Debit cards look like credit cards, but they work like a personal check. Your purchase is instantly deducted from your checking account. (This is bad news for you weasels who love to write a check on Tuesday and deposit the money on Wednesday.) Both Visa and MasterCard offer debit cards. They're accepted all over the world, everywhere a regular Visa or MasterCard would be welcomed—but they cost as little as a dollar a month. Debit cards are a major convenience if you want to keep yourself credit-card free.

Rebuilding your credit won't take forever, and it will give you a chance to organize your financial life more to your advantage in years to come. On the other hand, if you survey your situation and realize that it's too serious to repair, maybe you need to wipe out the past and just start again. You'll find out how in the next chapter, on declaring bankruptcy.

CHAPTER 12

Bankruptcy: Starting Over, Sort Of

If you're like a lot of us, even the word bankruptcy makes you feel
like a loser. If a lot of your money problems are caused by student
loan debt, it's worse. You ask yourself: how could I have been so stupid? Who did I think was going to pay this money back? When did
all my high hopes turn into . . . this?

Hey. Get over it. In your heart you know you've been doing the
best you can. You didn't come into this world knowing how to handle money. And if your student loan is a horror story that's just now
sinking in on you, you're not alone. Thousands of students borrowed
more than you did. However bad you're feeling right now, they're
feeling worse.

Since I'm not an attorney, I can't give you legal advice about
whether bankruptcy is for you. But I hope that if the need arises, this
chapter will give you the tools to ask smart questions about bankruptcy and your student loans. There's one thing I *can* tell you: Your
situation may feel uncomfortable right now, but it's not hopeless.

CAN I GO BANKRUPT ON MY STUDENT LOAN?

If you're drowning in debt, you may need to declare bankruptcy.
That's neither good nor bad. It's just a fact. Here's another fact. When
it comes to your student loan, you can't count on bankruptcy to res-
cue you. It may help, but perhaps not the way you wish and hope.

Thanks partly to our older brothers and sisters who used bankruptcy to weasel out of their obligations, the law is now set up so that going bankrupt on a student loan can be very tough. That doesn't mean it's impossible. *But for the first seven years after it comes into repayment, discharging your loan is pretty much out of the question, unless your circumstances are extremely severe.* You and your lawyer have to prove that repaying the loan would cause you *undue hardship*.

You don't get to decide what undue hardship means. The judge does that, by applying a set of specific legal standards to your situation. We'll explain those standards later. But for now, just remember that in order to argue that paying your student loan would cause you undue hardship, you have to be really poor, unable to provide yourself with the basic necessities. Moreover, the judge has to be convinced that your situation probably won't improve in the future.

Partly because individual cases can vary so much, popular books on bankruptcy can be totally confusing on the subject of student loans. For instance, some books list student loans simply as "nondischargeable debts," which might lead you to think that you owe the debt for life, no matter what. But that's not true.

A Seven-Year Wait—or Longer

If you wait seven years before you file, your loan definitely *can* be discharged in bankruptcy.

There is a big catch, though. Instead of seven *consecutive* years after your loan came into repayment, the law says that the time during which your loan payments were in deferment status—or, in some cases, during a forbearance—does *not* count as part of the seven years. In other words, you might think your seven years are over, only to find that your loan holder figures you've got another two or three years to go. That's another reason you shouldn't try to do your own figuring when it comes to going bankrupt on your student loan. Getting a knowledgeable attorney can mean the difference between a successful proceeding and a nasty, expensive defeat.

You're tough enough to survive it all, I'm sure. But bankruptcy is a big deal. Its effects will be with you until ten years from now, when you're in a whole new phase of your life—one where you're older and you want things to start making sense. All through those years, you may have to explain your story to strangers who have the power to rent you an apartment or sell you a car. They'll get to size you up. If they decide you're not reliable enough to do business with, you'll have to accept that.

Have You Tried Every Loan Repayment Option?

Knowing how long it follows you, do you have to declare bankruptcy? Maybe not. Even if bill collectors are driving you berserk over credit cards and other consumer debts, you don't have to go bankrupt. There are less radical ways to make them stop. Unless your finances are a ghastly, unsalvageable mess, Direct Lending's Income Contingent Repayment plan should give you enough breathing room to deal with your student loan while paying down your other debts. And it will injure you far less in the long run.

But if your consumer debts are hopelessly out of control, bankruptcy will bring all the craziness screeching to a halt. The minute you file bankruptcy papers, the people you owe have to stop hounding you. You're protected from creditors by what's called an *automatic stay*. Nobody can foreclose on your mortgage, repossess your car, shut off your lights—or intercept your tax refund to pay off your student loan, at least for a while.

You can choose either of two ways to declare bankruptcy. Chapter 7, liquidation, can wipe out almost all your debts right away. (This can include your student loan, but only after your seven-year wait is up—or only if you can prove undue hardship.) Chapter 13, debt reorganization, gives you several years of reduced payments that you negotiate through a court-appointed trustee, after which most of your remaining debts are forgiven. Though you'll still owe your student loan (unless the seven years have expired or repayment would cause you undue hardship), this will pare back your consumer debts so you can handle the student loan better.

Unless you try to lie about your money situation, your bankruptcy motion won't be denied. It's your legal right to declare yourself insolvent. In fact, our founding fathers specified debt forgiveness as one of the promises that would separate hip young America from tired old Europe, where if you couldn't pay your bills, they threw you into debtors' prison—not exactly the best place for you to get yourself on track again.

Whatever its drawbacks, bankruptcy will give you a new start. Getting yourself back on track is what it's all about.

In the next few pages, I'll give you a whirlwind tour through the basics of bankruptcy. We won't get into the fine points, partly because there are already about a gazillion good books on the subject. Besides, I don't want you to rely on this book. If you think bankruptcy is the path for you, I hope you'll hire an attorney to take you through the process. Particularly if you want to include your student loan in the festivities, you'll need somebody knowledgeable on your side.

What They Said Versus What We Heard

For us student borrowers, the topic of bankruptcy brings into stark relief the complete communication gap that exists between us and the lenders we're borrowing from. This "language barrier" comes from the weird nature of student loan debt. We all think we agree on what it is, but that's just because we don't listen very hard to the people on the other end of the transaction.

Deep down in our hearts, we students tend to think of a student loan as something like a scholarship. Yeah, sure, we want to pay it back. But if we can't pay—especially if we're doing the best we can to find work—they'll understand, right?

Way wrong. Your lenders do not have the faintest sense of humor about this. To them, you borrowed $20,000, and you *will* give it back. It's easy to call them heartless. On the other hand, be honest: how do you feel when somebody borrows and won't pay you back? As the great Richard Pryor once said, "When a man dies owing you money, it makes you want to dig him up and kill him again."

And besides, the law says your lender has to "diligently" attempt to collect its money. So it's not about heartlessness. Refuse to pay your student loan, and you're calling the law down on your head.

If you don't believe it, ask Kelly.

KELLY'S STORY: SHE DID IT HER WAY

Kelly's dream of an education became a nightmare. Year by year, her student loan situation worsened until, far from pursuing her plan to become a professor of cultural anthropology, she found herself in the midst of a Chapter 7 bankruptcy proceeding.

Kelly tends to cry when she talks about it. "I'm an honorable person," she says. "I've always paid my debts." Kelly borrowed about $20,000 in loans from 1981 to 1984 in order to earn a Ph.D. With a particular interest in all things Celtic, she actually traveled to Ireland to carry out a research project.

Kelly didn't see the sights in Ireland, though, because Kelly is blind. Kelly's disability set her on a collision course with her lenders. It's not that she's self-pitying. But she figured that in her case, it was just common sense for her lenders to leave her alone until she could get her career off the ground—even though that process was taking a discouragingly long time.

"Frankly, I'm not going to get hired as a waitress or a sales clerk," she matter-of-factly observes. "The unemployment rate for people with disabilities is 70 percent. My dilemma was either to try to get a job in my field, where I genuinely thought I had the best chance of getting employed, or paying back the loans in the amount demanded. But I couldn't do both, because in order to keep myself marketable, I needed to go to meetings, do research, keep myself current in my field."

Used to beating the odds in other areas of her life, Kelly gambled on her education. She now admits she may have been too optimistic. "I took out the loans fully expecting that I would have a job when I got out of school," she says. "I knew that it would be tough. I also felt that I would beat the odds, pay back the loans. It didn't work out that way."

For two years after graduation, Kelly used her unemployment deferments as she searched for work in her field. There were no bites, but she did get promising nibbles from a top university, and she still believes that with persistence, she'll be employed.

But when her unemployment deferments ran out, Sallie Mae,

which by then held her loan, was not interested in Kelly's plan or Kelly's timetable. They wouldn't offer what she wanted, which was a waiver on the interest piling onto her loans. The chancellor of Kelly's university even wrote to Sallie Mae and asked for lowered payments or a concession on her compounding interest. No deal, of course. (By this time, you know why. It's the law. Kelly, like lots of us, didn't quite believe that.)

In 1993, Sallie Mae did offer what it could—the opportunity for a loan consolidation. Kelly was outraged. "I looked at the little table that they had," she remembers. "I got so angry when I realized that $20,000 or $30,000 over thirty years might end up being $80,000 or something. I didn't know what my financial prospects would be, and it would have been tough to make the payments even at the lower rate. Consolidating might have been smart for them, but not terribly smart for me. My gut said, Don't do it." Kelly sighs. "Whether that was wise or not, I don't know."

Kelly Learns About Default

With Kelly in defiance, her loans defaulted and reverted back to her guarantor, New York State Higher Education Services Corporation (NYSHESC). Soon she was learning how it feels to be on the receiving end of what federal regulations call "diligent collection efforts."

"I got threatening letters, thrice-weekly phone calls, sometimes with the volume turned all the way up—electronic phone calls," Kelly says. "They were from Sallie Mae and then from NYSHESC. One took over where the other left off."

Kelly visited the Consumer Credit Counseling Bureau, where she was told—erroneously, as you now know—that guarantors can never compromise on price. As NYSHESC stepped up its collection efforts, Kelly also got legal representation for a while from Student Legal Services at her college. But their time and expertise were limited.

Eventually Kelly worked out an agreement with the New York agency. She'd document her income and expenses, and pay $50 a month. Then one little thing—a simple thing—went wrong.

"The old repayment agreement expired on September 29," Kelly

remembers. "The new agreement went into force on October 3. In
the meantime, I got a bill for $300 plus—the full monthly amount. I
wrote back and said, 'I've done my part, I've sent everything in.' I
kept sending in the $50 and asked for an explanation." Why did this
happen? Kelly still doesn't know. No one would tell her. Instead, she
recalls, "The next letter I got just said, 'If you don't send us the full
amount of these defaulted loans, we're going to notify our representatives.'" Kelly was about to get stomped by the FFELP monster.

If you've been through this trauma with your lender, you'll never
forget. Some irrational problem hits, and it's as if the world has
gone crazy. Nothing has changed that you can see, yet suddenly
you're in worsening trouble, and nobody seems to be able to tell
you why.

For Kelly, the process has been devastating. "It's been a terrible
three years," she says. "I haven't been able to work. I've been in
therapy. I wrote to Sallie Mae, the Department of Education, my congressman. I wrote to President Clinton. I did my dissertation on
Northern Ireland, and at that time, I knew the administration was
considering getting involved in the peace process. I asked if I could
come aboard and help."

Trying to Barter

Sounds a bit unrealistic, doesn't it? But do you see what Kelly was
doing? She was acting like a good student. She was offering, in
effect, to make up her debt by doing extra credit work. This is the
kind of gesture we students keep making over and over when our
debts overwhelm us. We try to barter, using the education we bought.
This is sweet, but a complete waste of time. The lenders advanced us
money. They want money back.

Kelly finally found a lawyer who agreed to represent her for a
small fee. Early in 1996, he advised her to file Chapter 7 bankruptcy. He saw the situation as she did: the debt—nearly $30,000 by
now—was not just seven years old, but eleven years old. Certainly it
should be dischargeable. Besides, with her physical disability, the
only practical thing Kelly could do was keep job-hunting in her field.
Her sole income was a monthly Social Security disability check,

along with a small monthly allowance from her parents. Without landing an academic post, she would never have the money to pay back the loan. So Kelly and her lawyer figured she also met the definition of undue hardship. Neither Kelly nor her lawyer believed that NYSHESC would contest the case.

The New York guarantor surprised them, however. It retained lawyers and announced that it would fight. As a guarantor, NYSHESC was required by law to "diligently" contest the loan's dischargeability unless seven years had definitely passed (or unless the loan was so small that chasing after it would leave the guarantor even further in the hole). By NYSHESC's calculations, Kelly had been given 57 months worth of deferments and forbearances over the years, so her seven years wouldn't really be up until late in 1997. Then came the shocker, as far as Kelly and her attorney were concerned. NYSHESC rejected the idea that paying the loan would cause Kelly undue hardship.

Courtroom Drama

Kelly's bankruptcy hearing turned out to be a bad day, especially when she realized another likely reason why the guarantor's lawyers had decided her case was worthwhile. True, Kelly didn't have the money to pay her debt. But her parents most definitely did.

Kelly didn't like to trade on the fact that she was the daughter of a wealthy family. She considered her modest monthly allowance a temporary necessity that she would accept only until she could become self-supporting through her own work. Kelly felt she couldn't ask her parents to bail her out of debt.

But NYSHESC's attorneys argued that Kelly's argument didn't fit the facts. Since she received a regular income from her folks, she obviously wasn't independent. And through them, she had the means to pay, even if it bruised her pride. As she ruefully admitted later, Kelly wasn't prepared to be met with stiff arguments from the opposing attorneys and no sympathy whatever from the judge. "This has made my life a hell," she remembers saying. She also recalls the judge's response: "Yes, but who do you think is going to pay this debt?"

Accepting the Debt

How did Kelly's case turn out? Her parents settled out of court. The guarantor knocked a significant percentage off the bill in return for a lump-sum payment. Now Kelly owes the money to her parents.

Of course, when all this started, Direct Lending's Income Contingent Repayment wasn't available. Even if it had been, that wasn't what Kelly wanted. She didn't want a lifetime of debt hanging over her head. She wanted her creditors to write off her debt, as if they had cosigned Kelly's career gamble and they expected all along to lose their investment if the gamble didn't pay off.

Kelly may have been naive on this particular subject. Yet she has also been smart enough, and brave enough, to refuse to let her disability keep her down; to travel, to earn academic distinction, to contribute. Kelly's the kind of person we usually congratulate. If she wasn't prepared to acknowledge the reality of her student loan debt then, she certainly is now. "If my story can help someone figure out what to do when the system goes wrong," she says, "then that'll be wonderful."

That's really the lesson here. Deep down, aren't you a little bit like Kelly? When you take out a student loan, you promise to repay a sum of money you can hardly picture. As you sign your name, you think, "If I can't pay this back, what'll I do?" Here's what you tell yourself: "I'm not some deadbeat. My intentions are honorable. I'll do the best I can, and if I can't pay, then I'll just . . . go bankrupt."

As you can see, that's no answer. Yes, going bankrupt is your right under the U.S. Constitution. And the past three years have seen a rise in successful student-loan bankruptcy proceedings. Still, bankruptcy is no fun. If you file to discharge your student loan and the loan holder opposes you, nobody is going to congratulate you on your big educational achievement. Your honor is going to be questioned. You're going to be made to feel like a deadbeat. And you may lose.

WHAT BANKRUPTCY CAN DO—AND WHAT IT CAN'T

In the broadest terms, you might say bankruptcy is good to get some debts off your back, postpone others, and help you hang onto possessions you'd lose otherwise.

Things bankruptcy can do

- Relieve you of your obligation to pay most of your debts, in what's called a "discharge."

- Keep your house or trailer from being foreclosed on by the lenders, which gives you time to concentrate on making back payments.

- Save your car or other valuable property from being repossessed, or even get back property that was repossessed.

- Keep you from being harassed by collectors, or having your wages garnished (or both).

- Stop your utilities from being cut off, or get them turned on again after you've already lost them.

- Negotiate lower payments (maybe) on debts like car loans.

- Give you a chance to defend yourself against bogus claims by people who say you owe them money when you don't.

Things bankruptcy can't do

- Can't discharge some of the big debts you'd most like to be rid of: child support, alimony, some student loans, criminal fines, and some taxes.

- Can't force creditors to let you keep property (collateral) on a secured loan like a car loan or a mortgage, unless you choose to keep paying that particular debt.

- Can't protect friends or family who cosigned on your loans. If your sweet Aunt Tessie cosigned the loan for your truck—and you go bankrupt—collectors will be dogging her for the rest of the money. Don't treat Aunt Tessie that way.

- Can't protect new debts you incur after you've already declared bankruptcy.

DON'T FILE IF IT WON'T HELP

Before you get into this, take a minute and get straight with yourself about several very basic preconditions.

1. How many of your debts are dischargeable? If more than half your debts fall into the nondischargeable category in the list above—student loans (sometimes), child support, alimony, taxes—bankruptcy won't give you the relief you expect. (Since there are exceptions in all these cases, a good attorney might help you beat the odds. But you can't depend on the decision going your way.)

2. For a while after filing for bankruptcy, you're not likely to receive any credit. Can you really, truly live on what you bring home in your paycheck?

3. Are you willing to see some of your possessions taken away? (This may not happen, but under Chapter 7 bankruptcy, the law says it can.) That's the deal you make in bankruptcy.

4. Can you stand the intrusiveness of this whole ordeal? No matter which path to bankruptcy you choose, lawyers will be rummaging through your private and personal financial records. You'll find out fast that this feels like having a stranger root through your underwear drawer.

And if you go Chapter 13, for a period of years, most of your debts will be paid through a court-appointed trustee. This is like living on an allowance from your Mom, but worse. She at least used to keep a spare $10 in her purse if you ran a little short on Friday night.

How will this Affect Your Future?

Naturally you're worried about how this big, scary step might affect people's impressions of you. Will you lose their respect? Will they decide you're trash? Will they take advantage of you in their future business dealings with you? Relax. Unless you tell them, they probably won't know.

Will going bankrupt now have a dreadful effect on your credit rating? Well, if you're looking at bankruptcy, your credit rating's probably pretty bad already. Bankruptcy won't make it all that much worse. Besides, the sooner you get this chapter behind you, the sooner you can start paying your debts on time and therefore getting some good news on your credit report for a change.

HOW'S YOUR TIMING?

Naturally, you want to file for bankruptcy when it will do you the most good—meaning when you owe the largest amount of debt. So if you know you've got to have some expensive medical procedure, or if it's the middle of the month and you know you can't pay your next month's rent, wait until after you've incurred these debts before you file. This is not dishonest; it's intelligent. It won't help anybody, including your creditors, if you consciously leave one of your debts out of the total you include in your bankruptcy.

Weasel Alert

If, on the other hand, you think bankruptcy is your big chance to furnish a house, buy a car, go on vacation, and escape without paying a dime, you're being really stupid. Maybe this hasn't occurred to you, but nothing we do is invisible. If six months before you file, you do your imitation of *Twister*—you know, roar through a shopping mall and pick up everything in your path—a bankruptcy trustee will see through you in a second. And guess what? You and your bankruptcy will be bounced right out of court. (Or the bankruptcy may go forward, but you'll still owe these debts, even after the bankruptcy.)

BANKRUPTCY LANGUAGE (TERMS YOU'LL WANT TO KNOW)

Like every other area of your life that relates to credit, money, and the law, bankruptcy comes with its own vocabulary. It may all sound like gibberish at first, but it's important to understand the language of bankruptcy, because these concepts really don't have equivalents that can be expressed in other words.

Here's a quick tour through the words you need to keep up with this discussion.

Lien: The creditor's right to take your property and sell it in order to collect a debt. If a car dealer sells you a Jeep on credit, your contract gives that dealer the right to repossess your Jeep and sell it to somebody else if you don't make your payments. This means the creditor holds a lien (or "security interest") on your Jeep. Filing bankruptcy will normally not eliminate most types of liens, but it may give you tools to deal with your debts better—without losing your property.

Collateral: Property put up by a borrower as security for a loan. For instance, if you owned a house, you might use that as collateral to get a small-business loan. If you don't pay the loan, your creditor gets to sell your house.

Equity: The amount of money your property is presently worth, minus the amount of any loan that uses that property as collateral. Say you bought a $10,000 car with a $9,000 loan. Say the car is now worth $6,000, and you still have $5,000 to pay off on the loan. Your equity is now $1,000.

Here's why equity is such a big deal in bankruptcy. You get to keep what is called "exempt property" of a certain dollar value. In computing how much you can keep, the dollar value is not based on the purchase price you paid, but on the equity you've got now. Obviously this is a big difference, in your favor.

The Mysteries of Exemption

When you file a Chapter 7 bankruptcy, your equity in all the property you own is divided up and declared either exempt or nonexempt. Property that's nonexempt is up for grabs. The bankruptcy court is free to sell it and divide the proceeds among your creditors, to pay back what you owe them, unless you buy the property back yourself.

Exemptions are preset by law. They're expressed as a certain dollar amount's worth of a thing you get to keep. For instance, the federal bankruptcy code allows you a $15,000 homestead exemption. (State law establishes certain exemptions, too.)

It can be hard to grasp how this number is figured, because it's all calculated on your equity in your home, not the home's value. Here's an example: say you originally bought your house for $50,000, with a $45,000 mortgage. Let's say the house is now worth $55,000, with $42,000 still left on the mortgage, because you've paid off $13,000 of the principal. Your equity in the house is $13,000. Okay. If you were going bankrupt, and the court sold your house in order to get money for your creditors, the house would bring $55,000. Of that price, $42,000 would have to go to the bank that holds the mortgage, leaving only $13,000 left over.

This means you get to keep your house in a Chapter 7 bankruptcy (as long as you take care of the bank holding the mortgage). Why? Selling it wouldn't do you or the creditors any good. By law, you must be allowed to keep $15,000 worth of home. That $15,000 is exempt. The bank would get the remaining $42,000. Your creditors wouldn't get anything. So they have no right to force a sale.

Note: At our stage of life not many of us have a yacht or a summer home or a BMW to hold onto. If you do have a big piece of property to protect, you simply bypass Chapter 7 bankruptcy in favor of Chapter 13, in which none of your possessions is threatened. On the other hand, if you couldn't decipher this example, go straight to the next section.

HOW TO FIND AN ATTORNEY

If you didn't understand before why it's wise to hire a bankruptcy lawyer, I hope you're starting to get the picture. The bankruptcy code is complicated. Not only is there a set of federal exemption laws, but each state has exemption laws of its own. And nearly half of all Americans have the right to choose whether to go bankrupt under federal rules or state rules.

Knowing what property you can keep—and how to keep it—can make the difference between a devastating experience, or the fresh start bankruptcy was meant to be. Besides, bankruptcy varies from court to court and judge to judge.

When in the Jungle, Travel with a Guide

You can hire an attorney who's already represented someone whose judgment you respect. Or you can shop for a bankruptcy attorney through a lawyer referral service, which you'll get by calling your local bar association. Or you look at the list from which the Bankruptcy Court in your area names trustees. Bankruptcy attorneys often serve as trustees (except, naturally, when conflicts of interest arise). If you're a very low-income person, some legal aid organizations will assist you at no charge.

Once you find a lawyer, set up a consultation and let him or her explain what he can do for you. Treat this initial consultation like a job interview—and remember that you're doing the interviewing. Don't sign any forms or make any commitments. Shop around until you find a lawyer who's comfortable to talk to, who'll answer your questions, and who'll spend time with you personally, not push you off on an assistant.

A simple personal Chapter 7 bankruptcy generally costs between $500 and $1,000. Low-cost bankruptcy specialists will charge a little less. Simple Chapter 13 cases cost a little more.

Don't be surprised by wide swings in attorney fees. Some lawyers charge a flat fee; others charge by the hour. Advance payments differ from lawyer to lawyer, but except for some Chapter 13 bankruptcies, you'll have to pay something up front. (Attorneys involved in

Chapter 13 will sometimes take payments as part of your negotiated debt adjustment plan.)

Avoid lawyers who specialize in either Chapter 7 or Chapter 13. Your lawyer should be open to whichever solution is best for you.

Finally, make your lawyer give you a definite date by which your bankruptcy petition will be filed, and hold him to it. Delay is a very big deal to you. If it's not important to him, he shouldn't be representing you.

CHAPTER 7 OR CHAPTER 13?

Now that you know the lingo, and some of what's at stake for you, let's go step by step through your two choices of bankruptcy. Remember, in Chapter 7, you liquidate your debts; in Chapter 13, you reorganize.

Chapter 7 works best if most of your property is exempt under your state or federal law; if most of your debts are unsecured; and if most are dischargeable under Chapter 7. Your student loan debt may or may not be dischargeable.

Chapter 13 is a better option if somebody's just about to foreclose on your house or repossess your car. (Under Chapter 7, these creditors have to pause in their efforts, but not for long.) Under Chapter 13, you get real time to catch up on these big debts without losing your possessions, and you may get the amount you owe reduced. Your student loan is not dischargeable under this plan, but relief on your other debts can help you pay it off.

Finally, Chapter 13 presents one really fabulous advantage: if you file Chapter 7, you have to wait six years before you do it again. But after you've filed either a Chapter 7 or Chapter 13, you don't have to wait six years before filing Chapter 13. Although bad faith may lead to its being dismissed, there are no fixed limits to how often you can file a Chapter 13 bankruptcy.

Chapter 7: I Quit!

In a Chapter 7 liquidation, you just call it quits—you ask the judge to wipe out most of your debts. This is obviously a pretty radical thing to do, and in return for that privilege, you give a court-appointed trustee the right to inventory your possessions and see what can be sold in order to pay off your creditors.

This doesn't mean the trustee can sell off your winter coat. Typically, the food and shelter and clothes and tools you need in order to work and live on a basic level won't be taken away from you. In fact, notes the National Consumer Law Center, "for many low-income persons, exemption statutes will permit retention of all their assets" in a Chapter 7 bankruptcy. In other words, if you have limited equity in your possessions, you may not have to give up anything you own.

What debts will you be rid of? Unsecured debts: credit cards, phone and utility bills, and medical bills. Also commonly included, though not necessarily unsecured, are debts for household goods, jewelry, and other personal property.

For most of us, the credit card debt is key. Medical debt, especially medical debt you shouldn't owe, is another good reason to consider Chapter 7. (After my friend Lulu had $23,000 worth of back surgery, her employer's cut-rate insurance company went out of business and left her holding the bill. Lulu discovered that Chapter 7 can be a thing of beauty.)

Major possessions you're paying off month by month are a different story, though. Your car is probably the best example. It's a secured debt, meaning the dealer who sold you the car has the security of knowing he can haul off the car and resell it if you won't pay.

If you're still paying your car note, you can't just tell the car dealer, "Know what? Changed my mind." You'll wake up and find your driveway empty.

Your Student Loan and Chapter 7 Bankruptcy

By now you know that it's your right to have your student loan discharged in Chapter 7 bankruptcy, *if* your loan has been in repayment more than seven years, or *if* you can prove that repaying the loan would cause you *undue hardship*.

Keep in mind, though, you may not encounter sympathy in the courtroom when you're seeking a discharge based on undue hardship. Some judges are quite turned off by ex-students complaining about undue hardship in paying for their educations. It's those clashing definitions of student loans again. Yeah, say students, we wanted the loans. We said we'd put up with poverty in order to pay them back. But we didn't realize it would be like this. Judges, on the other hand, deal with real poverty all the time. Compared to that, what we student debtors put up with is mere inconvenience.

A seven-year wait seems simple enough, right? But when do the seven years start? Generally, your seven years begins after your six- or nine-month grace period, on the day your very first loan payment was due. So at the earliest, you'll wait almost eight years after graduation before you can safely discharge a student loan in bankruptcy.

But that's not all. From that seven-year period you also have to subtract every deferment and often any forbearance you've ever had. And if you consolidated your loans, as so many of us have, you probably went back to square one.

Undue Hardship: The Hurdle You're Not Meant to Leap

As we've said, in order to discharge a student loan that's been in repayment less than seven years, you have to prove that repaying the loan would cause you *undue hardship*. And what's that, exactly?

If your situation is just sort of bad, or even if it's awful but might get better, you probably won't pass the undue hardship test. The case law says undue hardship has to involve more than whether you can pay right now. There must also be no real prospect of improvement in your future. Here's how it goes, according to the National Consumer Law Center's *Consumer Bankruptcy Law and Practice*:

> "Although most [courts] . . . agree that 'undue' means more than the 'garden variety' hardship that arises from the expense of future payments, each judge seems to bring a unique set of values to the process of defining and implementing the applicable standard."

In revising and tightening the law, Congress has been very clear that bankruptcy judges should discourage any middle-class students who might be skipping out on paying their loans just before latching onto those prosperous careers that college is supposed to bring them.

Over the years, various courts have struggled to define the concept of "undue hardship." Many now use a three-prong test to determine whether student loan repayment would cause undue hardship. All three prongs (conditions) have to be met before you get an undue hardship discharge.

1. The ability-to-pay prong: Here, the judge looks at your income vs. your expenses, also taking in all the other financial circumstances you bring to the inquiry. Can you continue a minimal standard of living while repaying the student loans?

2. The ability-to-pay-in-the-future prong: The judge must decide how much money you're likely to have in the future. Unless you're disabled, the court may find that someday you'll have the money. Since there's no statute of limitations on student loan debt, "someday" could mean when your parents die and leave you money or property in their will.

3. The good-faith prong: Now the judge goes through your records to see whether you've ever really cared about repaying your loan. If you've looked for a higher-paying job in order to make payments; if you've put yourself on a reduced budget; if you've kept in regular contact with your loan holder, it'll be obvious. If you've never actually paid your monthly note, don't expect a good outcome here.

There's a part two to the good-faith prong, too: *The judge has to look over all your debts and be convinced that you're not trying to go bankrupt mainly to get rid of your student loan.*

Some courts are now taking a middle position. Instead of discharging a student loan or not discharging it in bankruptcy, some courts will discharge part of the loan, such as the back interest or collection fees, and require you to pay the rest.

Unconscionable HEAL Loans

Ironically, the standard for discharging a HEAL (health profession) loan in bankruptcy is much tougher than the Johnson test for other federally guaranteed loans. *For the first five years after your HEAL loan enters repayment, there's no such thing as a hardship discharge.* And even after five years, you have to prove that it would be *unconscionable* for your lender to make you pay. According to the law, that means "results lying outside the limit of what is reasonable or acceptable, to that which is shockingly unfair, harsh, or unjust."

Poor Harderison Edward Malloy. He kept trying to make it through medical school, but he kept flunking out. Still, he did succeed in running up $90,000 worth of loans, including $32,228 in HEAL loans. Without a degree, Malloy wound up working as an assistant activities director in a nursing home, making $11,533.80 a year. His loan payments were brutal. Malloy's mother was buying his clothes, because after he paid his student loan bills, he was left with exactly $10 a month in salary. After his tax returns were confiscated a few times, Malloy filed for Chapter 7 bankruptcy.

On Malloy's first go-round in bankruptcy court, he was relieved of all his debts. But the U.S. Department of Education appealed that even though Malloy had been allowed to discharge his Stafford loans, he should still pay his HEAL loans—and the district court agreed.

Why? To be relieved of his Stafford loans, Malloy only had to prove repayment would cause him undue hardship. But to get free of his HEAL loans, he had to prove it would be *unconscionable* to make him pay. According to that standard, the district court ruled that Malloy's situation was tough, but not tough enough to justify writing off his debt. Ten bucks a month in spending money, for the next decade or so? That's bad, sure. But according to the courts, it's not unconscionable.

Getting a Determination Whether Your Loan Is Discharged in Bankruptcy

Oddly enough, *a bankruptcy judge won't decide whether your student loan is discharged through the bankruptcy unless you ask.* If nobody asks the judge, then the lender will probably assume the loan is not discharged and keep pestering you to pay. At a later date, you can go back to the bankruptcy judge or another judge to decide whether your student loan should have been discharged in your bankruptcy.

By far the smartest thing to do is to *ask the judge during your bankruptcy proceeding to rule that your student loan is discharged in your bankruptcy*. If your loan is over seven years old and there's no question of a deferment, forbearance, or consolidation, then your lender is likely to agree to the discharge. But if you're seeking a hardship discharge or if there is a question as to counting the seven years, the matter should be formally presented to the court. The loan holder will probably object, and there will be some legal maneuvering before the judge to decide who wins the dispute.

This is yet another good reason to hire a lawyer with experience specifically in student loan bankruptcy. "Even lawyers who specialize in bankruptcy tend not to be up on the area of student loans," cautions attorney Elizabeth Imholz. "It's kind of an arcane area. It's complicated, and the regulations are always changing."

Despite all these obstacles, bankruptcy may help you. Even if you can't get rid of your student loan, wiping out your other debts will make your loan payments more manageable in a hurry. There's nothing mysterious about how to file for bankruptcy. We'll go through the process quickly here, but for more detail, you can consult one of several good books on the subject.

Please remember while you're reading: as always, this book offers only one piece of legal advice—get a lawyer!

Chapter 7: How It Works

First, you fill out forms: a two-page initial petition; a statement of financial affairs; a statement of your intentions about how you want to handle certain debts; and a set of schedules that list all your debts, property, income, and expenses. If you've got an attorney, he or she will file this for you. As of this writing, filing a petition costs $175, which you can pay in installments.

Filing the petition activates the automatic stay. Now (in almost every case) your creditors are forbidden to take collection actions against you, or sue you, or seize your property. If a creditor violates the stay, your attorney may be able to use the violation to your advantage.

The court appoints a trustee, usually a lawyer, who's there to represent the interests of your unsecured creditors. The trustee handles the actual process of your bankruptcy, collecting whatever property of yours can be sold, supervising the sale, parceling out the proceeds to your creditors, and finally reporting back to the court.

But before any of that happens:

The trustee mails notice of a meeting of creditors. All your creditors will get this notice. Now's the time when they get to file claims and complaints against you.

If the meeting of creditors sounds dramatic, it really isn't. It's conducted by the trustee, usually in an office, not a courtroom, and the creditors rarely show up. The trustee will ask you questions, in order to learn enough about your situation to decide what should be done. After all the stress that went into your decision to declare bankruptcy, it may even seem like an anticlimax.

You make peace with your creditors. Your various obligations are handled differently. With secured debts like your Jeep, you have three choices. You can give the Jeep up, pay off the value of the Jeep so you own it outright, or agree to keep paying this one debt and not consider it as part of your bankruptcy.

In the course of deciding how to handle your various obligations, your judge needs to be asked to rule that your student loan is dischargeable in this proceeding.

Your property gets labeled exempt and nonexempt. You keep whatever's exempt, and any property that's nonexempt is turned over to your trustee, who will give notice of intent to sell it. Anybody, starting with you, gets a chance to object before the sale happens. You can avoid turning over your prized possessions if you pay their nonexempt value to the trustee in cash. (After all, your stuff's being sold only to raise cash to pay your creditors. If you can hand over the cash instead, that's less trouble for everybody.)

You get your discharge. In most cases, nobody will object to your case being settled, and you'll receive your discharge order (meaning your debts are now discharged) in the mail. Once you've got this order, the temporary protection of the automatic stay now protects you forever, at least in terms of these debts.

Are you finished? Probably. Every now and then creditors may try to collect again, usually because their record-keeping is lousy and they don't know you already dealt with them in bankruptcy. Even if you have to take them to court, they'll be forced to get off your back.

Chapter 13: Give Me Time, and I'll Fix This

Now that you've experienced liquidation under Chapter 7, you can see it feels pretty radical. Your reaction probably depends on how much you have to lose. If you work at a Starbuck's and all you own is a boom box, Chapter 7 is for you. Who cares, right? But if you've just bought your first new car and your first real set of bedroom furniture, and you want to keep them, then you don't want to liquidate. You want to reorganize your debts, so you can stay on the path you've set for yourself.

Chapter 13 gives you the one thing you need most: time. Just as in Chapter 7, your property has to be inventoried and valued, and your creditors must be paid at least the cash value of your nonexempt property. But under Chapter 13, you can choose to pay them off out of your future earnings, a little at a time, over the next three to five years. And exempt or nonexempt, your property stays with you.

All you need to file Chapter 13 is "regular income." That doesn't have to be salary from a job. It could also be government benefits, alimony, or any other check that arrives on a regular schedule.

Your Student Loan and Chapter 13 Bankruptcy

Until recent years, Chapter 13 was the bankruptcy of choice for students, because our loans were declared discharged at the end of our three-year debt adjustment schedule. Forget about that now, though. Now student loans under Chapter 13 are viewed just like the same loans under Chapter 7: what's left of the loan after your three-year debt adjustment period is dischargeable only if the loan has been in repayment more than seven years, or if you can convince a judge that paying would cause you undue hardship.

Still, Chapter 13 does give you some advantages in terms of your student loan, if only because for the next three years you'll pay only what you can afford on your student loans. Then too, nobody can send you intimidating collection letters or garnish your wages while you're in Chapter 13. All collection efforts must stop. So you've got at least three years of peace and quiet.

But you still owe the student loan debt.

Does Your Student Loan Debt Come First?

Although it's counterintuitive, in a Chapter 13 bankruptcy, your best strategy is to pay as much of your student loans as possible over the life of your three-year plan. You have to pay only so much to *all* of your unsecured creditors (including your student loan lender). If you pay more on your student loans, you'll have to pay less on your other debts. Since these other debts will be discharged in bankruptcy, while your student loans may not, it usually makes sense to pay as little as possible on these debts and as much as possible on your student loans. Then, at the end of your plan, you'll have less to pay on your student loans—and nothing to pay on your other debts. Think of it as your Visa bank paying off your student loan for you.

It's quite complicated to accomplish this strategy. You can try to treat your student loans differently than your other debt in your Chapter 13 plan; you can try to pay off your student loan outside your Chapter 13 plan; or you can work on various other strategies. The bottom line is that your attorney will have to figure out what your bankruptcy court will buy.

Chapter 13: How It Works

First, you file the papers. Just as with Chapter 7, a Chapter 13 bankruptcy begins when you file a two-page petition, your financial schedules, a statement of financial affairs, a list (with addresses) of your creditors, and a statement of compensation of your attorney. This time, the filing fee is $160. Here again, you can pay in installments.

You also file a Chapter 13 plan. This is where things change. A Chapter 13 plan is your description of when, how, and how much you're going to pay your creditors. If you can't get the plan together at first, you'll have fifteen days to make and file one.

The automatic stay goes into effect. That means if the Toyota dealer is about to repossess your 4Runner, he has to stop. And here's a genuinely great feature of Chapter 13. Under this automatic stay, the Toyota dealer can't try to collect from Aunt Tessie, who cosigned your loan.

A trustee is appointed. In addition to the tasks performed by a Chapter 7 trustee, a Chapter 13 trustee will eventually collect payments from you, send money to your creditors, and show up at any hearings dealing with you and your plan. Since you'll spend at least three years handing this person anything extra in your paycheck, don't count on being fond of him. Just aim for politeness. And remember, if you're having a really bad time with the trustee, you can always appeal to the bankruptcy judge.

You start making payments. You have to begin making plan payments within thirty days after you file. Your payments are held by your trustee until the court approves your Chapter 13 plan. After that, you can have your monthly payments to the trustee automatically deducted from your paycheck if you want.

The meeting of creditors. This is where your trustee will familiarize himself with your case. A big topic will be whether you can really make the payments you're proposing. It won't be a big humiliate-you fest, so don't be scared. Everybody in the room will be trying to make this work as smoothly and painlessly as possible.

The confirmation hearing. Held either the same day or soon after the meeting of creditors, this is where your creditors a chance to object to your plans for repaying them. What's the point? Once you and your creditors agree on the terms you set here, you're all bound by the agreement.

If you can't complete your Chapter 13 plan, you'll go in one of four directions:

Hardship discharge: If you've experienced serious financial deterioration, and the problems aren't your fault, federal bankruptcy law says you get a hardship discharge.

Modification: If new problems come up for you, you can modify your payment plan to address them, but your trustee and your creditors may object. If they do, the court decides whether you get to change your plan or not.

Conversion: You can change your Chapter 13 to a Chapter 7 bankruptcy. This will probably get you just about the same result as a hardship discharge. If you have nonexempt property, it will be liquidated—sold—and then you'll get a discharge.

Dismissal: You can dismiss your Chapter 13 case and go back to scraping by just as you did before. If you've got property you want to keep, that might be best. At least some of your debts should be less pressing by now.

What Happens When You Complete Your Chapter 13 Plan?

You get your discharge. For what it's worth, a Chapter 13 discharge is broader than the one you'll get with Chapter 7. In Chapter 13, you'll be free of all the same debts as in Chapter 7, plus debts incurred through fraud or false pretenses, and claims for willful and malicious injuries.

When your discharge is given, a notice will be mailed to you, your attorney, your creditors, and your trustee. Soon after that, the trustee files a final report, and your case is closed. Almost certainly, you'll still owe your student loan.

DO NOT ATTEMPT THIS AT HOME

Now that you've read the basics on bankruptcy law and your student loans, you may be getting the sinking feeling that there's a lot more to know. You're absolutely right. That's why, one final time, I urge you to consult an experienced lawyer with all your questions about your individual case. His or her good advice can make all the difference if and when you file.

That said, I also hope you won't let your own fear cheat you out of your legal right to declare bankruptcy and start over, if that's what you truly need to do. In bankruptcy, as in every other area of handling our student loans, we need to stand up for ourselves, not hide our heads and be ashamed. Nobody has ever seen student loans of the size we're dealing with now. Even the congressmen and congresswomen who write our laws don't always understand what we're up against, partly because we don't tell them.

Anyway, if you're like most of us, reading about bankruptcy is one thing. Actually filing is the last option on your list. You'd prefer to find a way to live peaceably with your loan. Can it be done? If you're willing to change some of your ideas about money, it often can.

CHAPTER 13

You Will Get Over This: Getting Your Finances Back on Track

Wow. We've come a long way together. By now you understand that if you borrowed a large student loan, that loan will be your companion for many years to come. You can't escape, unless you want escaping to become your life's work. But you can get on with things. You can put your loan in perspective and start looking forward.

As I've been saying throughout these pages, it's very possible to live in harmony with your debt. And that doesn't always mean pleasing your student loan holder, or your parents, or MasterCard.

This is your life. You're in charge. Nobody gets to bully you. The people you owe will be happy to tell you about your responsibility to them, but it's your job to be responsible to yourself. That means finding your own balance, one that honors your student loan debt but also makes you available for happiness, now and ten years from now.

This chapter will introduce you to two very different philosophies for living with your student loan. Both approaches have helped lots of people get their lives back on track after a big dive into debt. Even if neither feels right for you, the discussion will give you a place to start. Your personal life-and-debt strategy may contain little bits of all these programs—or none.

Before we go on, remember, the suggestions here are just that—suggestions. They're not punishments. You're not a bad person. You're not a loser. You're just checking out some choices you might make.

GETTING DOWN TO BUSINESS ABOUT PAYING YOUR LOAN

First, just to be fair, let's look at your financial future from your lender's perspective. Here are the facts: you borrowed money to buy an education. Now you've got the education, it should be your priority to pay the money back. As one lender told me, "It's time to get down to business and pay that loan." Hard to argue with that, isn't it? (Later in the chapter, we'll argue anyway.)

In your lender's philosophy—traditional American business philosophy—you should take a whole series of actions in order to repay your loan in the next few years. Though we may not all believe this is the most enlightened path, there's no denying that it works, and it may well work for you.

"Getting down to business" means paying off your student loan as soon as possible, but in a larger sense, it means coming up with a straightforward plan to secure your future. The goal is simple. You spend less than you make, you get your debt under control, you start saving money, and you invest what you save.

You have to work toward your own financial freedom. In business terms, that means learning how to take better care of yourself than you can if you're living paycheck to paycheck. Instead of paying interest out, you want interest coming in. You want your money to be making money. Until you're there, you can't be free.

If your loan is manageable, you know what to do. Hunker down and pay it fast. If you can get the job done within ten years, you have a much better shot at the big possessions most of us want: a house, a second car, a ski vacation, a trip down the Nile.

What makes your loan manageable? Figure it this way: if your payment is 10 percent or less of your monthly income, you really could be dealing with it, unless you've got some special circumstance. (No, you weasels, a new-car note does not qualify as a special circumstance.)

On the other hand, if your loan is too big to be manageable, you've got to get creative. As you've seen, when it comes to student loans, bankruptcy won't necessarily help you. And while Direct Lending's Income Contingent Repayment plan will keep you afloat, it's also a huge Band-Aid that doesn't solve your underlying problem. Unless you're paying your monthly interest and a little bit more, your debt situation is getting deeper.

It's not complicated. To pay your student loan debt, you have to make and set aside more money—or live on less.

TACKLING YOUR DEBT BY YOURSELF

Here's how lenders tell you to handle your student loan debt. "Just make a budget . . . and stick to it!" Of course, like Nancy Reagan's famed antidrug slogan "Just say no," this advice is completely useless if you're actually having a problem. But maybe you're one of the few and proud who can engineer a big financial change all by yourself.

My friend Alan paid back his $10,000 student loan in four years flat. Know how he did it? As a waiter, he got his pay in cash. He'd go home and separate the cash into envelopes. One of the envelopes was his student loan money—a nice, plump envelope. Another envelope was his living money. A not-too-fat envelope. Alan would count the two. If the student loan payment was short, the living money envelope got a little bit skinnier. Before the day was over, Alan got that loan payment out of the house and into the bank—and mailed a check off to his lender.

This may make no sense to you, but it worked for Alan, maybe because it made his effort visible. He could see what he was doing, and he could see that it was getting him somewhere. Alan repaid his loan while he was young, while he had the heart. He did it, and now he's past it.

The challenge of paying back a student loan is that you can't see where the money's going or what you're getting in return. It's invisible, like the thousands of dollars' interest you pay on your credit cards.

Which is why Sallie Mae's CEO, Lawrence Hough, is very okay with pressing students to get those checks in the mail. "Borrowers can always prepay their debt and save substantially on interest," he notes. "But that's not human behavior. The practice is, the car breaks down, and you buy more car than you need. You decide to invest in real estate so you won't have to rent, and you buy a condominium or whatever. It's a society of hard consumer-goods investment, and if you can get credit at some point—well, prepayment just doesn't seem to happen very often."

Your Personal Tool Kit

To get a handle on your student loan debt, you need to get a clear picture of your expenses versus your income. This is easier than ever before, thanks to the FFELP industry's newfound desire to promote customer goodwill.

If you have access to the Internet, boot right up and head for Sallie Mae's ultra-fabulous website, *www.salliemae.com*. There you'll find a sophisticated batch of interactive calculators. Once you plug in the numbers for your particular situation, Sallie Mae does the math. How much do you spend each month, versus how much you take in? You'll know in a flash. You can also see all the what-ifs. Which expense is making your student loan payment impractical? If you're on a ten-year repayment plan, would it help to consolidate? What if you went back to school and got another loan? What would your payments be?

If you don't need necessarily need specifics about your student loan—if you're looking to get a handle on your personal finances as a whole—several computer programs will help.

If you don't have a computer, you're not shut out. Practically any financial workbook at your local bookstore has a preprinted balance sheet you can copy. Failing everything else, a pencil and a blank sheet of paper will do. The trick, of course, is to actually make yourself fill out the paper. You can count on feeling pretty resistant to all this at first. Working with your own budget is like going to the gym—nothing but aches and pains until you hit your groove. Later on, however, it'll make you feel devastatingly sexy, financially speaking.

Here's how you begin. Get the box of files where you keep your bills. They'll give you a lot of the numbers you need. Now, write down what you spent this month in the following categories.

Housing
Food
Phone
Utilities
Transportation (including bus fare or gas and car insurance)
Clothes
Laundry
Medical
Dental
Odds and ends for yourself
Entertainment
Other debts
Student loan payment

Big Mac Attack

If you don't know how much you spent this month, break down the month into weeks, then days. For instance, you probably have no idea how much you spend each month on food. But if you buy groceries every Sunday afternoon, and you're always shocked when the bill tops $50, you know you're spending at least $200 a month in the supermarket. Same with lunch during the week. Do you always go to McDonald's and get a $3.99 Big Meal? Then your weekly Big Meal bill is $19.95. (That's 5 days @ $3.99 a day.) Knowing that, you can see that your monthly tab at McDonald's is $79.80. (That's right, 4 weeks @ $19.95 a week.)

Now you know you're spending at least $280 a month on food, and that's before you buy one bag of pretzels or go out for even one dinner at a nice restaurant. Suddenly it's clear, isn't it? Counting everything you spend on lunches and dinners and snacks, you're probably shelling out $400 and more for food each month. And you could probably cut that figure down by $100 without going hungry or even becoming a social troll.

Would $100 extra in monthly income help you pay your student loan? You tell me. But right now, that's not the point. Don't judge yourself, and don't tell yourself you have to make any changes. You're just gathering information, that's all. Fill in numbers for extras as well as essentials. Don't cheat yourself. You're looking to enjoy life, not drag yourself along.

Now total up your expenses and subtract them from your income. What's the news? Are you bringing in enough money to cover your loan payment? Or are you going to have to come up with a more creative plan?

If your debt is big, you may need assistance—not just in creating a personal repayment plan, but in adjusting to the plan once you've made it. You may choose to do without some things you're used to, in return for knowing that every month your debt is bleeding you a little less. True, revising your money intake downward is frightening. But the funny thing is, once you settle into your new path, life gets okay again. You're still eating, you still see movies, your neighbor's car alarm still wakes you up just as you were drifting off to sleep. It's the same life. Honest. The difference is, you're making progress.

CONSUMER CREDIT COUNSELING: PUTTING YOUR CARDS ON THE TABLE

Strange but true, if you want to get your student loan debt under control, you have to attack your consumer debt first. That means clothing, car, food, and (red alert!) credit cards. Unless you're living pretty large, you can't hope to shell out $400 in consumer debt each month and still have another $400 for your student loan. Direct Lending's Income Contingent Repayment plan will help you get your balance. But for long-term relief, you've got to get your consumer debts down to zip, so you can make large enough student loan payments to actually shrink what you owe.

How do you make that happen? Try asking for help.

You can start with Consumer Credit Counseling Service. This national organization, founded in the fifties, has over twelve hundred locations. Look in the phone book or call information, and you'll find an office near you. At CCCS, you'll get a one-on-one introductory session with a counselor who'll suggest a debt repayment plan. Be advised, however, the priority here will be paying the bills to your creditors' satisfaction.

"People come in to see us because their creditors are forcing them to," explains Dara Duguay, Director of Education for CCCS's busy operation in Los Angeles County. "Well, not forcing," she corrects herself, "but strongly suggesting it. Let's say you stop paying your Visa bill. A collector from Visa will probably tell you to come see us."

This doesn't mean CCCS won't treat you with concern. "We're a free service," Duguay says. "We've got injunctions against some organizations with names very similar to ours that charge many hundreds of dollars to counsel people. We've seen some 800 numbers, or places where they do just mail counseling. We feel it's most effective to come in on a one-on-one basis and sit down with a counselor and really discuss all your options."

Duguay is up front about who runs her operation. "Our primary supporter is the creditors," she says. "They give us voluntary contributions. If you get in trouble with Visa and file bankruptcy, Visa won't get anything back. But if you come to us, we show you how to manage your money better. We put you on a debt-repayment program, and eventually Visa will get paid. So it's a win-win situation."

Do students use CCCS? All the time. "We usually see people in their mid-twenties, because that's when the problems arise," Duguay reflects. "They can get their first credit card when they're eighteen, but it takes years for the debt to build up to the level where they can't repay. Usually by the time we see them they've gotten to the point where they can't make a minimum payment. You can charge a thousand dollars; a $20 minimum payment isn't hard to come up with. But by the time your debt has increased to $10,000—that's when we see people."

Students are sliding into debt younger than ever before, and Duguay sees a big reason why. "I graduated in 1986, and I couldn't get a credit card to save my life. But nowadays, when I speak on college campuses, I see credit card companies with booths all over the place. All you need to get one is a student ID.

"Last fall," she continues, "we had a booth at freshmen orientation events at several campuses. There were credit card booths everywhere, with very long lines, giving away free gifts. Nobody was waiting in our line. Seniors would come up to us and say, 'God, I wish I'd known about you guys. I'm in trouble.' But the freshmen didn't want to come to our booth. They wanted a credit card."

Young students, sighs Duguay, just don't understand what happens in debt. "If you charge up $1,700 at 18 percent as a college freshman, by the time you finish paying off that card with minimum payments only, you'll have had time to get three BAs and two master's degrees." Duguay also sees kids misled by the false affluence of the characters they watch on TV. "When I speak in high schools, I tell them that the average student with a high school diploma is going to make $1,000 a month," she says. "That's the reality, but they don't believe it. They're all going to be football stars and get record deals. College students are the same way. They think they're going to be making a ton of money, so repaying their student loans won't be a problem. They don't understand."

CCCS Debt Repayment: How It Works

Though you may hesitate before getting your records together and making an appointment at CCCS, nothing too scary happens when you get there. You won't be bound to do anything. In fact, you can leave and never come back, though you'll leave with a better understanding of your situation. Here's exactly how it goes.

"When you come for an appointment—usually referred by a creditor or a friend who's been to see us in the past—we'll spend the whole hour going through your budget, which hopefully you've filled out in advance," says Duguay. "The budget lists all of your sources of income, your expenses, and all of your debts. We spend the majority of the time going through your expenses, seeing if there's any way we can cut back, looking at the wants versus the needs, like do you have to eat out ten times a week, or could you stop charging $10,000 a month at Nordstrom's department store. We see if there's fat we can cut. After we do that, we see if you have money left over to send your creditors.

"Most people come to see us because they've gotten so overextended that they can't even send the minimum payments," Duguay continues. "So we see how much money is left over. In many cases we can negotiate smaller payments with the creditors. If we put you on a debt-repayment program, they'll cooperate by either not charging you interest, lowering your interest rate, or waiving late fees and penalty fees. You can eventually get yourself out of debt, even though you're making smaller payments than they usually ask for."

Chopping up the Credit Cards

Customers who enroll in CCCS's Debt Management Plan start by closing all their charge accounts. This is nonnegotiable. The next step is the one that hurts—chopping up the credit cards.

"On my desk is a jar, like a flower vase, that's full of cut-up credit cards," Duguay says. "That's maybe a day's work from one of our counselors, cutting up people's credit cards. The average American has ten credit cards now. We counsel people all the time with forty, fifty, sixty credit cards.

"Debt Repayment is totally voluntary. We don't force people," Duguay continues. "But if they choose to enter the program, we cut up all their credit cards right here in the office. You can't keep charging if you want to get out of debt. We close all their accounts, and they live on a cash-only basis, which is hard if you're not used to it. But in approximately three years, people are debt-free, at least with the consumer debts they brought to us. I'd say roughly 20 percent of the people we see go on this program. Nationally, the number is about 30 percent. It's a wonderful program."

So Sorry, So Long: Recommending Bankruptcy

Radical as Debt Management under CCCS can be, Duguay cautions that it may not be drastic enough. "We send a small percentage of people to a bankruptcy attorney. It's too late, they've waited too long. Some people can't go on the debt repayment plan because they don't have any money to send their creditors. They're way over their head!"

"But most of the people we see can solve their situation on their own. We recommend things they can do to increase their income or cut back on their expenses. We had one couple that came in. They were living in a penthouse apartment right on the beach. Their rent was $3,200 a month. 'Move inland, cut your rent,' we suggested. 'You'll solve all your problems.' They said, 'Yes, but we like to hear the ocean in the morning.' Our counselor suggested that they tape the sound of the ocean. A simple answer to their problem!"

Still, Duguay says, she encounters lots and lots of static. "All day long our counselors hear 'I don't want to give up my maid; I need my gardener; we don't cook, we have to go out to eat.' People resist giving things up, but if they're willing, they can solve their own problems."

Helping You Track Down Your Loan

CCCS can also help with a debt problem that's not so easy to solve on your own: where's your defaulted FFELP loan, and how did it completely ruin your credit rating?

CCCS counselor Judy Hoover has learned all too much about how a student can be haunted by the snowballing effects of an old, sometimes forgotten, student-loan debt. With the FFELP system forever tossing loans from lender to collector and back again, it can be years before a student is aware that his or her loan has been listed in default. By then, tracking down the truth—not to mention the loan— is a job for a real detective. Hoover is an ace.

"Students will come in with a credit report from Experian or Equifax, and there'll be twelve student loans on it," Hoover explains. "That doesn't mean they took out twelve student loans. What happens is, the student doesn't pay the lender—say, Citicorp. Citicorp turns the loan over to the guarantor. So now it's on the credit report twice. Then the student doesn't pay the guarantor, which turns the loan over to a collection agency. Now the same loan is on the student's credit report three different times. If you have four student loans, you could have twelve student loan debts showing up on your report. A creditor may not take the time, as I do, to sort through and say, 'Which one is this?'

"I ask the student, 'Do you still have the original payment agreement, the promissory note?'" Hoover laughs. "Most of them don't even remember what they signed. So I figure out where the loan is, then trace it back to the original lender, to see who we should start repaying. I've tracked down a lot of loans."

Our Old Friends, the Collection Agencies

Hoover often tries to get students' loans consolidated with Sallie Mae or Direct Lending. But that's a tough battle too, because consolidating may cut into the profits of the collection agents who are holding your loan.

"Once these loans go into collection," Hoover notes, "most people don't have a clue as to how much interest collection agencies can add. That's why collection agencies are reluctant to even give students permission to do a consolidation," says Hoover. "I've told kids, 'You fill out the form for Federal Direct Loan Consolidation. If a collector says you're not allowed to do it, tell them it's BS, and do it anyway!'

Automobile showrooms tend to be where students learn the truth about their defaulted loans. Hoover's seen it often: "The kid is just about to buy a car. The auto agency pulls a credit file, and all of a sudden somebody tells the kid, 'We can't lend you money for a car, you have $35,000 worth of student loans on your record.' The kid says, 'Of course I don't, that's ridiculous.' But then he looks at it, and that's what it says. The loan may be on there four times, and there may also be these 43 percent collection fees, added on through the years.

"This 43 percent added is a crime," Hoover says flatly. "Nobody really knows about it. There hasn't been any public awareness. Some students come in to see me just dumbfounded, literally in tears. They don't know what to do, and they begin to think, 'This is impossible for me to pay off!'"

Yet with bankruptcy a long shot except under certain circumstances, student loans must generally be paid off, as Hoover well knows. "You just have to find a way to pay it," she says. "Adjust your expenses, get money from your parents. You may have to get a second little job and dedicate that whole income to repaying the loan. But you have to pay it. It'll never go away."

Summing Up the CCCS View of the Debt World

Summing up, you might say CCCS represents the Arnold Schwarzenegger approach to paying off your debt. ("*Hasta la vista*, baby." Explosion follows.) It's all about getting tough. This may work great for you. If you like a good fight, you'll appreciate CCCS's straight talk and tough budget, and the feeling of taking command of your debts and knocking them out one by one.

On the other hand, CCCS may give you a major case of the twitches. It's not that the counselors aren't empathetic, as you've seen. But you should also remember where they're coming from. Their goal is to get you to accept what your creditors have in mind for you. If you'll do that, the creditors will bend a little bit.

But you know what? That whole model of debt repayment just may not work for you.

Maybe there's something about the setup you can't and won't accept. If so, there's another philosophy of dealing with your debt. It's not easy either, but it may be more right for you.

DEBTORS ANONYMOUS: SURRENDERING FEAR, INVITING PROSPERITY

Ever hear of debting? That's right, "debting," as a verb. You're debting when you buy something on credit, not exactly sure of the balance on your credit card, not exactly knowing how or when you'll pay it off. This gives you a weird, indefinable anxiety. Do you have the money? Do you not? Are you okay?

You could easily find out your balance. But that's not what you choose to do. You "shut your eyes" and buy something else. . . on credit. In Debtors Anonymous—a twelve-step program that helps people make peace with their finances—that's called *compulsive debting*. It comes from being afraid of looking at your money situation. Instead of seeking out the facts, you'd rather just worry and not quite know. That's called *terminal vagueness*.

We're not talking secured debt, where you have to return the thing you bought if you don't pay. The debt we mean is unsecured, where you paid "imaginary" money for an intangible service that can't be taken back.

The Vaguest of All Vague Debts: Your Student Loan

It's very doubtful that you're a true compulsive debtor. But I'll bet you can relate to what we're talking about. Because you're already up to your elbows in a terminally vague and anxiety-provoking debt—your student loan.

You borrowed it with no idea whether you could pay. You've spent weeks and months trying to ignore it. You fight the urge to throw out each and every letter from your loan holder. You can't believe how big it is. And you can never clear it up, because you can never give your education back. How's that for vague?

Before you read any further, let me promise you that I'm not going to try to "convert" you to DA or any other special group. Very few people are real compulsive debtors. But if—like Judy Hoover's clients at CCCS—you're faced with the overwhelming anxiety of a student loan debt you can't pay, you deserve to hear how DA would advise you.

The DA Way: Life, Not Debt

CCCS tells you to fight your way out of hock. Scrimp and save. Focus on the debt, debt, debt. DA says, Stop fighting. Let the debt wait a while. Focus on your life. Develop yourself spiritually and financially. Attain clarity about your own relationship to money. If you're painstaking, you'll become a person who can support an abundant life—and that will include repaying the debt.

Is this just too warm and fuzzy? Actually, attacking your debt this way is hard, because you're asked to give up worrying and take it on faith that you'll be okay—and if there's one area where we're not used to practicing faith, it's money.

Here's the other tough thing. *Like CCCS, DA asks you to stop using unsecured debt, and that means cutting up your credit cards.*

Are all these people crazy? What are you supposed to do without credit? Well, that's not a decision anybody makes easily. But on the other hand, remember, it's probably been years since you saw your whole paycheck. A big chunk of it may have been vanishing into credit card bills.

DA: How to Begin

A recovering debtor from southern California, Michael is delighted to share his experience for this book. But first he makes sure to distinguish Debtors Anonymous from business-based debt counseling programs like CCCS.

"In DA we don't have a budget," he says. "We make a spending plan. A budget is synonymous with sort of holding your head under water. A spending plan is more like freeing you up to earn. That's been the biggest solution for most of the people in DA I know. Earning is the solution to compulsive debting."

Describing how DA works, Michael begins by telling about the feeling of being in debt way over your head. "It's paralyzing," he says. (Can you relate?) When you first decide to confront your debt situation, he suggests, you can start to lift your own depression by doing just a few simple things each day. Odd as it may seem, the first thing you can do is start writing down what you spend every day. "How stupid," you say. "Like that'll help." But it does. It will make you feel more in control. Also, in a couple of weeks you'll have real information about what you're spending—and you may find that you've been cheating yourself.

Michael and his friends in DA have found that when people are in enough debt—when they're scared enough—they tend to do two things. They "hide" what they're spending from themselves by not recording purchases. And because this leaves them anxious, they skimp on taking care of themselves. I'm not talking about extravagances, like a trip to Cancun. (That's for later.) I mean things like a haircut that doesn't make you look like one of the Three Stooges.

Cheating Yourself Leads to Money Binges

Skimping on ourselves often doesn't produce the results we wanted. We plod along, feeling deprived, until—aagh!—we have a credit card meltdown. We're walking past the sporting goods store and see a pair of running shoes on sale. Once we're inside and trying them on, the feeling of actually buying something, of not being deprived, goes right to our heads. Suddenly we just don't care. That credit card whips itself out, and we go home with a tennis racquet, a jogging suit, and a Soloflex machine.

What Michael and his friends are doing in DA is really simple. Each is looking for his or her *comfort level* with money—no more, but no less. If that level doesn't conform to the wishes of their creditors, they write a straightforward letter and explain their position:

> Dear Mr. X:
>
> I'm sending you X dollars. I'm not in a position to pay more at this time, but I acknowledge my debt to you, and I will pay it. I'll keep in touch with you and give you regular updates on my progress.

In return for asking this much consideration from their creditors, Michael and his friends follow three personal rules: they don't lie; they don't go bankrupt; and they don't use credit cards. It may sound suspiciously New Age to you, but if you do these things—all of them, not just some, you weasels—you will start to feel less frustrated and more in control. And once you start to feel control, you may find yourself developing what DA calls the *willingness to earn*.

This term is not really as obvious as you think. Isn't everybody willing to earn? Well, most of us are willing to show up in an office and do enough of what we're told to keep our paychecks coming. But you can do that and still feel like a loser—hopeless, saddled with this unpayable debt, too lame to have become Tiger Woods or Billy Corgan or Jenny McCarthy. If you're convinced you can't win, you'll do the least that's asked of you. And sure enough, you won't make much money.

If you're a large-loan student debtor, you've got to do what it takes to feel like a winner, partly because you're going to have a very hard time cutting back expenses enough to pay off the debt. You really need to increase your earning power instead.

Considering your situation, it wouldn't be surprising if you'd been depressed about money for a while without knowing it. In that case, the following list of tip-offs may help you get a sense of where you are. In his best-selling book, *How to Get Out of Debt, Stay Out of Debt, and Live Prosperously,* author Jerry Mundis gives a vivid picture of symptoms like these:

SCARED OF MONEY? TEN WAYS TO TELL

1. Do your bills creep up on you without your knowing? Are you always getting late notices? Remember, your credit card will slap maybe $20 late charges on you if your payment comes in late. Twenty bucks late payments on four credit cards equals maybe half your monthly student loan payment. Even if your payment is huge, finding $200 to send in is easier than finding $280. So why wouldn't it occur to you to get your credit card payment in on time?

2. Do you avoid opening your mail? Come on, it's not that you're so busy. You're scared. Aren't you? In your fear that you'll reach into that envelope and pull out a "snake," a bill you can't pay, you may be cheating yourself out of something good. Mundis tells a great story of a woman who got an envelope from the IRS, buried it in a stack of papers, and finally worked up the courage to look at it months later. What was inside? A refund check.

3. Do you pretend to have more money than you really do? The object of this game is to see a big balance in your bank account when you take cash out of the ATM. Considering how psycho this is, it's kind of amazing how many of us do it. The pretend game goes like this. We could save money on interest by writing a check when the credit card bill actually comes in. But we hang on to the money, even for a few days. Why? So we'll see a bigger total in our bank account. It makes us feel better.

4. Do you refuse to keep a running balance of your money? You don't balance your bank statement at the end of the month. You say you're too busy. Or you know your money situation is bad, and you don't want to know how bad. You know how much you've got, more or less, you tell yourself. You carry the number in your head. Actually, what you carry in your head tends to be more money than you've really got.

5. Are you always looking for the lowest down payment and the longest repayment term? Buying this way is a lot more expensive than putting a chunk of money down and keeping your payments low. You already know this. You wouldn't do it if you had the money to do it differently. But you don't have the money, because you've got ten or fifteen other little drains going on your monthly check. Little installment payments look harmless by themselves. They're not.

6. Do you always charge instead of paying cash? Little stuff. Dinner. A pair of shoes. You used to write a check and pay for these. But gradually you've started to put them on your credit card. This makes them a lot more expensive, but it allows you to look at that falsely reassuring bank balance all the time.

The accompanying symptom here is that when you pay on that charge card, some invisible hand propels you to write a check no larger than the minimum payment. Buying the shoes in the store, you tell yourself, "I'll go right home and send in a check to the credit card company." (Have you ever done that? Do you know anyone who has?)

7. Do you think you're a hero for paying your bills? Well, you aren't. You moved into the apartment, so you pay the rent. You ate the steak, so you pay the tab. There's no big mystery about it. You're no hero for paying your bills. All you're doing is buying continued access to all the nice things you've already been using. You have to pay your bills. It's a universal law, and it's not changing any time soon.

8. Do you hate talking about money? Is talking about money like discussing the details of your love life? Not done by nice people? If you've been trained this way, you're going to have to get used to "talking dirty." Not talking about money is the very best way to keep yourself feeling vague and fearful. It's also the only way a smart person like you could possibly fool yourself about what's in your own bank account. When it comes to your student loan, this is particularly damaging, because you tend to think everybody else is coping better than you are. Not true!

9. Do you feel better with lots of small balances on lots of credit cards? This is more lying to yourself. If you're looking at a smallish total when your credit card bill comes around, you don't really owe much, though you owe the same amount on another six cards. You only let yourself acknowledge one at a time.

10. Do you just throw up your hands and say you can't understand all this money stuff—somebody else will have to do the details? Sorry, but this just means you don't want to know. Think about it. Never do you get to feel safe or secure. You can never trust yourself to handle any situation. Is it really more comforting not to know your own story?

What Could I Do Differently—Not That I Want To!

It's highly doubtful that you just read through this list and said, "Thank heaven, somebody's finally put into words how messed up I am." It doesn't work like that. If you're hearing these ideas for the first time, it will probably take you a while to decide you don't like where you are, and you want to make a change. Are there practical actions you can take to make yourself feel better without turning your whole life upside down? Absolutely. We'll talk about strategies for your student loan in a bit, but right now let's look at your debts in general. Or rather, let's look at you.

TIPS TO GET YOUR MONEY ON TRACK

1. Who are you now? You're not your debts, though you may have forgotten that. You're someone with a future that's already bringing you new adventures and surprises—one of which will be what happens with your debts. You'll pay them, or negotiate an agreement. Or some strange thing you can't foresee will change the whole ball game. As my friend Sherry told me when I was having a black moment about my own student loan, "You're not going to die owing this debt." I didn't believe it. Now, a few years later, I do. Things change. So will you. Stick around and see.

2. Forget tomorrow. You're okay today. True, you may owe four quatrillion dollars to Sallie Mae. On the other hand, you don't have to pay it all right now. You can worry about the future, but what's the point? That's just inventing trouble that hasn't happened yet. Just for today, you have to admit you've got shoes, clothes, a roof, food, and at least a chunk of an education. So you're actually doing pretty well.

3. Put your bills in a friendly box, one that really feels cheerful. If it has fun memories for you, so much the better. Is it flowered, plaid? A *Star Trek* lunch box? An old Barbie tote bag? Whatever. It has to make you feel like you want to burst out laughing.

4. Don't touch your bills for one whole month. They've been doing fine this long; they'll do fine a little longer. By the time you're ready to call your creditors, you'll be in a different place financially. And emotionally and psychically as well.

5. Write down everything you spend. This includes every cup of coffee, every stick of gum. Also that excellent marijuana you're getting from your cousin Wayne. This record is for your eyes only, so make it down and dirty. You want to know how much you're really spending, because you probably don't have a clue. Each week, then each month, you enter the numbers in your computer, or add them up in your notebook. Remember, you aren't bad or wrong for spending money! Nobody wants to take anything away from you. You're just trying to see where your money is going. In fact, you may find you're depriving yourself unfairly, and you'll have to pay yourself more.

6. Keep in touch with your creditors. You already have experience at this, from dealing with your student loan. The same rules apply to other debts as well. Don't make your creditors come to you. If you move, let them know. If you can't make a payment, call and tell them. Explain that you plan to pay, but you can't right now. Tell them when you'll be in touch again. Keep your word. Sounds easy, doesn't it? It isn't, of course. But you can do it.

7. About those credit cards. Chop 'em up. I know you won't do this without a fight, so here's an alternative. Get a safe deposit box, which is just a few bucks a month. Keep your credit cards in there.

Then your cards will actually be serving the purpose you claim you need them for: they're there in case of emergencies.

One more time: *Why is it better to do without credit cards? Because interest is a drain on your income.* It's like having a wound that just keeps bleeding. It makes you financially anemic. Don't you want to be strong and healthy and run and play with the other children?

8. Save something. Anything. Michael from DA has a great idea. He keeps several savings accounts, one for each of his big goals. These goals aren't all serious, by the way. One account is his vacation fund. "It really feels good to put money in there," he says. "It reminds me that I may be working really hard, but some of it's just for Michael—just for me."

Whether you're saving for a vacation or gathering an emergency "layoff fund" in case you finally have to slap your boss after all, it's marvelous to have money of your own. There's nothing like it. It gives you power in this world. If you can't save much, that doesn't matter. The money really does add up.

I have a one-gallon can in my house. Every time I put my jeans in the wash, I take the change out of my pocket and throw it in the can. Once a year I take the can to the bank—and come home with $200. If that's what happens when you save quarters and pennies, imagine the results with dollar bills . . . or fives.

TIPS FOR TAMING YOUR STUDENT LOAN

You have to start by believing your efforts to work on your loan will help, even if they won't solve the whole problem today. Like throwing change in my gallon can, you can develop a set of habits that do a little bit every time to bring your loan under control.

1. Send your tax refund to your student loan holder every year. Your loan holder comes after your tax return if you're delinquent. But even if you're in good shape, can't you volunteer to send your refund in? Think about it. If you're young and on a salary, your tax return is probably the only chunk of money you'll see all year. If you sent it off as soon as it came, would you miss it? Well, yes, but you're also okay without it. Meanwhile, that money could do you some real good with your loan. If you're paying at least your interest every month, then you can apply this chunk of cash to your principal. If your refund is big enough—say, $1,500 or more—you can even ask to have your monthly payments refigured and reduced.

Even if you're paying less than your interest, sending the money will help. By reducing your unpaid interest, you'll slow the rate at which your debt is growing larger. So you reduce the difficulties of paying when your income improves.

Taking charge of your loan is like getting a huge ocean liner to stop and turn around. It only happens a little at a time.

2. Get a second job. Sure, this sounds awful. But does it have to be? You already hang out somewhere on Saturdays. Is it someplace you might get paid to be? If you're a bartender, you'll get to chat with those same lowlifes you love to watch football with. If you're a gym bunny, you can run around in your tights, plus sign up new members on commission. If you love to read, you can take one of those solitary jobs, as a weekend security guard, or a hotel desk clerk. The more mindless, the better.

If you're a high-strung creative type, you can definitely get a freelance business going. There's a whole unofficial, cash-only economy made up of folks who need little art or copywriting jobs done, and who don't have the budget to come see you at your ad agency during the week. And of course, if you can really jockey a computer, you don't need job-hunting advice from the rest of us.

If you want to make progress with a big loan, and you don't make a big salary, accept that you're going to have to moonlight. You're going to have to make an extra effort to retire this debt. We're not pretending that you wanted it this way. But since this is your challenge, you need to cultivate the willingness to earn your way out of it. Here's the place where you can really use the skills college taught you. Here's your chance to test your talents in the world, not the classroom. Who knows? Your efforts now might form the seeds of your own business later on.

3. Let your lender take your payments straight from your bank account. It's easier to make a payment if you never see the money. (Besides, in return for permission to access your account, several FFELP lenders will give you better interest rates.) Unfortunately, we haven't evolved far enough so that you're entitled to have your employer subtract your student loan payments from your salary before taxes, as you can with money for medical expenses. But if student advocates have their way, pretax withholding will be the next big thing. So will having your employer match your student loan payments monthly, as a perk.

4. Enjoy your life as it is. This is your challenge. In a very real and practical way, paying off your student loan is a spiritual adventure. You went into this whole thing on faith, didn't you? You chose to believe that four (or six or eight) years of college would provide you with the tools to change your life. Don't lose sight of that now. Your story is far from over. The hell with anybody who says you have to be punished for doing your best to get an education. Do your best to honor your debt, but better to let the debt go than to let it sour your life. You know what? It's not the end of the world!

I had a wonderful accountant in New York City. At tax time one year, she slapped her calculator around and pronounced that I owed several hundred dollars. I gave her a major dirty look. "Please," she laughed. "If it can be fixed with money, how bad could it be?"

KEEP YOUR HEART ALIVE

To deal with repaying a big loan, you need hope. And to have hope, you must act in a way that brings hopeful things to you. In the midst of all your plots and plans about making extra money and keeping up with your career, don't forget to take care of your inner health too.

1. Don't be alone. Honey, owing this much money is depressing. You may want and need therapy along the way. Good for you. Go get it. What you've got to do is hard; it's a challenge. But so what? Life is a challenge. As it happens, you're up to it. Above all, talk about your student loan. By hiding the fact that we owe, we miss the fact that practically everybody our age is worrying about a student loan debt too. If we stopped hiding, we'd see how we can work together and try to improve this situation for ourselves.

2. Have a student loan buddy, somebody from your class. Somebody it's okay to talk—really talk—money with. Preferably, they should be able to read legal jargon better than you. And it helps if they'll pick up the phone in the middle of the night.

3. Keep exploring your field. Even if you couldn't get work as a researcher and had to take a telemarketing job, keep going to the library and reading the journals. Or tutor a student younger than you. (This has the added advantage of keeping you up with what's happening.) Don't give up your dream yet, okay? Not all opportunities happen in the first year after you leave school.

4. Laugh. That's the way to heal. They can't take your education back. Use it, okay? That's the best revenge.

NEVER GIVE UP

Since we left school, my classmates and I have learned that when it comes to living with our student loans, we're in charge. Nobody else knows what we should do—not our government, our lenders, our schools, or even our parents. We were naive to think that the whole billion-dollar student loan machine roared along exclusively for our benefit.

In taking advice from people who stood to profit by our actions, we sometimes bought more education than we needed. If we had known then what we know now, would we have behaved differently? I have to admit, I wouldn't. Despite the outrageous cost, education was what I wanted, and I've learned to accept what I did to get it.

But that doesn't mean we should all just sit back and let this crisis keep escalating. Since you and I have been through the fire, we

282 THE GUERRILLA GUIDE TO MASTERING STUDENT LOAN DEBT

should be leading the debate about how to restore higher education to the days when it brought Americans together rather than pushing us apart. In our last chapter, you'll get a glimpse of the future as some of our leaders see it. I'll also give you an idea what you can do to pass your valuable experience along.

CHAPTER 14

Talk Back: Remaking the Future

So. We're finally here. It's our last chapter together. If I've done my job, you're no longer scared of your loan debt. You understand how to take care of yourself—and maybe you've even got a little energy left over to try to change our loan situation for the better. On the other hand, you also understand that all of the interlocking and interrelated problems regarding student loans make progress pretty hard to come by.

Still, good things are happening. Before we start talking about how you and I can change the world, let's check in and see what's already being done to help us. Throughout this book, you've heard a variety of really smart thinkers repeat the same stubborn and solution-defying set of problems. *One:* the cost of college is going to keep rising. *Two:* we don't need more loans, we need more grants. *Three:* we can't get more grants, so we have to keep pumping out more loans.

Doesn't anybody have an idea how to solve this? Actually, people do. Some of the thinkers who spoke with me for this book are trying to make loans themselves work better, and others are attacking the problem of how to help us repay the loans we've got. Here's a look at what's going on, in the words of some of the student loan world's movers and shakers.

ANN COLES
Vice President for Information Services, TERI:

"It would help to shift some of the financial self-help from loans to work, and to provide incentives to employers who participate in employment opportunities and cooperative education programs. The best example is Northeastern University in Boston, which originated the co-op concept back around the turn of the century.

Co-op students are on campus for, say, three months and off campus for three months. When they're off campus, they're working full time in jobs related to their major; so they're getting job experience and they're earning money, some of which they can save to pay for their college tuition when they're back on campus. In particular areas like business and engineering, the co-op jobs pay extremely well. Of course, not only are students making money, but they're building work history and experience, which will make them more competitive for jobs later on. Many co-op students end up working for their employers when they graduate."

EARL ESTERLY
Vice President, Van Ru Collection Agency:

"I like the idea that the funds for student loan programs come from the private sector. That prevents someone in Washington from saying, 'We are spending $28 billion in student loans this year. We've attacked Social Security, we've attacked the Department of Defense, we've done some things with health care. Now it's time for education to take a hit. Therefore, this year we're cutting the program back to $25 billion. That means there's $3 billion of needs that won't be met.'

"I have a colleague at a guaranty agency who's actively working on a program with the Feds where a guarantor and the other participants in the program are going to be rewarded for their ability to make loans and prevent them from going into default. We really do ourselves immeasurable damage all along the line when we have a defaulted student loan, and not just fiscally. Putting twenty-three-year-old kids into collections—what a way to get started in life."

JOE FLADER
Legislative Director for Rep. Tom Petri:

"You should be able to simply pay your loan along with your federal income taxes each year; have your loan payments withheld just like taxes. The IRS is already in the student loan collection business. They're in this refund capture game. And they're also subject to getting involved in wage garnishment, which is very bureaucratic and, I would think, a mess from their point of view. And we say to them, 'Look, if there isn't any separate accounting of the money, then what does it matter to you? You just run this information into the student loan accounts. You get back a small number of student borrowers who underpaid. You go after them for underpayment of taxes, which you already have a system for doing.'"

TED FREEMAN
CEO, TERI:

"When we know a student will have trouble repaying a federal subsidized Stafford loan, we should be giving that student a scholarship. We have a Pell Grant program that's been authorized for years and years, but we've never given the maximum Pell Grant to anybody because of funding.

"We're telling too many young people that you have to go to a traditional college to make it in life. We've got to change that. A colleague of mine predicts that within ten years, we will have 50 percent fewer undergraduates enrolled in traditional education than we have now. Higher education does not have to mean a four-year undergraduate program. As a matter of fact, I don't want my plumber to have that degree, because then he's going to have to charge me extra money to pay off his student loans. Everybody needs education beyond high school, but what's wrong with a community college? There are an awful lot of courses in trades, for plumbers, electricians, car mechanics. We're convincing everybody up front, 'Oh, you don't want to be a car mechanic, you can't make a whole lot of money being a car mechanic.' My God, we need car mechanics!"

MILTON FRIEDMAN
Economist:

"I think the student loan program is a disgrace and should be killed. Government has no more business being a banker—making loans to individual students—than it has making blue jeans. The government is a lousy businessman. There's only one thing the government does very well: take money from some people and give it to other people.

"Student loans have increased the demand for education, and that raises the price. If government subsidized buyers of chocolate, don't you think the price of chocolate would go up? Why is it different for colleges? It isn't. At the higher level, education is simply an investment. People go to college in order to earn a higher income. Why should the people who don't go to college subsidize the people who do?"

LAWRENCE A. HOUGH
CEO, Sallie Mae:

"I think our investors believe that, over time on a competitive basis, we'll beat Direct Lending. And secondly, I think many of them believe that the government, at some point, will decide this is not an appropriate role for government. Perhaps it's at the time in which we've got a taxpayer population that owes the government $150 billion, $200 billion worth of loans. And politicians decide that's not such a good idea."

DIANE VOIGT
Retired Chair of the Direct Lending Task Force:

"My personal guess is that we are going to see very, very few loans written off at the end of twenty-five years. The Republican contention is that someone will deliberately lead a life of abject poverty in order to get out of paying their student loan. I don't think a lot of those people are out there. I'm not going to say, 'Wow, I've got a student loan, I'm going to have to go work at McDonald's for twenty-five years so I don't have to repay it.' That's foolish."

ELIZABETH IMHOLTZ
Consumer Activist and Attorney:

"I'd like to see improvements on notices for students, so that they don't get into overborrowing, or they at least have the opportunity to understand the limitations of the borrowing and what their rights are. Also I have another thought that I'm considering suggesting: an ombudsman's office within the Department of Education for students. It's gotten so complicated, and with the two student loan programs, there are a lot of snags in the system and places where people can really get lost and have trouble straightening it out. But I don't want to argue to set up something that becomes meaningless in the bureaucracy."

DIANE SAUNDERS
Vice President for Communications and Public Affairs, Nellie Mae:

"Businesses need to get involved and offer students loan repayment as an employment benefit. Every twenty-something knows the traumas of downsizing. They've seen firsthand what it's done to their families. Consequently, they have no loyalty. Their belief in the corporate hierarchy is not there. They want to move up the ladder quickly—or leave. But with student-loan repayment as a corporate benefit, you can get the best and the brightest, and keep them.

"You can do this in two ways. You can give an annual bonus, which would give your employee the opportunity to buy down his or her student loan debt in lump sums. Or, with a minor legislative change, you could offer a monthly student-loan repayment feature as a part of a pretax 'cafeteria plan.' Your employee could automatically deduct loan payments every month before his or her taxes were figured, and you could match the payments. This wouldn't necessarily cost extra money but would be a replacement benefit. Where an employee with a family might prefer dependent health care, a recent graduate might prefer a loan-repayment option."

HOW IS FFELP SERVING US NOW?

FFELP, that old rascal, has turned over a charming new leaf. By year's end 1996, the industry had introduced several major changes designed to bring more order to its far-flung national network of participants. The CommonLine Network, designed to standardize the loan application process via the Internet, went online in 1995 and was expanded in 1996. FFELP's thirty-six guarantors also adopted the Common Manual, one rulebook by which they all agreed to be governed. New software programs let you fill out one standard application form and then have your loan money delivered electronically, just as with Direct Lending.

Thus, for schools and students who for years had squawked in vain about overcomplicated FFELP paperwork, Direct Lending is a big hero just because it scared the bejeepers out of FFELP. "I think Direct Lending is the best thing that could have happened to the guaranteed student loan program, because now one program wants to look better than the other, and that's a good thing," says attorney Elizabeth Imholtz. "They are vying with each other to look more consumer-friendly, and we have been able to achieve some very nice things for consumers through that competition."

Wags might say most of that stuff was just basic civility that was long overdue, but FFELP's other innovation is more like grace under fire. As we've mentioned, a number of secondary markets and guarantors now offer real price breaks for students who stick with FFELP. Perks like waivers of up-front borrower fees and lowered interest rates in return for on-time payments can mean hundreds of dollars coming your way. A typical offer might give you a two-point interest reduction if you make your first forty-eight payments on time. (A word to the wise, from Marilyn McKay, marketing and sales director of the California Higher Education Loan Authority [CHELA], one of the largest secondary markets: "When they say forty-eight payments on time, they mean on time." A day late in four years, and you can say goodbye to the two-point interest reduction.)

HOW IS DIRECT LENDING SERVING US NOW?

As for Direct Lending, at the end of its first two years in operation, the program had a volume of $16 billion, about 34 percent of the overall loan business for 1996. In the first year of its existence, it won huge compliments from financial aid administrators. But opponents of the program were gleeful in 1996 when, sure enough, an administrative snafu at the much-maligned Education Department caused nine hundred thousand students to receive their notifications of financial aid late.

Still, says Direct Lending's Elizabeth Hicks, "We're now the largest lender in the entire country, larger than any of the FFELP lenders. There aren't many companies that in two years' time go from zero market share to something in the 34 percent range, right? That would be quite an accomplishment for someone trying to break into the beverage market."

At this point, it seems doubtful that either FFELP or Direct Lending is going to be able to knock its opponent out of the running any time soon. But with Reauthorization of the Higher Education Act on the congressional agenda every five years, it's safe to say that both sides will keep on slugging.

It's a little tough to make predictions about what will happen next, but probably by the time you join me in this discussion, some of the following suggestions will be law, or on their way to being law. Others may have imploded, exploded, or just scuttled under the carpet and quietly breathed their last. So use this list as a place to start, okay? You're a student loan expert now, and you can look these things up for yourself.

HOW WILL THE PROGRAMS COMPETE IN THE FUTURE?

As long as their programs coexist, it's safe to say FFELP and Direct Lending will wrangle on "level playing field" issues. In public, players on both sides say they just want the game to be equal. (This is sort of hilarious, since folks on each side seem to be talking cooperation at the front door and then whacking each other in the alley.) Nevertheless, when the rival loan programs make their case to you, the customer, they want to look equally attractive. What would this include?

1. Income Contingent Repayment: This is the biggie, of course. FFELP wants the right to offer it. As long as only Direct Lending can offer the true option of paying a small percentage of your income, FFELP lenders know that all the interest breaks in the world won't make a difference to those of us whose loans are over a certain insane total. Regarding the loan forgiveness part of the deal, the FFELP industry's idea so far is to service the loan and collect the interest over twenty-five years, then ask the government to pay any excess loan left over. Doesn't this mean that the FFELP lender would get all the ice cream and hand the government the dirty dishes? FFELP lenders don't think so.

2. Negotiable perks: Just as FFELP can't offer ICR, so Direct Lending can't offer negotiable interest rates. Certainly the idea of a government lending program starting to do things more like a commercial lender is not so easy to picture, but who knows?

3. The twenty-five-year income-contingent tax bite: Remember how you'll be taxed on any amount left over after you've been making income-contingent payments on your loan for twenty-five years? Both sides dislike this provision, but for very different reasons.

For some advocates of Direct Lending, this tacked-on punishment is just kind of silly. If you were so broke for twenty-five years that you couldn't pay your loan, does it make sense that you could pay a big chunk of tax all at once? No way. In coming years, they're hoping to get this dropped.

For FFELP, the twenty-five-year forgiveness-plus-taxable-income idea is also stupid, but for them it's because they see shipwreck ahead—huge tax write-offs, billions and billions of dollars' worth, and helpless, innocent taxpayers paying for the indiscretions of feckless young people. They'd like to see the whole idea of income-contingency redesigned, so that there were more specific safeguards—for lenders, not borrowers.

4. The switcheroo: Under the law as of this writing, you can go from FFELP into Direct Lending, but you can't go back. It's like Dorothy leaving Oz. What that means is that if your circumstances improve, and you'd like to get back to the land of FFELP's reduced interest, you can't. This makes lenders wild-eyed, and by the time you read this, smart money says they will have changed it.

STUDENTS VERSUS DEBT

As the perpetual FFELP–Direct Lending mud-wrestling bout contin-ues in the background, we students will continue to push our own agenda. At least, I hope so. Groups I've spoken to plan to keep ham-mering on some of the following questions:

1. Where are the grants? Since every professional in higher educa-tion talks about how much we need grants, what would it take for Congress to fund them? This is a question, I can safely say, that will still be being asked whenever you read these pages.

2. How can we avoid raising debt limits? Where in years past, stu-dents have lobbied for higher loan limits, our Washington student spokespeople are now starting to say, That's it. We're maxed out. We have to think of another way to go about this.

3. Why does college cost so much? On this question, students and the Republican Congress are in perfect agreement. Look for some distinguished academic feet to be held to the fire at congressional hearings during the next few years.

4. What can employers do? Knowing that the answers to these first three questions probably won't be all that satisfactory, students will be seeking tax incentives that would make it easier for us to attend graduate school part time, and more appealing for our employers to help us. Remember when interest on our student loans used to be tax-deductible? Student activists would like to see that again.

5. How can we create better loan-forgiveness programs? Government programs that let you work off part of your loan (by teaching in a deprived area, and so on) have often flopped because they didn't offer enough loan forgiveness, and because they were so poorly publicized that nobody knew how to join. Look for students to push for a lot more creativity from government in this area.

HIGHER EDUCATION PROFESSIONALS VERSUS DEBT

The best education professionals are realizing that American students are going to keep right on being fed to the debt monster unless somebody does some better studies to show what's actually happening to us. Nellie Mae has actually put in motion a major national study to show all of its sampled students' debts, from Stafford loans to Visa cards—a landmark action that hopefully will lead to more of the same.

HOW DO I GET INVOLVED WITHOUT GIVING UP TOO MUCH TIME?

Get on your computer and surf, surf, surf. The whole brawling and contentious world I'm talking about is right there, arguing all day and all night on the Net. You can get at least a fair idea of what's going on without ever leaving your chair. More than that—and here's the important part—you can make a difference, just by joining one or more of Washington's grassroots student organizations. Even if you don't actively do anything with them, your name will help.

If your time is limited, but you want to keep tabs on whether your loan terms are going to change, start with the granddaddy of the student websites, maintained by the *National Association of Graduate and Professional Students (NAGPS)*. If you check in here once every month or two, you'll definitely know what's what in Washington. Of roughly twenty links, two ongoing favorites are The Student Aid Crisis Page, which gives you a meticulously updated picture of who did what to whom in Congress; the NAGPS Reference Shelf, which will send you to just about every other website you're interested in; and Join a NAGPS E-mail List!, which allows you to zap your congressperson with a piece of your mind without even looking up their E-mail address. NAGPS will download your letter and send it right over to Capitol Hill. That's gracious living!

If you want background information on the other two most active student grassroots organizations in Washington, they're available to you on the Internet as well. *United States Student Association (USSA)* has lots of interesting, old-style leftie history to report, starting with its formation in the forties, and carried through in its commitment to diversity and social issues today. *U.S. Public Interest Research Group (U.S. PIRG)* has campus organizations you might be interested in, and even if you're not, U.S. PIRG's Washington office can help you stay current with what's going on during the 105th Congress.

The National Association of Graduate and Professional Students (NAGPS)
http://nagps.varesearch.com/nagps/nagps-hp.html

United States Student Association (USSA)
http://www.essential.org/ussa/

U.S. Public Interest Research Group (U.S. PIRG)
http://www.igc.apc.ord/pirg/
Many lenders listed at the back of this book have informative websites.

Many lenders listed at the back of this book have informative websites. Meanwhile, for any and all business-type stuff, you might start by checking out Sallie Mae's gorgeous website. In line with the corporation's "plan ahead" philosophy, this site has several interactive calculators for those of us who are a bit math-challenged. Want to find out how much interest you'll rack up if you ask for a three-month deferment? Sallie Mae's calculator will tell you. If you feed it your total loan amount, it'll also tell you what your monthly payments will be, whether on a ten-year schedule or the endless consolidation route. There's also solid advice on making a budget for a school semester.

Sallie Mae
http://www.salliemae.com

If you don't have a computer, you're not out of luck. Most of the people you want to deal with have 800 numbers, and they love to send out written information about themselves. Whatever's left to learn about them, a trip to the library will do it. Follow their exploits in back issues of the *Washington Post*.

PLEASE . . . VOTE!

If I haven't harangued you enough in these pages, let me try one more time. This issue, the issue of our student loans, can be your starting point to learning to listen and lend your voice to our nation's debate about how we'll live and how we'll deal with the problems that confront us. This is your job as an American, and there's no getting around it. If you don't make the effort to keep up with what we're doing as a nation, then you have absolutely no right to complain the next time some idiot fouls up your student loan business.

Please make the decision to listen, to learn, and above all, to vote.

I CAN DREAM, CAN'T I?

Throughout this book, I've tried to give you practical help, stuff you could use in the world as it is, not as we'd like it to be. But I think you and I ought to aim higher than just the practical. Before we part company, let's imagine for a minute: not what we think we can have, but what we ought to have—and, finally, what we wish for.

We students deserve a few courtesies and considerations we aren't getting. Actually, they're more than courtesies, they're rights. We ought to be treated better, and here's how such treatment might start.

1. A national network of lawyers to defend us, at prices we can afford, when someone in the student loan industry makes a mistake at our expense.

2. The right to know who we're talking to when we're dealing with employees of our loan holders. The right to speak to that person by name, and call that person again if necessary.

3. More studies on debt — our real debt, not just the undergraduate numbers that form the basis of the public loan conversation.

4. The ability to sign over our income tax returns every year, giving our refunds as lump-sum loan payments. If the IRS can process these when we're in default, why can't we do it voluntarily?

5. The right to comparison shop, using a reference book — a catalog — of which consolidator offers what, with competitors lined up next to each other on the page. If we're going to have competing lenders, let's go whole hog.

Those are rights I think we ought to have. But I also have a couple of wishes, a couple of dreams. Since the Reagan years, we have been publicly subscribing to the idea that education benefits the individual, not society. This is like saying that learning to fly only benefited the Wright Brothers. Education is more beneficial to society than most things we'll ever do, and common sense is all it takes to tell you so.

Bill Clinton, in his days as a presidential candidate, foresaw a national service situation where we would all pay down our loans while we were doing something crucial: meeting and talking to and sharing with each other.

Is it completely out of the question for us to explore doing what Clinton wanted — national service in exchange for loans? Have we really thought of all the angles? Does it have to be AmeriCorps or nothing? Why can't we work off loan debt on weekends and in semi-annual boot camps, as with the National Guard?

When I assess the value of my college education, I feel a spiritual debt to the inspired people that I met there, not just a financial debt to the bank that enabled me to go. Both components were necessary, each impossible without the other. It just seems right to give service in order to repay. I can't pretend to be an economist. If experts tell me America doesn't have enough money to support a service-for-loans program, I have to believe it's true.

But this whole education was about wishing. I don't plan to stop now.

One thing is certain. As you and I carry our student loan debts into a new century, we're going to have to use all our energy toward making this strange situation work for us, not against us. Whether through national service or just encouragement and fellowship, we have to remember that we're not alone. This is our life, loans and all. This is our America. Let's take our place in it, noisily. We already paid our dues.

Appendix 1

Sallie Mae
Deferment Guide

REPAYMENT LIMIT—ALL BORROWERS

Benefit	Perkins	Stafford* and Unsubsidized Stafford	SLS***
Standard	10 years	10 years**	10 years**
With Sallie Mae's SMART LOAN Account	up to 30 years	up to 30 years	up to 30 years
Interest rate	3%, 4%, or 5%	7%, 8%, 8%/10%, 9% or variable, capped at 9% (as of 7/1/94) based on the 91-day T-Bill	12%, 14% or variable, capped at 11% (based on 52-week T-Bill)
Repayment usually begins	6 months after leaving school for borrowers pre 7/1/87; 9 months after leaving school for borrowers post 7/1/87; available only to (prior) borrowers (see p. 308 for definition)	7% loans = 9–12 months after leaving school; all others = 6 months after leaving school	with last disbursement of the loan, but borrowers may be able to defer payment until leaving school

*Certain of these loans may be converted to a variable rate. Borrowers should check with their lenders.

**Select Step® Account (graduated repayment) lets borrowers reduce intial monthly payments. Income Sensitive Repayment lets borrowers reduce initial monthly payments and lets them extend their repayment term.

PLUS	HPSL	HEAL and HEAL Relief® Account	SMART LOAN® Account
10 years**	10 years	up to 25 years****	—
up to 30 years	up to 30 years	—	up to 30 years
12%, 14% or variable, capped at 10% or 9% (as of 7/1/94) based on 52-week T-Bill	3%, 5%, 7%, or 9%	variable, based on 91-day T-Bill; maximum rate of T-Bill + 3.0%	equal to weighted average of the interest rate of loans consolidated, rounded up to the nearest whole percent
with last disbursement of loan	1 year after leaving school	9 months after leaving school, a qualified internship/residency program, or fellowship/educational activity	within 60 days after consolidation

***After July 1, 1994, no new SLS loans were made. The SLS program was eliminated by merging the program into the Unsubsidized Federal Stafford loan program.

****Graduated Repayment lets borrowers reduce initial monthly payments. Income Contingent Repayment lets borrowers reduce initial monthly payments and lets them extend their repayment term.

DEFERMENT OPTIONS—
"PRE"/"PRIOR" BORROWERS

Principal Payments May Be Deferred While Borrower Is:	Perkins	Stafford and Unsubsidized Stafford	SLS
Attending school full time	yes	yes	yes
Attending school at least half-time	yes	available only to "prior" borrowers (see p. 308 for definition) who take out a Stafford/GSL or SLS loan for the deferment period	available only to "prior" borrowers (see p. 308 for definition) who take out a Stafford/GSL or SLS loan for the deferment period
Unemployed	yes; interest will continue to accrue and be payable by borrower	up to 2 years	up to 2 years
Serving in the Armed Forces, Public Health Service, Peace Corps or VISTA	up to 3 years; only NDSL loans made after 9/30/80 are eligible for Public Health Service deferment	no more than 3 years for Armed Forces, Public Health Service, and NOAA service combined	no more than 3 years for Armed Forces, Public Health Service, and NOAA service combined
On active duty in the National Oceanic and Atmospheric Administrative Corps	up to 3 years; available only to "prior" borrowers (see p. 308 for definition)	no more than 3 years for Armed Forces, Public Health Service, and NOAA service combined; available only to "prior" borrowers (see p. 308 for definition)	no more than 3 years for Armed Forces, Public Health Service, and NOAA service combined; available only to "prior" borrowers (see p. 308 for definition)

PLUS	HPSL	HEAL and HEAL Relief® Account	SMART LOAN® Account
yes; parent and/or student	yes—for loans made after 11/4/88—must be attending health professions school	yes	yes
available only to "prior" borrowers (see p. 308 for definition) if parent and/or student who take out a Stafford/GSL or SLS loan for the deferment period	no	no	yes, if the borrower has taken out a Stafford/GSL or SLS loan for the deferment period
up to 2 years	yes; employment/disability periods are treated as forbearances; interest may accrue and be payable by borrower	no	up to 2 years
no more than 3 years for Armed Forces, Public Health Service, and NOAA service combined; only loans made prior to 8/15/83	up to 3 years; service in VISTA not eligible for deferment	up to 3 years in each; Armed Forces, National Health Service, or Peace Corps	no
no	up to 3 years	no	no

DEFERMENT OPTIONS—"PRE"/ "PRIOR" BORROWERS (continued)

Principal Payments May Be Deferred While Borrower Is:	Perkins	Stafford and Unsubsized Stafford	SLS
Serving an internship required to receive professional recognition and begin professional practice	up to 2 years; only loans made after 9/30/80	up to 2 years	up to 2 years
Serving in an internship or residency program leading to a degree or certificate awarded by a school, hospital, or health care facility	up to 2 years; then forbearance for balance of internship/residency	up to 2 years; then forbearance for balance of internship/residency	up to 2 years; then forbearance for balance of internship/residency
Studying in approved graduate fellowship program	no	yes	yes
Participating in a fellowship training program or full-time educational activity related to the health profession for which borrower is preparing	no	no	no
Temporarily totally disabled or unable to work while caring for a disabled spouse (or dependent for Stafford, SLS, PLUS borrowers effective after 10/17/86)	up to 3 years of combined eligibility for borrower, spouse, or dependent for NDSL loans made after 9/30/80	maximum cumulative time limit of up to 3 years of combined eligibility	maximum cumulative time limit of up to 3 years of combined eligibility

PLUS	HPSL	HEAL and HEAL Relief® Account	SMART LOAN® Account Principal
up to 2 years; only loans made prior to 8/15/83	up to 5 years	unlimited if borrower has loans that were disbursed prior to 10/22/85 — up to 4 years if borrower's loans disbursed on or after that date — must be in field related to health education	no
no	yes, and if participating in advanced health professional training	unlimited if borrower has loans that were disbursed prior to 10/22/85 — up to 4 years if borrower's loans disbursed on or after that date	no
yes; parent and/or student	no	no	yes
no	up to 2 years if prior to or within 12 months after completion of advanced professional training — deferment for loans made after 10/21/85	up to 2 years for loans made after 10/21/85	no
maximum cumulative time limit of up to 3 years of combined eligibility	yes; employment/disability periods are treated as forbearances; interest may accrue and be payable by borrower	no	maximum cumulative time limit of up to 3 years of combined eligibility

DEFERMENT OPTIONS—"PRE"/ "PRIOR" BORROWERS (continued)

Principal Payments May Be Deferred While Borrower Is:	Perkins	Stafford and Unsubsidized Stafford	SLS
Parental leave while borrower is pregnant/caring for own newborn or adopted child	up to 6 months; not working/attending school; enrolled at least half-time at some time during 6 months preceding leave; available only to "pre" borrowers (see p.308 for definition)	up to 6 months; not working/attending school; enrolled at least half-time at some time during 6 months preceding leave; available only to "pre" borrowers (see p.308 for definition)	up to 6 months; not working/attending school; enrolled at least half-time at some time during 6 months preceding leave; available only to "prior" borrowers (see p.308 for definition)
Mother of preschool children entering/reentering work force at no more than $1.00 above minimum wage	up to 1 year; available only to "prior" borrowers (see p.308 for definition)	up to 1 year; available only to "prior" borrowers (see p.308 for definition)	up to 1 year; available only to "prior" borrowers (see p.308 for definition)
Full-time volunteer for a tax-exempt organization	up to 3 years for NDSL loans made after 9/30/80	up to 3 years	up to 3 years
Teaching full-time in public or non-profit elementary/secondary school in teacher-shortage area	no	up to 3 years; available only to "prior" borrowers (see p.308 for definition)	up to 3 years; available only to "prior" borrowers (see p.308 for definition)
Studying in approved rehabilitation program for the disabled	no	yes	yes
Grace Period After Deferment	6 months	6 months on loans made before 10/1/81; none post 10/1/81, except for some Desert Shield/Storm borrowers	no, except for some Desert Shield/Storm borrowers

PLUS	HPSL	HEAL and HEAL Relief® Account	SMART LOAN® Account
no	no	no	
no	no	no	no
up to 3 years; only loans made prior to 8/15/83	no	up to 3 years if volunteer under Title I of the Domestic Volunteer Service Act of 1973	no
no	no	no	no
yes; parent and/or student	no	no	yes
no, except for some Desert Shield/Storm borrowers	no	9 months for borrowers who have not entered repayment prior to a deferment period	no

DEFERMENT OPTIONS—
"NEW" BORROWERS

Principal Payments May Be Deferred While Borrower Is:	Stafford, Unsubsidized Stafford, and Perkins	PLUS[1]
Attending school full-time	yes	yes
Attending school at least half-time	yes	yes
Unemployed	up to 3 years	up to 3 years
Studying in an approved graduate fellowship or rehabilitation program for the disabled	yes	yes
Economic hardship	up to 3 years	up to 3 years
Chiropractic school graduates	no	no
Practicing primary care after completion of internship/residency in osteopathic general practice, family medicine, general internal medicine, preventive medicine or general pediatrics	no	no

[1] PLUS deferments are based on the parent borrowers' eligibility for the deferment.

[2] HPSL deferment options unchanged from "Pre"/"Prior" Chart.

[3] A "new" HEAL borrower is one who signs HEAL promissory notes on or after October 13, 1992. The deferment eligibility for chiropractic school graduates and practicing primary care is for loans made on or after 10/13/92 and not just for new borrowers. Other standard HEAL deferments apply as indicated on chart.

HPSL[2]	HEAL[3] and HEAL Relief® Account	SMART LOAN® Account[4]
—	yes	yes
—	no	yes
—	no	up to 3 years
—	no	yes
—	no	up to 3 years
—	up to 1 year	no
—	up to 3 years	no

[4] Consolidation loan applications received on/after 1/1/93 and before 8/10/93 are eligible for interest subsidy during deferment. Applications received on/after 8/10/93 are eligible for interest subsidy during deferment if the consolidation loan includes *only* Federal Stafford loans for which the federal government paid interest during the in-school, grace or deferment periods.

KEY NOTES

- All loans may be prepaid without penalty. Debt canceled upon death or total disability of borrower.
- Partial or full cancellation of Perkins loans may be allowed for certain types of public service.
- Under certain circumstances military personnel may have their Stafford and SLS loans and consolidation loans repaid by the Secretary of Defense.
- Income sensitive/income contingent or graduated repayment is available to borrowers when they enter repayment.
- With HEAL Relief, borrowers can consolidate all of their HEAL loans—including loans not serviced by Sallie Mae—into one new loan with opportunities to lower the interest rate, saving thousands of dollars.
- Borrower classifications:

    "Pre" Borrower—is one with outstanding Stafford or SLS loans made for enrollment before 7/1/87 or disbursed before 7/1/87.

    "Prior" Borrower—is one who had no outstanding Stafford, SLS, PLUS, or consolidation loans on the date he or she applied for the loan and whose first disbursement was after 7/1/87 and before 6/30/93.

    "New" Borrower—is one who had no outstanding Stafford, PLUS, SLS, or consolidation loans on the date he or she applied for a new FFELP loan.

KEY TERMS:

Accrued interest—Interest that accumulates on the unpaid balance of your loan principal.

Capitalization of interest—Addition of unpaid interest to the principal of your loan which increases both your total debt and monthly payments.

Deferment—A period of time during which borrowers do not have to make loan payments because they are engaged in an activity specified as eligible for deferment such as full-time student status or post-graduate training (see chart). On some loans the federal government pays the interest during a deferment. On others, the interest accrues and the borrower is responsible for paying it. Most deferments must be requested; they are not automatic. To obtain a deferment you must file a deferment form with every loan holder for each loan for every year that you are eligible for a deferment. If you are not in repayment, this means getting in touch with the lender(s) 30 to 60 days before your grace period expires. In the case of HEAL loans, if you decide to go directly into a deferment after graduation, you need to contact the lender to make arrangements so that your loans don't go into repayment status.

Forbearance—A temporary adjustment to repayment schedule for cases of financial hardship. A forbearance must be requested, it is not automatic. Because you pay less (or nothing) during periods of forbearance, it takes longer to repay the loan. This means interest accrues on the loan for a longer period, thereby reducing payments over the short term, but increasing your total loan cost. It may also mean capitalization of accrued and unpaid interest during this time, thus increasing both the balance owed on the loan and the monthly payments required after the forbearance period has ended. With Stafford loans the forbearance period is unlimited for medical residency training after deferments are exhausted and for up to three years when the borrower is having economic hardship. With HEAL loans, a forbearance is granted during periods when the borrower is unable to make scheduled payments due to economic hardship, limited to two years, at the option of the lender (may be extended beyond two years with government approval).

Appendix 2

Directory of

Guaranty Agencies

Data Content Updated May 1, 1996

ALABAMA

Alabama Commission on Higher
  Education
P. O. Box 302000
Montgomery, Alabama 36130-2000
(334) 242-1998
(334) 242-2416
(800) 843-8534 (in state)

ALASKA (FEDERAL LOANS)

USA Funds, Inc.
P. O. Box 6180
Indianapolis, Indiana 46206-6180
(800) 382-4506
(317) 849-6510
(800) 428-9250
(800) 824-7045
  (repayment/deferment info)
www.usagroup.com

ALASKA (STATE LOANS)

Alaska Commission on
  Postsecondary Education
Alaska Student Loan Corporation
3030 Vintage Boulevard
Juneau, Alaska 99801-7901
(907) 465-2962
(800) 441-2962 (out of state)

ARIZONA

USA Funds, Inc.
P. O. Box 6180
Indianapolis, Indiana 46206-6180
(800) 382-4506
(317) 849-6510
(800) 428-9250
(800) 824-7045
  (repayment/deferment info)
www.usagroup.com

ARKANSAS

Student Loan Guarantee Foundation
of Arkansas
219 South Victory Street
Little Rock, Arkansas 72201-1884
(501) 372-1491
(800) 622-3446

CALIFORNIA

California Student Aid Commission
P. O. Box 510845
Sacramento, California 94245-0845
(916) 445-0880
(800) 367-1589 (defaulted loans)
(916) 322-9277 (billing problems)

COLORADO

Colorado Student Loan Program
Suite 425
999 18th Street
Denver, Colorado 80201-2440
(303) 294-5050
(800) 727-9834
www.cslp.org

CONNECTICUT

Connecticut Student Loan Foundation
525 Brook Street
P. O. Box 1009
Rocky Hill, Connecticut 06067
(860) 257-4001
(800) 237-9721
(800) 345-6055
www.cslf.com

DELAWARE

Delaware Education Loan Services
Carvel State Office Building
Fourth Floor
820 North French Street
Wilmington, Delaware 19801
(302) 577-6055
(800) 292-7935
www.state.de.us/high-ed/
commiss/webpage.htm

DISTRICT OF COLUMBIA

American Student Assistance
330 Stuart Street
Boston, Massachusetts 02116-5292
(617) 426-9434
(800) 999-9080
www.amsa.com

FLORIDA

Florida Department of Education
Office of Student Financial
    Assistance
325 West Gaines Street
1344 Florida Education Center
Tallahassee, Florida 32399-0400
(904) 942-4662
(800) 366-3475

GEORGIA

Georgia Student Finance Commission
Suite 200
2082 East Exchange Place
Tucker, Georgia 30084
(770) 414-3000
(800) 776-6878
www.gsfc.org

HAWAII

USA Funds, Inc.
P. O. Box 6180
Indianapolis, Indiana 46206-6180
(800) 382-4506
(317) 849-6510
(800) 428-9250
www.usagroup.com

IDAHO

Northwest Education Loan
   Association
500 Coleman Building
811 First Avenue Seattle, Washington
98104
(206) 461-5300
(800) 562-3001

ILLINOIS

Illinois Student Assistance
   Commission
1755 Lake Cook Road
Deerfield, Illinois 60015-5209
(708) 948-8500
(800) 477-4411
(800) 934-3572 (defaulted loans)

INDIANA

USA Funds, Inc.
P. O. Box 6180
Indianapolis, Indiana 46206-6180
(800) 382-4506
(317) 849-6510
(800) 428-9250
www.usagroup.com

IOWA

Iowa College Student Aid
   Commission
200 10th Street, 4th Floor
Des Moines, Iowa 50309-3609
(515) 281-4890
(800) 383-4222
www.state.ia.us/government/icsac/
index.htm

KANSAS

United Student Aid Funds, Inc.
P. O. Box 6180
Indianapolis, Indiana 46206-6180
(800) 824-7044
(317) 849-6510
(800) 428-9250

KENTUCKY

Kentucky Higher Education
   Assistance Authority
Suite 102
1050 U.S. 127 South
Frankfort, Kentucky 40601-4323
(502) 564-7990
(800) 928-8926
www.kheaa.state.ky.us

LOUISIANA

Louisiana Office of Student Financial
   Assistance
P. O. Box 91202
Baton Rouge, Louisiana 70821-9202
(504) 922-1012
(800) 259-5626

MAINE

Finance Authority of Maine
1 Weston Court
State House Station 119
Augusta, Maine 04333
(207) 287-2183
(800) 228-3734 (within Maine)
www.famemaine.com

MARYLAND

USA Funds, Inc.
P. O. Box 6180
Indianapolis, Indiana 46206-6180
(800) 382-4506
(317) 849-6510
(800) 428-9250
www.usagroup.com

MASSACHUSETTS

American Student Assistance
330 Stuart Street
Boston, Massachusetts 02116-5292
(617) 426-9434
(800) 999-9080
www.amsa.com

MICHIGAN

Michigan Guarantee Agency
P. O. Box 30047
Lansing, Michigan 48909-7547
(517) 373-0760
(800) 642-5626

MINNESOTA

Northstar Guaranty, Inc.
P. O. Box 64080
St. Paul, Minnesota 55164-0080
(612) 290-8795
(800) 366-0032
www.northstar.org

MISSISSIPPI

USA Funds, Inc.
P. O. Box 6180
Indianapolis, Indiana 46206-6180
(800) 382-4506
(317) 849-6510
(800) 428-9250
www.usagroup.com

MISSOURI

Coordinating Board for Higher
 Education
3515 Amazonas Drive
Jefferson City, Missouri 65109
(800) 473-6757
(573) 751-2361
www.mocbhe.gov

MONTANA

Montana Guaranteed Student Loan
 Program
2500 Broadway
Helena, Montana 59620-3103
(406) 444-6594
(800) 537-7508
(800) 322-3086 (defaulted loans)

NEBRASKA

Nebraska Student Loan Program
P. O. Box 82507
Lincoln, Nebraska 68501-2507
(402) 475-8686
(800) 735-8778
www.nslp.com

NEVADA

USA Funds, Inc.
P. O. Box 6180
Indianapolis, Indiana 46206-6180
(800) 382-4506
(317) 849-6510
(800) 428-9250

NEW HAMPSHIRE

New Hampshire Higher Education
    Assistance Foundation
44 Warren Street
P. O. Box 877
Concord, New Hampshire 03302
(603) 225-6612
(800) 525-2577
www.nhheaf.org

NEW JERSEY

Office of Student Assistance
4 Quakerbridge Plaza CN543
Trenton, New Jersey 08625
(609) 588-3200
(800) 356-5562
(800) 792-8670
www.state.nj.us/treasury/osa

NEW MEXICO

New Mexico Student Loan Guaranty
    Corporation
P. O. Box 27020
Albuquerque, New Mexico 87125-
7020
(800) 279-3070
(505) 345-8821

NEW YORK

New York State Higher Education
    Services Corporation
99 Washington Avenue
Albany, New York 12255
(518) 474-5592
(800) 642-6234

NORTH CAROLINA

North Carolina State Education
    Assistance Authority
P. O. Box 2688
Chapel Hill, North Carolina 27515
(919) 549-8614
(800) 544-1644

NORTH DAKOTA

Student Loans of North Dakota
    Guarantor
P. O. Box 5524
Bismarck, North Dakota 58506-5524
(701) 328-5600
(800) 472-2166
www.banknd.com

OHIO

USA Funds
P. O. Box 6180
Indianapolis, Indiana 46206-6180
(800) 382-4506
(317) 849-6510
(800) 428-9250
www.usagroup.org
or:
Great Lakes Higher Education Corp.
2401 International Lane
Madison, Wisconsin 53704
(800) 236-5900
(800) 236-6600
www.glhec.org

OKLAHOMA

Oklahoma State Regents for Higher
  Education
P. O. Box 3000
Oklahoma City, Oklahoma 73101-
  3000
(405) 858-4300
(800) 247-0420
(800) 442-8642

OREGON

Oregon State Scholarship
  Commission
Suite 100
1500 Valley River Drive
Eugene, Oregon 97401
(541) 687-7400
(800) 452-8807
www.teleport.com/~ossc

PENNSYLVANIA

Pennsylvania Higher Education
  Assistance Agency
1200 North Seventh
Harrisburg, Pennsylvania 17102
(717) 257-2850
(800) 692-7392
www.pheaa.org

RHODE ISLAND

Rhode Island Higher Education
  Assistance Authority
560 Jefferson Boulevard
Warwick, Rhode Island 02886
(401) 736-1100
(800) 922-9855

SOUTH CAROLINA

South Carolina State Education
  Assistance Authority
Suite 212
Interstate Center
P. O. Box 210219
Columbia, South Carolina 29221
(803) 798-7960
(800) 347-2752

SOUTH DAKOTA

Education Assistance Corporation
115 First Avenue, SW
Aberdeen, South Dakota 57401
(605) 225-6423
(800) 592-1802
www.eac-easci.org

TENNESSEE

Tennessee Student Assistance
  Corporation
404 James Robertson Parkway
Suite 1950
Parkway Towers
Nashville, Tennessee 37243-0820
(615) 741-1346
(800) 342-1663 (within Tennessee)
(800) 447-1523 (within Tennessee)
(800) 257-6526 (outside Tennessee)

TEXAS

Texas Guaranteed Student Loan
  Corporation
P. O. Box 201725
Austin, Texas 78720-1725
(512) 219-5700
(800) 845-6267
(800) 252-9743
www.tgslc.org

UTAH

Utah Higher Education Assistance
  Authority
P. O. Box 45202
Salt Lake City, Utah 84145-0202
(801) 321-7200
(800) 418-8757
www.utahsbr.edu

VERMONT

Vermont Student Assistance
  Corporation
Champlain Mill
P. O. Box 2000

Winooski, Vermont 05404-2000
(802) 655-9602
(800) 798-8722
www.vsac.org

VIRGINIA

Educational Credit Management
Suite 300
411 East Franklin Street
Richmond, Virginia 23219
(804) 644-6400
(888) 775-3262

WASHINGTON

Northwest Education Loan
  Association
500 Colman Building
811 First Avenue
Seattle, Washington 98104
(206) 461-5300
(800) 562-3001

WEST VIRGINIA

West Virginia Education Loan
  Service
P. O. Box 591
Charleston, West Virginia 25322
(304) 345-7211
(800) 437-3692 (within West
  Virginia)

WISCONSIN

Great Lakes Higher Education
  Corporation
2401 International Lane
P. O. Box 7658

Madison, Wisconsin 53704
(608) 246-1800
(800) 236-4300
(800) 944-0904 (defaulted loans)
www.glhec.org

WYOMING

USA Funds, Inc.
P. O. Box 6180
Indianapolis, Indiana 46206-6180
(800) 382-4506
(317) 849-6510
(800) 428-9250
www.usagroup.com

AMERICAN SAMOA

USA Funds, Inc.
P. O. Box 6180
Indianapolis, Indiana 46206-6180
(800) 382-4506
(317) 849-6510
(800) 428-9250
www.usagroup.com

NORTHERN MARIANA ISLANDS

USA Funds, Inc.
P. O. Box 6180
Indianapolis, Indiana 46206-6180
(800) 382-4506
(317) 849-6510
(800) 428-9250
www.usagroup.com

FEDERATED STATES OF MICRONESIA, MARSHALL ISLANDS, REPUBLIC OF PALAU

USA Funds, Inc.
P. O. Box 6180
Indianapolis, Indiana 46206-6180
(800) 382-4506
(317) 849-6510
(800) 428-9250
www.usagroup.com

VIRGIN ISLANDS

Great Lakes Higher Education
   Corporation
2401 International Lane
P. O. Box 7658
Madison, Wisconsin 53704
(608) 246-1800
(800) 236-4300
(800) 944-0904
www.glhec.org

GUAM

USA Funds, Inc.
P. O. Box 6180
Indianapolis, Indiana 46206-6180
(800) 382-4506
(317) 849-6510
(800) 428-9250
www.usagroup.com

PUERTO RICO

Great Lakes Higher Education
  Corporation
2401 International Lane
P. O. Box 7658
Madison, Wisconsin 53704
(608) 246-1800
(800) 236-4300
(800) 944-0904 (defaulted loans)
www.glhec.org

Directory of Secondary Markets

**ALABAMA HIGHER
EDUCATION LOAN
CORPORATION**

100 N. Union Street
Montgomery, AL 36104-3702
(334) 242-1998
(800) 843-8534 (Alabama)
(800) 624-8393 (out of state)

**SOUTHWEST STUDENT
SERVICES CORPORATION**

1201 S. Alma School Road,
Ste. 11000
Mesa AZ 85210
(602) 461-9830

**ARIZONA STUDENT LOAN
FINANCE CORPORATION**

P. O. Box 25366
Tempe, AZ 85285
(520) 623-5873
(800) 545-6765

**ARKANSAS STUDENT
LOAN AUTHORITY**

101 E. Capitol, Ste. 401
Little Rock, AR 72201
(501) 682-1258
(800) 443-6030

**CHELA (CALIFORNIA
HIGHER EDUCATION
LOAN AUTHORITY)**

388 Market Street, Ste. 1250
San Francisco, CA 94111
(415) 391-3131

CALIFORNIA STUDENT AID COMMISSION

P. O. Box 510845
Sacramento, CA 94245-0845
(916) 445-0880
(800) 298-9490
www.csac.ca.gov/

COLORADO STUDENT OBLIGATION BOND AUTHORITY

1981 Blake St., Ste. 201
Denver, CO 80202
(303) 295-1981
(800) 448-2424

CONNECTICUT STUDENT LOAN FOUNDATION (CALS)

525 Brook St.
P. O. Box 1009
Rocky Hill, CT 06067
(860) 257-4001
(800) 237-9721

SALLIE MAE

1050 Thomas Jefferson St. NW
Washington, DC 20007
(202) 333-8000
(800) 292-6868 (customer service)
(888) 272-5543 (centralized customer service)
www.salliemae.com

GEORGIA STUDENT FINANCE COMMISSION

2082 East Exchange Place, Ste. 200
Tucker, GA 30084
(770) 414-3000
(800) 776-6878
www.gsfc.org

STUDENT LOAN FUND OF IDAHO MARKETING ASSOCIATION

6905 Hwy. 95
P. O. Box 730
Fruitland, ID 83619
(208) 452-4058
(800) 528-9447

ILLINOIS DESIGNATED STUDENT ASSISTANCE COMMISSION

1755 Lake Cook Rd.
Deerfield, IL 60015
(847) 948-8500
(800) 934-3572 (default)
(800) 447-4414 (preclaim)

INDIANA SECONDARY MARKET FOR EDUCATION LOANS

P. O. Box 826
Indianapolis, IN 46206
(317) 469-2000
(800) 635-1867

IOWA STUDENT LOAN LIQUIDITY CORPORATION

900 Equitable Bldg.
604 Locust St.
Des Moines. IA 50309
(515) 243-5626
(800) 243-7552

KENTUCKY HIGHER EDUCATION ASSISTANCE AUTHORITY

1050 U.S. 127 South
Frankfort, KY 40601
(502) 564-7990
(800) 928-8926

LOUISIANA PUBLIC FACILITIES AUTHORITY

2237 S. Acadian Thruway, Ste. 3650
Baton Rouge, LA 70808
(504) 923-0020
(800) 228-4755
www.lpsa.com

MAINE EDUCATIONAL LOAN MARKETING CORPORATION

P. O. Box 549
Augusta, ME 04332
(207) 623-2600
(800) 922-6354
www.m-e-s.com

NEW ENGLAND EDUCATIONAL LOAN MARKETING CORPORATION

50 Braintree Hill Park, Suite 300
Braintree, MA 02184
(800) EDU-LOAN
(800) 634-9308 (customer service)
www.nelliemae.org

MICHIGAN HIGHER EDUCATION STUDENT LOAN AUTHORITY

608 W. Allegan
Lansing, MI 48933
(513) 373-3662
(800) 877-5659

MINNESOTA HIGHER EDUCATION SERVICES OFFICE BOARD

550 Cedar St.
St. Paul, MN 55101
(612) 296-9665
(800) 657-3866
www.heso.state.mn.us

MISSISSIPPI HIGHER EDUCATION ASSISTANCE CORPORATION

P. O. Box 5006
Jackson, MS 39296-5006
(601) 981-9425
(800) 986-4322
www.mheac.com

MISSOURI HIGHER EDUCATION LOAN AUTHORITY

1215 Fern Ridge Pkwy., Suite 208
St. Louis, MO 63141
(314) 469-0600

MONTANA HIGHER EDUCATION STUDENT ASSISTANCE CORPORATION

P. O. Box 5209
Helena, MT 59604-9947
(406) 444-6597
(800) 852-2761

NEBRASKA HIGHER EDUCATION LOAN PROGRAM

P. O. Box 62505
Lincoln, NE 68501
(402) 475-7272
(800) 667-7906
www.ne-epc.com

NEW HAMPSHIRE HIGHER EDUCATION LOAN CORPORATION

44 Warren Street
Concord, NH 03302
(603) 225-6612

NEW JERSEY HIGHER EDUCATION ASSISTANCE AUTHORITY

4 Quaker Bridge Plaza
Trenton, NJ 08625
(609) 588-3300
(800) 792-8670
www.state.nj.us/treasury/osa

NEW MEXICO EDUCATIONAL ASSISTANCE FOUNDATION

P. O. Box 27020
Albuquerque, NM 87125
(505) 345-3371
(800) 279-3070

COLLEGE FOUNDATION, INC.

P. O. Box 12100
Raleigh, NC 27605
(919) 821-4771
(800) 722-2838
www.cfi-nc.org

INDUSTRIAL COMMISSION OF NORTH DAKOTA

Box 5509
Bismarck, ND 58502
(701) 328-5657
(800) 554-2717

OHIO STUDENT LOAN FUNDING CORPORATION

1 West Fourth St. #200
Cincinnati, OH 45202
(513) 579-3595

OKLAHOMA STUDENT LOAN AUTHORITY

P. O. Box 18145
Oklahoma City, OK 73154
(405) 858-4300
(800) 456-6752

PENNSYLVANIA HIGHER EDUCATION ASSISTANCE AGENCY

P. O. Box 2461
Harrisburg, PA 17102
(717) 720-2850
(800) 692-7392
www.pheaa.org

RHODE ISLAND STUDENT LOAN AUTHORITY

560 Jefferson Blvd.
Warwick, RI 02886
(401) 736-1190
(800) PLUS-LOAN
www.risla.com

SOUTH CAROLINA STUDENT LOAN CORPORATION

P. O. Box 21337
Columbia, SC 29221

(803) 798-0916
(800) 347-2752

SOUTH DAKOTA STUDENT FINANCE CORPORATION

105 First Ave. SW
Aberdeen, SD 57401
(605) 622-4400
(800) 592-1270

TENNESSEE STUDENT ASSISTANCE CORPORATION

404 James Robertson Pkwy.
Parkway Towers, Ste. 1950
Nashville, TN 37243-0820
(615) 741-1346
(800) 257-6526 (out of state)
(800) 447-1523 (in state)

ABILENE HIGHER EDUCATION AUTHORITY

Box 3424
Abilene, TX 79604
(915) 672-6172

BRAZOS HIGHER EDUCATION AUTHORITY

P. O. Box 1308
Waco, TX 76703
(817) 753-0915

CENTRAL TEXAS HIGHER EDUCATION AUTHORITY

P. O. Box 8500-152
San Marcos, TX 78666
(512) 392-6200
(800) 359-5111

GREATER EAST TEXAS HIGHER EDUCATION SERVICING CORPORATION

P. O. Box 4940
Bryan, TX 77805
(409) 774-7590
(800) 829-4599

NORTH TEXAS HIGHER EDUCATION AUTHORITY

201 E. Abram, Suite 800
Arlington, TX 76010-1196
(817) 265-9158
(800) 366-4372

PANHANDLE PLAINS HIGHER EDUCATION AUTHORITY

2306 6th Ave., Box 839
Canyon, TX 79015
(806) 655-2821
(800) 736-5727

SOUTH TEXAS HIGHER EDUCATION AUTHORITY (COSTEP)

P. O. Box 6500
McAllen, TX 78502
(210) 682-6371
(800) 949-6371

TEXAS HIGHER EDUCATION COORDINATING BOARD

P. O. Box 12788
Capitol Station
Austin, TX 78711
(512) 427-6340
(800) 242-3062
www.thecb.state.tx.us

STATE BOARD OF REGENTS OF THE STATE OF UTAH

355 West N. Temple #3, Triad 3,
   Ste. 550
Salt Lake City, UT 84180
(801) 321-7201
(800) 418-8757

VERMONT STUDENT ASSISTANCE CORPORATION

P. O. Box 999
Winooski, VT 05404
(802) 655-4050
(800) 798-8722

NORTHWEST EDUCATION LOAN ASSOCIATION (STUDENT LOAN FINANCE ASSOCIATION)

500 Coleman Bldg., Suite 11
811 First Ave.
Seattle, WA 98104
(206) 461-5454
(206) 461-5470
(800) 732-1077

WEST VIRGINIA REGIONAL OFFICE OF PHEAA

P. O. Box 591
Charleston, WV 25322

(304) 345-7211
(800) 437-3692 (in state)
(800) 692-7392 (out of state)
www.pheaa.com

WYOMING STUDENT LOAN CORPORATION

P. O. Box 209
Cheyenne, WY 82003
(307) 638-0800
(800) 999-6541

INDEX

Gooding, William, 99–100
grace period, and repayment, 96, 107, 178
GradAssist Loans, 149
GradEXCEL loans, 149
Graduating into Debt, 7
grants, 32, 291
Great Returns Program, 145
Great Rewards Program, 145, 178
GSL (Guaranteed Student Loan) Program, 52–57, 59, 63
guarantors. *See* guaranty agencies
guaranty agencies, 45–47, 66
   audits of, 46, 76–78
   and debt collection, 184–85
   definition of, 68–69
   and delinquency, 170–71
   directory of, 310–18
   and FFELP, 45–47, 66
   financial practices of, 71–79
   legal powers of in default, 186
   lobbying efforts by, 78
   non-profit, 74
   and outside collection agencies, 187–88
   regional, 158
   and secondary markets, 75
   state-run, 74
   as student loan police, 75
   timetables for, 184–85

hardship, as deferment, 115, 121, 127–28, 239, 248–50, 257
Harvard University, 28
HEAF (Higher Education Assistance Foundation), 76
HEAL loans
   See also FFELP
   and bankruptcy, 250–51
   case study of, 250–51
   deferments for, 303, 305, 307
   definition of, 124–26
   repayment of, 299, 301
hearings, requesting, 192–93
Hicks, Elizabeth, 289
Higher Education Act (1965), 52, 175
Higher Education Amendments (1992), 170, 196
Higher Education Assistance Foundation. *See* HEAF
Hoover, Judy, 268–69
Hough, Lawrence A., 48, 65, 85, 159, 262, 286

How to Get Out of Debt, Stay Out of Debt, and Live Prosperously (Mundis), 273–75
HPSL loans, 124–26, 299, 301, 303, 305, 307

ICR. *See* Income Contingent Repayment
Imholtz, Elizabeth, 174, 198–99, 252, 286–87, 288
incentive programs, 145–46
income
   calculation of for repayment, 144
   compared to loan debt, 22
   disposable, 189–90, 197
   median American, 20–21
Income Contingent Repayment (ICR)
   as bankruptcy alternative, 234
   and consolidation, 176, 196, 199–201
   definition of, 135–38
   and Direct Lending, 43, 81–83, 133
   future of, 289–90
   historical and political background of, 81–87
   and loan management, 261, 264
   and record keeping, 163
Income Sensitive Repayment (ISR), 81, 131, 141–45, 163, 199–201
income tax refund interception, 143, 191–93, 202
income-to-debt ratio, 224
inflation, effect on student loan programs, 55
The Institute for Higher Education Policy, 7
insurance fees, 68
interactive calculators, 262
interest, 18, 194
   benefits, 8, 178
   calculation of, 8, 117, 215–17, 262
   on defaulted loans, 114, 194
   definition of, 209
   effect of consolidation on, 131
   effect of debt payment delay on, 107
   effect of deferment on, 117–21
   effect of forbearance on, 116
   effect of loan surfing on, 150
   effect of postponing payment on, 117–18
   effect of subsidized loans on, 107
   notices in default, 181
   and principal, 154, 194, 214
   rates for banks, 68, 211

military personnel, Perkins loans cancel-
lations for, 123
military service, as deferment, 119, 124
minimum loan payment, 198
minimum payment, credit card, 216
M.I.T. *See* Massachusetts Institute of
Technology
moonlighting, and second jobs, 279
Mundis, Jerry, 273–75
NAGPS. *See* National Association of
Graduate and Professional Students
Nassirian, Barmak, 56–57, 71, 74, 86
National Association of Graduate and
Professional Students (NAGPS), 6,
95, 292–93
National Consumer Law Center (NCLC)
and bankruptcy, 248
and loan consolidation, 200
and minimum loan payments, 198
publications of, 176, 201–2, 249
and tax refund interception, 193
National Defense Education Act (1958),
51
national interest rate, 211. *See also* inter-
est
National Oceanic and Atmospheric
Administration Corps, 119, 125
national service, 88, 90, 96, 295. *See also*
volunteer service
NCLC. *See* National Consumer Law
Center
negative amortization, 136
Nellie Mae (New England Education
Loan Marketing Corp.), 6, 13, 75,
149, 159
New York State Higher Education
Services Corporation (NYSHESC),
237
NGAPS. *See* National Association of
Graduate and Professional Students
Nicholson, Roy, 77
notices
collection, 169–70
to collection agencies, 203
of default, 181–82
and Department of Education, 190–91
in garnishment of wages, 189
in income tax interception, 191
to lender from borrower, 179
from lenders, 169–70
required from collection agencies,
187–88

Nursing Loans, 149
NYSHESC. *See* New York State Higher
Education Services Corporation

104th Congress, and student loans,
94–102
OpLoans, 149
origination fees, 68
"Overlap Group," 28
overlimit fees, 218
Oxendien, Larry, 76

parental deferment, 120
Parent Loans for Undergraduate
Students. *See* PLUS
payments
inability to pay, 109, 185–87
late credit, 224
minimum, 179
monthly, 19
partial after default, 194–95
reasonable and affordable, 177, 182,
197–98, 203
Pell, Claiborne, 54
Pell Grants, 54–55, 66, 96
Pennsylvania Higher Education
Assistance Agency (PHEAA), 186
Periodic Rate, credit card, 216
Perkins, Carl D., 51
Perkins loans, 51, 96, 109, 158
cancellations of, 122–24
case study of, 158
deferments for, 119–21, 302, 304
and False Loan Certification, 124
and hardship, 128
repayment of, 298, 300
petitions, bankruptcy filing, 252,
255–56
Petri, Tom, 73, 74, 85, 87, 100, 284–85
PHEAA. *See* Pennsylvania Higher
Education Assistance Agency
P.L.A.T.O. Loans, 149
PLUS loans, 57, 119–21, 134, 299, 300,
303, 305, 306. *See also* FFELP
preconditions, for bankruptcy, 242–43
prepayment, of loans, 178
primary care medical practitioners, deferments for, 126
prime rate, 211. *See also* banks; interest
Princeton University, 28
principal, and interest, 154, 194, 214
private loans, 148–50

troubleshooting, 155–71. *See also* contact information
trustee, court-appointed, 248, 252–53, 256
TRW. *See* Experian
tuition
  bargaining for, 27–28
  expenses associated with, 8–9
  increases in, 55
  statistics on, 8

unemployment, as deferment, 120, 126–27
Unfair and Deceptive Acts and Practices (NCLC), 176
United States Student Association (USSA), 94–95, 292
University of Pennsylvania, 28
University Support Services, Inc., 149
unsecured debt, 270–71
unsecured loans, 213
USA Funds, 13, 66–67, 77, 161
USA Group, 18, 27, 77, 167
USA Today, 8
U.S. Auditor General, 183
U.S. Bankruptcy Code, automatic stay provision of, 192
U.S. Census Bureau, 20–21
U.S. Congressional Opportunities Committee, 74

U.S. Department of Education. *See* Department of Education; Direct Lending
U.S. General Accounting Office (GAO), 46, 66, 77
U.S. Public Interest Research Group (U.S. PIRG), 70, 95–97, 293
U.S. Student Association. *See* United States Student Association
USSA. *See* United States Student Association
utilities, and bankruptcy, 241

VLoans, 149
Voigt, Diane, 48, 160, 286
volunteer service, 119, 123, 124–25

wages, garnishment of, 43, 143, 148, 180–81, 185–86, 188–91, 193, 202, 241
Waldman, Steven, 44, 88–91, 98
War on Poverty, 52–53
White House Daze: The Unmaking of Domestic Policy in the Bush Years (Kolb), 87
William D. Ford Federal Direct Loan Program. *See* Direct Lending
work-study, 52, 96

Yale University, 28